The Chechen Wars

THE
Chechen Wars

Will Russia Go the Way of the Soviet Union?

Matthew Evangelista

BROOKINGS INSTITUTION PRESS
Washington, D.C.

Copyright © 2002
THE BROOKINGS INSTITUTION
1775 Massachusetts Avenue, N.W., Washington, D.C. 20036
www.brookings.edu

Library of Congress Cataloging-in-Publication data

Evangelista, Matthew, 1958–
  The Chechen wars : will Russia go the way of the Soviet Union? /
Matthew Evangelista.
      p.   cm.
  Includes bibliographical references and index.
  ISBN 0-8157-2498-5 (cloth : alk. paper)—
  ISBN 0-8157-2499-3 (pbk. : alk. paper)
  1. Chechnëiia (Russia)—History—Civil War, 1994—Causes. I. Title.

DK511.C37 E94   2002
947.5′2086—dc21   2002013166

9 8 7 6 5 4 3 2 1

The paper used in this publication meets minimum requirements of the
American National Standard for Information Sciences—Permanence of Paper for
Printed Library Materials: ANSI Z39.48-1992.

Typeset in Minion

Composition by Betsy Kulamer
Washington, D.C.

Printed by R. R. Donnelley and Sons
Harrisonburg, Virginia

*In memory of
Galina Starovoitova,
1946–98*

Contents

Maps

Acknowledgments

My work on this topic began in the mid-1990s, when there had been only one post-Soviet war in Chechnya. Since then I have accumulated numerous debts in the course of writing about the first and second wars and their domestic and international implications for the Russian Federation. I am particularly grateful to the Carnegie Corporation of New York for providing a scholarship that allowed me the time to complete a draft of the manuscript and revise it during a sabbatical leave in Italy. The Corporation does not, however, take responsibility for any statements or views I have expressed. At the European University Institute near Florence I was fortunate to receive a Jean Monnet Fellowship and become affiliated with the Robert Schuman Centre for Advanced Studies and its European Forum. I thank Helen Wallace, the Centre director, Mark Pollack and Jan Zielonka, who ran the Forum with her, and many colleagues for their hospitality, collegiality, and valuable comments on my work.

Cornell University's Peace Studies Program awarded me a travel grant to conduct interviews in Russia and provided much moral support, for which I thank its directors at the time, Barry Strauss and Judith Reppy. I owe a great debt to the Program on New Approaches to Russian Security (PONARS) under the leadership of Celeste Wallander and Stephen Hanson. At PONARS conferences and in e-mail discussions I was able to present work in progress, pose questions, and engage in debate with world-class specialists on Russia who also happen to be some of the most helpful, interesting, and friendly people I know.

For research assistance, I thank Iuliia Korshunova, David Rivera, and Marat Umerov, whose help was invaluable in setting up interviews in Russia and transcribing them with great care and professionalism. I thank Sandy Kisner for transcribing interviews conducted in English. It has been a pleasure to work with the outstanding staff at Brookings: Christopher Kelaher, Janet Walker, Larry Converse, Tanjam Jacobson, and Vicky Macintyre. Thanks also to Philip Schwartzberg, who prepared the maps, and to Cornell's Department of Government for financial support for their preparation.

For comments on the manuscript, discussions related to it, and provisions of materials, I thank Mikhail Alexseev, Doug Blum, Georgi Derluguian, Yoshiko Herrera, Ted Hopf, James Hughes, Stuart Kaufman, Sarah Mendelson, Nikolai Petrov, Henry Shue, and Robert Bruce Ware. The extraordinary expertise manifested by these scholars is surpassed only by their generosity in sharing it with me. Reviewers for several presses provided me excellent criticisms and suggestions for revision. Some I have named above, but others—equally deserving of thanks—remain anonymous.

David Wippmann, my colleague in the Cornell School of Law, was kind enough to read and comment on my discussion of war crimes. As with the other readers, he bears no responsibility for my remaining errors—including calling Russia's military actions against Chechnya "invasions," a legal term that technically should not apply to a country's use of armed forces within its own territory. Many Chechens, of course, dispute Russia's legal claim to sovereignty over their territory—achieved initially by genuine invasion during the time of the tsars—but I employ the term in its common usage, rather than to make a legal point.

Parts of chapter 8 were presented at conferences at the European University Institute and the Catholic University of Milan. I am grateful to the organizers of those conferences—Thomas Risse, Peter Katzenstein, Peter Gourevitch, Robert Keohane, Jeffrey Checkel, and Vittorio Emanuele Parsi—and to participants who provided valuable comments.

As with most people who work on Russia, I owe a great debt to David Johnson of the Center for Defense Information in Washington, D.C. Johnson's Russia List (JRL) is an invaluable source of information, articles, translations, and discussion about Russian politics, available by e-mail subscription. Much of the material I used comes from Johnson's compilation, although I usually tried to cite the original source when I could get access to it. I would also like to thank Liz Fuller of Radio Free Europe/Radio Liberty (RFE/RL). Although I do not know her personally, her initials appear on many of the daily reports of events in Chechnya, without which it would have been very difficult to put together a basic chronology of the conflict. I also want to acknowledge that I could not have written this book without relying on the excellent work done by previous writers on the Chechen situation, including John Dunlop, Georgi Derluguian, Carlotta Gall and Thomas de Waal, Fiona Hill, Anatol Lieven, and Valerii Tishkov.

Finally, I would like to thank Klaus, Eveline, and Jana Eder for renting us their wonderful house, *Frassineto*—and Joanie, Clara, and Marielle for agreeing to live here with me. This area of Tuscany suffered enormously during the last year of World War II, as Italian partisans and Allied forces fought to drive out the German occupiers. Just a short drive from where I write, the Florence War Cemetery bears solemn testimony to the sacrifices of soldiers from the British Commonwealth. The last months of the struggle had much the quality of civil war as well, as communist partisans finally defeated the fascists who had brought such destruction upon Italy by their alliance with Nazi Germany. The beauty and tranquility of the countryside, and the material well-being and social comity of its residents, have helped ease these terrible events into history. My hope in finishing this book here is that one day Chechnya—and Russia as a whole—will enjoy such peace and prosperity and be able to forget the dark days that this book recounts.

NOTE ON TRANSLITERATION   Transliteration follows the U.S. Library of Congress system (without diacritical marks), except in the case of proper names and other words that have more widely used English versions (for example, Yeltsin, Chechnya, Grozny, Soviet). When quoting from other authors, I have revised their transliterations for the sake of consistency.

Molino del Piano
June 2002

1

Introduction

Chechyna, of course, is an extreme instance in the relations between Moscow and its regions. However, it serves as a warning that federalism may fail in the Russian republic just as it failed in the Soviet Union as a whole, ground up between the millstones of imperial centralism and ethnic particularism.

—Robert V. Daniels, 1997

In December 1994 the government of the Russian Federation launched a devastating war against the separatist republic of Chechnya. It lasted nearly two years, killed tens of thousands of people, and turned hundreds of thousands more into refugees. Despite a ground invasion and massive bombing of cities and villages (including vast destruction of the capital city of Grozny), the Russian armed forces failed to defeat the guerrillas. Chechen forces shocked and demoralized the Russian public by launching terrorist attacks on Russian territory. Finally they recaptured Grozny. Moscow withdrew its forces in humiliation, signing a peace agreement with the newly elected Chechen president, Aslan Maskhadov, that deferred resolution of Chechnya's status until the year 2001.

Chechnya had achieved de facto independence, but at tremendous cost. Would any of the other eighty-eight regions that make up the Russian Federation follow its example? Could Russia go the way of the Soviet Union and disintegrate into its constituent parts?

To many observers, Chechnya seemed a unique case. Only one other republic—Tatarstan—had joined it in refusing to sign the Federative Treaty that Russian president Boris Yeltsin proposed in 1992. But despite Tatarstan's own declaration of sovereignty, it managed to avoid violent conflict with Russia and to work out a modus vivendi. As a Tatar spokesperson told me in November 1998, the "lessons of Chechnya should be a warning to everybody": military conflict between the center and the regions "should not be repeated in any form."

Less than a year later, however, two such conflicts had broken out in the Russian North Caucasus. First, in August 1999 rebel forces, led by opponents of President Maskhadov, invaded neighboring Dagestan, ostensibly to liberate it from Russian rule and found an Islamic republic. Russian military forces and Dagestani villagers opposed the invasion. Then the Moscow government went a step further and began bombing Chechnya and sending in ground forces.

What had seemed unthinkable just months before was now a reality: renewal of the Chechen War and spillover of the conflict into Dagestan. How would this latest crisis in the North Caucasus affect the stability of the Russian Federation? Vladimir Putin, the former KGB agent appointed prime minister just as the new war began, had an answer: "I was convinced that if we didn't stop the extremists right away, we'd be facing a second Yugoslavia on the entire territory of the Russian Federation—the Yugoslavization of Russia." If Russia granted Chechnya independence, "immediately, dissatisfied leaders from different regions and territories would turn up: 'We don't want to live in a Russia like that. We want to be independent.' And off they'd go."[1]

Although Russian troops readily halted the incursion into Dagestan, their effort to impose control over Chechen territory got bogged down. The toll of civilian casualties mounted as Russian forces launched artillery and air attacks against Grozny and other population centers, provoking a wide-scale refugee crisis. As rebel fighters fled to the mountains, Russian army and police units set up "filtration camps" in the areas under their control to identify suspected "bandits" and "terrorists" among the remaining population. Evidence of torture and summary executions led to local protests and international accusations of human-rights abuses, but little change in Russian policy.

How could Russia's leaders have steered their country into such destructive and seemingly self-defeating wars, at a cost of tens of thousands of dead and wounded, Russian citizens nearly all? The secondary literature on the war of 1994–96 is already quite extensive, supplemented by firsthand reports, memoirs, and other documentation.[2] It all points to a troubling paradox: the outbreak of this war—as with many others—seems to have been simultaneously overdetermined (to use the social-science jargon) and avoidable. Among the main competing explanations for the war are the *strategic arguments*: Chechnya stands astride key transportation junctions, including the Rostov-Baku highway and Rostov-Baku railroad, the only links between northern Russia and Transcaucasia and the countries of eastern and southern Europe. It has also been an important center for oil refining and transit. Some Russian officials sought to justify the first invasion of Chechnya as being necessary to secure these facilities for the sake of the economic well-being of the rest of the country.[3] More cynical observers suggested that personal interests in controlling Chechnya's oil trade played a big role in both wars.

A broader strategic argument was based on the precedent that Chechen secession could set: that "the 'brushfire' of drives for independence may pick up elsewhere across Russia, leading to the eventual destruction of Russian territorial integrity."[4] This argument became the centerpiece of justifications by both Russian presidents for their pursuit of war in Chechnya.

Many analysts attribute the wars in Chechnya to the *historical and structural legacy of the Soviet system*. The more simplistic versions imply that the very existence of some 100 ethnic groups in the Russian Federation, whose aspirations were suppressed under the Soviet order, provides sufficient reason to understand the sources of such conflicts as the one between Russia and Chechnya. Indeed, the Chechen case provides an extreme example of the phenomenon. Having suffered mass deportation from their homeland on Stalin's orders during World War II, the Chechens retained a strong sense of ethnic identity and an abiding mistrust of Russia. Such explanations make the Chechen drive for independence appear natural and inevitable.

A more sophisticated explanation related to the Soviet legacy emphasizes the political structure, dating back to the Stalinist era, imposed on various ethnic groups. Here the stress is not on Soviet suppression of ethnic identity, but on the creation or fostering of that identity through the development of local institutions, formalization and teaching of indigenous languages, and encouragement of native culture—all within strict control of the Communist Party. In this interpretation, the Soviet Union was not so much the "prison house of nations" as the "hothouse" of nationalism. The point is that the Soviet authorities created the formal institutions of self-rule, which, although meaningless in the highly centralized and authoritarian Soviet context, provided the basis for assertions of autonomy during the post-Soviet transition.[5] The Soviet legacy also sowed the seeds of violent conflict in that many of the Soviet administrative boundaries separated ethnic groups in a fashion that fostered irredentism as the Union of Soviet Socialist Republics disintegrated.

In contrast to structural and historical explanations, those based on analysis of *leadership politics* and *personalities* highlight the idiosyncratic and contingent nature of the decisions to invade Chechnya. One view attributes the first war to a pathological decisionmaking process in Moscow. According to this view, Boris Yeltsin—ill, weak, and unpopular—sought to boost his "ratings" with a quick, victorious war against a people associated in the Russian popular consciousness with the worst excesses of the transition to capitalism: organized crime and violence. Surrounded by corrupt, self-serving advisers, he persuaded himself to undertake what soon turned into a hopeless quagmire.[6] The other side of the leadership perspective focuses on the erratic nature of the Chechen leader, General Dzhokhar Dudaev. He was extremely sensitive to perceived personal slights, and he tended to exaggerate the economic benefits that would accrue to an independent Chechnya, making him willing to take greater risks than the situation warranted. Lacking the political skills necessary to govern an impoverished, isolated ministate, the Chechen general felt more comfortable leading a war of national defense against Russian aggression.[7]

To the extent that observers favor a leadership- or personality-based explanation for the second war, they point out that the initial Chechen intervention into Dagestan was led by two highly unusual and charismatic figures: Shamil' Basaev and Khattab (nom de guerre of Habib Abd al-Rahman).[8] Their roles as self-promoting opponents of the elected Chechen president Aslan Maskhadov were probably more important to understanding the conflict than any commitment to Islamic revolution. Also relevant was the weakness of Maskhadov himself as a leader, a weakness that allowed Moscow to make the case that an invasion was necessary to restore order to a lawless territory.

On the Russian side, leadership- or personality-based explanations for the second war focus on the electoral ambitions of Vladimir Putin. Appointed prime minister when the war began, he saw his popularity soar the cruder his language became and the harsher his army's response to the Chechen situation. When Yeltsin resigned the presidency on the eve of the New Year 2000, he chose Putin as his designated successor. The popularity of the war made Putin unbeatable in the March 2000 presidential elections. Not surprisingly, he voiced no regrets about resuming the war, even though it meant breaking the peace agreements his predecessor had signed. "I do not have a second of doubt that we are doing the right thing," Putin maintained. "Maybe we should be even tougher."[9]

Toughness may not be the answer, but weakness was certainly part of the problem. As a number of analysts have pointed out, the Russian state was considerably weaker than its Soviet predecessor. The lack of "stateness" in contemporary Russia is part of the historical and structural legacy of the breakup of the USSR, and, in effect, provides a link between that explanation for the Chechen Wars and the one that focuses on leadership politics and personality.[10] If post-Soviet Russia had built the infrastructure of a "normal," law-governed state, the role of personal idiosyncrasies and Kremlin intrigues would not have been so significant and the influence of the "power ministries," dominated by military and secret-service personnel, would not have been so great. Moreover, the lack of functioning state institutions lay at the heart of Chechnya's inability to govern itself under the Dudaev regime, and after, and undoubtedly contributed to the escalation of violence and the outbreak of war.

In considering the first war, many analysts have drawn the paradoxical conclusion that Galina Starovoitova, the liberal Russian politician and human rights activist, expressed to me in an interview in November 1998, shortly before she was murdered: Chechnya was a unique case, containing an overdetermined number of strategic and historical-institutional factors pointing toward secession, but also one that did not need to result in war. She and others have pointed particularly to the fact that a face-to-face meeting between Yeltsin and Dudaev might have been enough for the latter to temper his demands and settle for something less than full independence for Chechnya.[11]

If the Chechen case was so unusual and the violent outcome avoidable, then it is not surprising that with the end of the first Chechen War, few observers anticipated another bout of violent secessionism in Russia. The consensus seemed, instead, to predict a gradual loosening of bonds between center and periphery in Russia and the uneasy relationship that has come to be known as "asymmetric federalism."[12] In the wake of the renewal of war in 1999, the pendulum swung back in the other direction. Alarmist predictions about a domino effect of separatism began to reappear, both in the West and in Russia.[13]

By far the most alarmist interpretations of the Chechen conflict have come from Vladimir Putin himself. "What's the situation in the North Caucasus and in Chechnya today?" he asked himself in an interview in early 2000. "It's a continuation of the collapse of the USSR."[14] Thus he justified a renewal of all-out warfare. "This is what I thought of the situation in August [1999], when the bandits attacked Dagestan: If we don't put an immediate end to this, Russia will cease to exist. It was a question of preventing the collapse of the country."[15]

I examine the various explanations for the outbreak of the two wars in the first part of this book. My analysis leads me to question the argument that beyond the case of Chechnya itself the territorial integrity of the Russian Federation was at stake. Chapter 2 presents a brief review of the history of Chechen-Russian relations and a narrative account of the origins of the first war based on the most recent sources, including a collective memoir of nine former Yeltsin advisers. Chapter 3 covers the period between the peace agreement of August 1996 that ended the first war and the outbreak of the second war three years later. If the first war could have been avoided by such measures as direct negotiations between Yeltsin and Dudaev, the road to the second war is likewise littered with missed opportunities of many kinds. Chapter 4 focuses on the outbreak of the second war, especially the machinations of Boris Yeltsin and his "family" of political cronies and relatives, as they sought to secure the position of the president's designated successor, Vladimir Putin. I seek to make sense of the various rumors concerning the origins of the invasion of Dagestan and the mysterious series of apartment bombings that terrorized Russian citizens and turned many of them into strong supporters of a renewed war effort. Although I analyze the origins of the two wars, I do not provide a military history of the wars themselves or a study of strategy and tactics, tasks that have been undertaken by several other authors.[16]

The second part of the book takes up the issue that seemingly drove both Yeltsin and Putin to unleash war on their own country: the apparent fragility of the Russian Federation. I examine the hard cases—the regions most often cited as likely to seek further autonomy or outright secession from Moscow—and find far less cause for concern than one would expect from the hyperbolic language of a Yeltsin or Putin.

In fact, across the political spectrum in Russia observers have identified the same core regions as being "at risk" for secession in the wake of the Chechen conflict. Galina Starovoitova, who once advised Yeltsin on ethnic affairs, predicted at the outset of the first war that the "crude use" of "notorious tools of imperial policy," would "produce mistrust of the center's policy and centrifugal tendencies." She expressed particular concern about the republics with large Muslim populations, such as Tatarstan and Bashkortostan. Vladimir Putin, while himself making the crudest use of Russian military "tools," justified the resort to force as a means of maintaining control of regions at risk of separation. "I have never for a second believed," said Putin, "that Chechnya would limit itself to its own independence. It would become a beachhead for further attacks on Russia." If the Chechen rebels had remained in power, "they would have swallowed up Dagestan, and that would have been the beginning of the end. The entire Caucasus would have followed—Dagestan, Ingushetiia, and then up along the Volga river to Bashkortostan and Tatarstan, reaching deep into the country."[17]

In chapter 5, I look at four cases of "regions at risk" of secession. First, I consider Dagestan, the republic, along with Ingushetiia, most immediately affected by the catastrophic events associated with the wars in Chechnya. Some 100,000 refugees fled to Dagestan in the wake of the first war, threatening to destabilize the delicate political balance between the thirty-odd ethnic groups living there. Why is it that Dagestan, the poorest region in Russia next to Chechnya itself, has not pursued secession and instead actively opposed efforts by Chechen militants to separate it from Russia in 1999?

The next case is Tatarstan. The "Tatarstan model" is often invoked as a peaceful alternative to what happened in Chechnya and as a harbinger of the asymmetrical federalism that came to characterize Russian center-regional relations. What were the keys to Tatarstan's relative success? Could they be more broadly applied? More than one observer has argued that Tatarstan, in its drive for autonomy from Moscow, came close to a violent conflict of the Chechen sort. What factors kept it from the brink?

A related and important case is Bashkortostan. Like its neighbor Tatarstan, Bashkortostan is rich in natural resources, relatively well developed in industry (including military production), and one of the few "donor" regions whose tax revenues are redistributed to the poorer areas of the federation. A number of observers have pointed to the danger that Bashkortostan and Tatarstan might join together to form the nucleus of a "Volga-Urals Republic" and assert independence from Russia. Such an entity would be a military-industrial powerhouse and could pose a real threat to the survival of the Russian Federation.[18] What has kept the two regions from pursuing such a course?

Next I turn to the Russian Far East, to the Maritime Territory—Primor'e—and to Sakhalin *oblast'*. Including these regions allows one to "control" for the effect of Islam and non-Russian ethnic identities on the prospects for separatism. Sakhalin and Primor'e are predominantly Russian, but they have had many reasons to assert their autonomy from Moscow. Their natural trade partners are in the Far East, and the exploitation of their resources (gas, oil, fish) has been hindered by Moscow's inter-ference or recalcitrance. The government of Sakhalin has objected to Moscow's efforts to negotiate the status of the disputed Southern Kuril Islands with Japan, without taking Sakhalin's interests into account. Pri-mor'e, in addition to the material factors involved in Sakhalin's case, raises issues of cultural influences and identity. Many observers have noted the distinctive, independent character of the Russians of the Far East and Siberia—as well as a historical precedent of the short-lived Far Eastern Republic of the early 1920s. If identity and material incentives play an important role in separatist movements, they should be evident in Sakhalin and Primor'e. If, on the other hand, there exist countervailing factors that contribute to the preservation of the Russian Federation despite strong fissiparous tendencies, the cases from the Russian Far East should reveal them.

Despite the arguably underappreciated durability of Russia's system of asymmetrical federalism, most Russian leaders have sought to reform it, primarily in a recentralizing fashion.[19] Vladimir Putin has gone the fur-thest, seeking to reinforce what he calls the "power vertical" and to insti-tute a "dictatorship of law." He has appointed former military, police, and intelligence officials to govern a new system of super-regions and has undertaken a high-profile attempt to bring wayward subjects such as Tatarstan, Bashkortostan, and Primor'e back into line—all in the interest of preserving the state. Chapter 6 reviews Yeltsin's approach to federalism and summarizes Putin's "cure," which could be worse than the disease. By insisting on putting his police officials in charge of the regions, Putin could undermine important bastions of stability, such as Ingushetiia. Indeed, Putin's regional reforms may be counterproductive: unnecessary for maintaining the integrity of the Russian Federation and likely to bring back some of the worst features of the Soviet era. Thus Russia could go at least some of the way of the Soviet Union, not by breaking up but by reverting to an overly centralized authoritarian regime.

The discussion of "regions at risk" and the danger of recentralization suggests that Russian leaders have overreacted to the threat of secessionism triggered by the wars in Chechnya. The domestic implications of Chechen secessionism were hardly as threatening as Yeltsin and Putin portrayed them. What of the international implications? From the first days of the first invasion, the Russian armed forces have violated the laws of war on a vast scale—with indiscriminate bombing of civilian population centers, torture, and execution of scores of Chechens caught up in sweep opera-tions and detained in concentration camps; massacres of villagers and townspeople, and numerous other depredations against refugees and innocent civilians. Has the international reaction to Russian war crimes reduced the country's international prestige to an extent that might hinder Russia's integration into international and European institutions, an explicit goal of both the Yeltsin and Putin regimes?

The question of Russia's international standing in light of extensive evidence of war crimes committed during the two campaigns against Chechnya is the subject of chapter 7. I review the body of international law applicable to internal conflicts such as the Chechen Wars, the understanding of those laws by Russian political and military officials, the interpretation of Russian behavior offered by Russian and Western journalists and specialists, and the Russian government's response to domestic and international criticism. I argue that a number of prominent Western observers of Russian politics have let Russia off the hook by misunderstanding the extent and gravity of Russian war crimes, whereas numerous Russian journalists and human-rights activists have been more critical. The Western tendency to play down Russian war crimes has provided a kind of protection for Russia's international standing.

In the wake of the attacks of September 11, 2001, Russia seemed likely to avoid any further criticism of its behavior in Chechnya. Western governments had already shown themselves willing to forgive Moscow's brutal means because they believed its ends—preservation of territorial integrity—were just. Now they appeared inclined to accept Putin's framing of the Chechen conflict as one of combating internationally sponsored terrorism. After September 11, Russia became a member in good standing of the international antiterrorist coalition, thanks to its support of the U.S.-led war against the Taliban regime in Afghanistan.

As chapter 8 describes, however, cooperation with the West in the struggle against international terrorism did not mean that Russia would automatically be welcomed into Western institutions, such as the European Union, the North Atlantic Treaty Organization (NATO), or the World Trade Organization. Nor in fact did it mean that Moscow would get a free pass on Chechnya. Even if Western governments contemplated a Realpolitik deal of silence on Chechnya in return for cooperation against al-Qaida (and some of them evidently did so), they could not prevent their own citizens or members of international organizations from speaking out about Russian abuses. Russia's integration into international institutions already faces many barriers. Doubts about the country's suitability, based on the government's conduct of the Chechen Wars and reluctance to prosecute war criminals in compliance with domestic and international law, are not at the top of the list of reasons to go slow—even though, arguably, they should be.

Chapter 9 summarizes my argument that Russia is unlikely to go the way of the Soviet Union and break up into its constituent units. More likely is at least a partial reversion to an authoritarian centralism reminiscent of the Soviet era, with restrictions on the media and on political activism. Such restrictions will make it all the more difficult for Russian society to recognize the costs of using excessive force to subdue Chechnya's aspirations for autonomy and to do something to reverse the unwise course that its leaders have pursued.

2

Yeltsin's War

Armed intervention is impermissible and must not be done. Were we to apply pressure of force against Chechnya, the whole Caucasus would rise up and there would be such turmoil and blood that no one would ever forgive us. It is absolutely impossible.

—Boris Yeltsin, August 1994

This was Yeltsin's private war because the government did not declare war and the parliament did not declare war. The entire war was carried out according to the commands and decrees of one political figure.

—Ruslan Khasbulatov, April 1996

The origins of the Russian invasion of Chechnya in late 1994 are complicated and still somewhat mysterious, despite the availability of memoir accounts, interviews, and some documents. In one respect, however, there is no mystery. This was Boris Yeltsin's war—to win, to lose, or to avoid altogether, if he had so chosen. In one volume of his memoirs, Yeltsin claimed: "I never shirked responsibility in the course of the Chechen campaign, even when other people gave the orders. I took responsibility upon myself." That characterization takes considerable liberties with the truth. In the midst of some of the toughest situations, when key decisions had to be made, Yeltsin would be traveling abroad or convalescing in a hospital. Indeed, at the very outset of the war, when Russian troops invaded Chechnya in December 1994, Yeltsin disappeared from sight in order to have an operation on his nose. Yet, even if only in retrospect, Yeltsin is willing "to take responsibility—for the storming of Grozny, for the bomb attacks, and for their cessation." That is as it should be.[1] The history of the conflict in Chechnya from 1994 to 1996, to the extent that one can piece it together, demonstrates that this was truly Yeltsin's war.

Background to War

Russia and Chechnya share a long history of conflict, from invasion and colonial rule during the Tsarist era through mass deportations and repression under Stalin. That shared history did not predetermine the outbreak of war in 1994, but it does go some way toward explaining the Chechens' desire for greater independence as the Soviet Union disintegrated. There is also, however, a long history of Russian-Chechen cooperation in the North Caucasus. During the Soviet era many Chechens received higher education, joined professions, and moved to urban centers outside their homeland. If not for the economic collapse of the USSR, many Chechens might have continued along this trajectory to a modern cosmopolitan life-style, leaving the ways of the guerrilla fighter in the distant past. Instead, the demise of Soviet order and the policies of Russian and Chechen leaders brought about the renewal of violent conflict. In this context, a brief history of Russian-Chechen relations provides a useful background to discussion of Yeltsin's war.

The Tsarist Legacy

Russia's first military encounter with Chechnya came in 1722, when Chechen fighters routed a cavalry force sent there by Peter the Great. Later in the century, Chechen resistance to Russian influence was led by Sheikh Mansur, a religious and military leader who launched a *gazavat*, or "holy war," against corrupt Muslims and Russian interlopers. Mansur's followers were dismissed by Russian military authorities as ignorant scoundrels and "ragamuffins," much as Russian leaders would use equally demeaning language two centuries later to characterize Chechens as bandits and terrorists.

The legacy of antagonistic relations between Chechnya and the Russian government contributes much to understanding the sources of the outbreak of violence in Chechnya in the 1990s. This is not to say that immutable ancient hatreds made conflict inevitable. Although Russia's strategic objective to control the North Caucasus region dates back two centuries, its methods have varied. Efforts at co-opting and integrating the peoples of the region alternated with heavy-handed repression that incited hatred. A constant theme has been the counterproductive nature of Russia's military actions. The blunt military instrument most often served to alienate potential allies and turn an indifferent population against the Russian authorities.[2]

The first serious attempt to subdue Chechnya followed in the wake of Russia's annexation of Georgia in 1801 and the outbreak of war with Turkey in 1807. Russian authorities advanced strategic arguments to justify expansion, particularly the need to secure the route from Vladikavkaz to Tbilisi, the capital of Georgia, through the Darial Pass. The effort to incorporate the mountain peoples of the region into the Russian Empire was led by General Aleksei Ermolov. The policies he pursued represent the worst of Russian approaches to the Chechens, and they set the precedent for subsequent crimes of the Soviet and post-Soviet eras. Under Soviet rule, the Communist Party tended to portray Ermolov as the symbol of an enlightened civilizing mission. The Chechens, some of whom sought to blow up a statue of the general in Grozny in 1969, knew better.

Ermolov advocated a strategy of economic warfare against the recalcitrant mountaineers, destroying their crops and burning their villages. His forces perpetrated massacres against unarmed villagers and carried out the first mass deportation of Chechens, including sending captured prisoners into exile in Siberia. Mountain peoples who had moved to the fertile land between the Terek and Sunzha Rivers were driven back up into the mountains, reversing a trend toward the more "progressive" economic and political practices that had followed the migration. As one historian puts it, "By forcing the Chechens back up into the inhospitable mountains, Ermolov returned them to an economically and socially primitive state, thereby ensuring the existence of a fierce and dedicated opponent for the Russian Empire over the next half century (and beyond)."[3]

Paradoxically, Ermolov's military and economic policies "led gradually to a consolidation of Chechen society." The destruction of Chechen villages and other "harsh punitive actions drove many Chechens into the arms" of Islamic leaders such as Kazi Mullah and the legendary Shamil'.[4] The Russian government during the tsarist era carried out three major deportations, setting the precedent for Stalin's genocidal actions against the Chechen people in the 1940s. The deportations failed to break Chechen resistance and instead contributed to an abiding attachment to the homeland and a smoldering sense of grievance. Chechens, whose primary loyalty was typically local, formed their sense of a "national" identity mainly in opposition to Russian offensives.

Deportations and Restoration

The Soviet era brought some measure of industrial and modern life to the Chechens along with the worst catastrophe of their history, the mass deportations to Central Asia and elsewhere ordered by Stalin in 1943–44. Indeed, the two issues are linked. As one account describes, the deportations "unwillingly dragged thousands of Chechens into the modern era, transforming them from a mountain farming people into a scattered diaspora."[5]

The proposal to abolish the Checheno-Ingush Autonomous Soviet Socialist Republic (ASSR) and expel its population was discussed at a meeting of the Politburo on February 11, 1943. The only disagreement came over whether to expel the people immediately or wait until Hitler's armies had been completely driven from the North Caucasus. No one opposed the deportation in principle. Nikita Khrushchev, who later criticized and reversed Stalin's decision, favored waiting for defeat of the Germans in the region. Anastas Mikoian expressed concern about the USSR's reputation abroad.[6]

At the height of World War II, the Stalinist regime carried out a number of such deportations on the basis of ethnic identity. Accusations of "mass treason" for collaboration with Nazi forces were based on dubious evidence. Many people were deported from regions that the German armies never reached, including Chechnya itself.[7] More than a million Soviet citizens of German ancestry (whose families had lived in Russia for generations) were sent from their homes in the Volga region and Ukraine to Siberia and Central Asia. Next Stalin's attention turned to the "small peoples" of the North Caucasus: the Karachai, Kalmyk, Balkar, and others.

The deportation of the Chechens and Ingush was the most ambitious operation after the Volga Germans. About 500,000 people were rounded up, starting in the middle of the night of February 22–23, 1944, and packed into trains. Some 12,525 railway carriages were used, fewer than expected: because so many of the deportees turned out to be children, they could be packed in more tightly than adults. The lack of food, toilets, or washing facilities produced an epidemic of typhoid. The harsh winter at their destination in Kazakhstan further decimated the population of deportees. Between the deportation itself and the conditions of exile, about a quarter of the deported population had perished within five years of their arrival, according to official statistics.[8]

In the mid-1950s, following Stalin's death, Chechens and others began making their way back to their homelands in the North Caucasus. Finally in 1956, Stalin's successors, led by Nikita Khrushchev, officially permitted the deported groups to leave their places of exile, but discouraged them from claiming their former property and tried to prevent them from returning to the sites of their (destroyed) ancestral villages in the mountains.[9]

In 1957 the Soviet authorities reestablished a homeland for the Chechens and Ingush. The Checheno-Ingush ASSR was created by transferring back territory formerly assigned to the Dagestan ASSR and the North Ossetian ASSR, as well as the area around the former capital of Grozny, which after the deportation had become a mainly Russian region (*oblast'*). Some of the territory of the Grozny *oblast'* that had formerly belonged to Checheno-Ingushetiia was transferred to Dagestan and Stavropol' district (*krai*).[10] Intentionally or not, the new arrangement led to a dilution of the Chechen population within the autonomous republic—41 percent, compared with 58.4 percent in 1939.[11] It also created conditions for competing territorial claims among the various other ethnic groups, leading to violence in some cases as the Soviet Union disintegrated.

The Chechens were not unique in their experience of harsh, even genocidal treatment and deportation under the Soviet regime. Yet "they were the largest nation on a compact territory to be deported and then allowed to return." Although other small deported groups attempted to mobilize on national grounds as the USSR broke up in 1991, it was the Chechens who had "force of numbers as well as the fresh historical grievance that pushed them into open separatism."[12]

The End of the Soviet Era

"The Chechen Republic's transition from spontaneous anticommunism to the idea and policy of state sovereignty was not smooth." That understatement comes from Taimaz Abubakarov, minister of economics and finance in the Chechen government of President Dzhokhar Dudaev during the first half of the 1990s. It encompasses several points that have characterized the debate over the sources of the first Chechen War.[13] First, a key factor in the political mobilization within Chechnya, as in much of the rest of the Soviet Union, was not only or primarily nationalism, but *anticommunism*. It is not so much the values theoretically associated with communism—such as collective property and egalitarian economic and social structures—that Chechens, along with most other Soviet citizens, found objectionable. Nor was it necessarily an ideological objection to the Soviet Communist Party itself. Dudaev, who joined the party in 1968 as a military officer and was considered by his subordinates to have been an extremely loyal member, never formally resigned.[14] For Dudaev and his fellow Chechens, the aspects of "communism" that elicited the most resistance were the hypercentralization and inefficiency of the political and eco-nomic system directed from Moscow, and the secrecy and hypocrisy of political life. Indeed, these were the main objections of Russians and non-Russians throughout the USSR.

With the advent of Mikhail Gorbachev's *perestroika* reforms, residents of Chechnya mobilized to support the goals of decentralization, economic change, and political activity that Gorbachev's program came to represent. Some of them seized on nationalist symbols, but others chose other ban-ners—such as the Green ecology movement—to oppose the structure of Moscow-dominated communist authority.[15] In 1989 that structure was represented by Doku Zavgaev, the first secretary of the Communist Party in the Chechen-Ingush Republic, in effect, the top leader and representa-tive of Moscow. Zavgaev, though an ethnic Chechen, was cautious in asserting Chechnya's rights. He was, however, apparently instrumental in advocating that Moscow promote for the first time ever a Chechen mili-tary officer to the rank of general. Thus Dzhokhar Dudaev owed his status as a Soviet general to his soon-to-be nemesis.[16]

In other regions of Russia, including autonomous republics such as Tatarstan, former communist leaders managed to reinvent themselves in the face of nationalist pressures and remain in control. Zavgaev, however, was outmaneuvered by his opponents among what Timur Muzaev, the most authoritative chronicler of these events, has called the radical nation-alists. First they formed the Vainakh Party, from the word Chechens use to refer to themselves and the Ingush, who speak a related language. Then they convoked a Chechen National Congress in November 1990 and invited the recently promoted General Dudaev—who had never lived in Chechnya—to head the nationalist movement.[17]

Responding to the radical nationalists three days after the close of the Chechen National Congress, the Supreme Soviet of the Chechen-Ingush ASSR issued a "Declaration of State Sovereignty of the Chechen-Ingush Republic." Despite the declaration, officials of the Supreme Soviet—the political institution still formally part of the USSR's system of govern-ment—intended that the republic maintain close relations with Russia. The radicals, now led by Dudaev, had other ideas. They favored secession and linking Chechnya to neighboring Muslim republics in a North Cauca-sus confederation. The first half of 1991 saw an increasing division between the radical nationalists determined to break with Russia and a more moderate wing of the Chechen nationalist movement. According to Muzaev, "The second session of the Chechen National Congress, sum-moned by Dudaev and his adherents in Grozny on 8–9 June 1991, marked the triumph of the radicals."[18] Renamed the National Congress of the Chechen People, its executive committee, with Dudaev as its head, emerged as the main rival to the Supreme Soviet.

Communist authorities in Moscow followed the developments in Grozny and accurately reported the goals of Dudaev's movement as the "self-dissolution of the current structure of the Supreme Soviet of the Checheno-Ingush Republic, carrying out new elections and the creation of a sovereign national state." But, at least judging by the Central Committee documents that have been declassified, the communist officials seemed more worried about the claims from Ingush political leaders for "restoration of the autonomous region [*avtonomii*] of the Ingush people and its original historical borders." They feared, presciently as it turned out, conflicts between Ingush and Ossets over the Prigorodnyi district—traditional Ingush lands that were then part of North Ossetiia—and the outmigration of Russian speakers (see map 2-1, p. 23).[19] Yet by and large Gorbachev's advisers in the Central Committee seemed more concerned about the heterodox nationalist proposals of the communist leader Doku Zavgaev— made, in part, in reaction to the more extreme positions espoused by his rival Dudaev—than about Dudaev himself.[20]

The big opportunity for the opponents of Moscow's rule came with the failed coup against Soviet president Gorbachev in August 1991. Zavgaev and the local communist authorities in Grozny had failed to condemn the coup plotters, who sought to reverse Gorbachev's reforms, especially his proposal for a new Union Treaty to create a less centralized, confederation of republics to replace the USSR. They thereby discredited themselves in the eyes of increasingly nationalist and anticommunist Chechens as well as among the supporters of Russian president Boris Yelstin, whose symbolic role in defeating the coup had made him a hero.

Demonstrations in Grozny apparently convinced Yeltsin's circle that Zavgaev and the Soviet-era authorities had to go. It is a matter of some dispute as to how widespread the opposition to Zavgaev actually was. Valerii Tishkov reports that the demonstrations in Sheikh Mansur Square (formerly Lenin Square) in Grozny did not have an obvious political objective: "These were not political actions, but rather a demonstration of solidarity, free spirit or libertarianism, and militancy, mobilized and directed by local leaders." Demonstrators were apparently paid "100 rubles per day (at that time a rather significant sum); livestock was specially slaughtered and meat was constantly being prepared in the Square. Men who were not otherwise employed (there were few women at the Chechen demonstrations)—basically the older generations—were the backbone of the demonstration and guaranteed its spirit by performing the traditional *zikr*" dance. On Russian television the same faces kept appearing at the demonstrations, ostensibly directed at the remnants of Soviet power.[21]

In the meantime, Dudaev's supporters seized government buildings and the radio and television center. They disrupted a session of the Supreme Soviet and caused the death of Viktor Kutsenko, the elderly head of the Grozny City Council and an ethnic Russian, who was either thrown out of a window or fell trying to escape.[22] In response to the demonstrations and violence, Zavgaev demanded that Moscow authorize forces to disperse the demonstrators and restore order, but Yeltsin's government decided otherwise.

On September 14, 1991, Ruslan Khasbulatov arrived in Grozny from Moscow. Khasbulatov, an ethnic Chechen, was chair of the Russian Supreme Soviet, parliamentary deputy from Checheno-Ingushetiia, and at the time still an ally of Yeltsin. He persuaded Zavgaev and the members of the Chechen-Ingush Supreme Soviet to abolish that body, to resign their positions, and to establish a temporary council that would rule until new parliamentary elections could be held on November 17.[23]

No sooner had Khasbulatov returned to Moscow than Dudaev and his supporters attempted to usurp power from the temporary council. They stormed the republic's KGB headquarters and seized its cache of weapons, reportedly with the acquiescence of Moscow authorities. At this point, according to Tishkov, "some misgivings began to appear among the Muscovite initiators of 'decommunization' of Chechnya about the increasingly independent behavior shown by Dudaev. As Khasbulatov later admitted, he 'spoke with Yeltsin about adding one more star to Dudaev's shoulder-strap and returning him to the army'" to get him out of Chechnya. In fact, the Russian air force chief Petr Deinekin evidently offered Dudaev promotion to a high command position if he would stay in the service. "The highest position for me," Dudaev reportedly answered, "is as an ordinary Chechen."[24]

With its support of Dudaev, and its abandonment of Doku Zavgaev, "Moscow played a decisive role in the overthrow of the old regime and in the coming to power of national-radical elements."[25] Another Russian political observer similarly argues that if Yeltsin's assistants, "responsible for nationalities problems had understood the nature of processes going on in the North Caucasus, they in turn would not have facilitated the rise of Dudaev to power in Chechnya. It's possible that there would have been no crisis, and no first or second war."[26] A well-informed Russian military official even speculates that, like communist-era leaders in Tatarstan and

Bashkortostan, who remained in power by embracing the rhetoric of nationalism and autonomy, Zavgaev could have done the same if not for Moscow's precipitate support of Dudaev. "It's possible that he would have calmly held power for more than another decade if not for the Muscovite purveyors of misfortune having planted the thought with the Chechens of the necessity of an obligatory change of the *ancien régime*."[27]

Dudaev took advantage of the "social anarchy" that prevailed in Chechnya, as one of his erstwhile supporters described it, but his actions were not widely popular.[28] In fact, they met opposition from a wide range of Chechen nationalist organizations. On September 25,1991, ten groups formed a round table to demand that Dudaev's executive committee halt its efforts to displace the temporary council and seize power.[29] They were too late. On October 8 Dudaev's National Congress of the Chechen People declared itself the sole authority in the republic. On October 19 Boris Yeltsin—the president of a Russia still formally part of the Soviet Union—wrote to the leaders of the National Congress demanding that they relinquish control of the government buildings they had seized, return weapons to the interior ministry, disarm the "illegally created armed formations," and hold elections as scheduled on November 17.[30]

Instead, Dudaev and his allies followed their own plan. They preemptively held elections on October 27 for parliament and the president. Accounts of the elections differ dramatically. Dudaev's executive committee claimed that 77 percent of the eligible electorate participated and that 85 percent voted for Dudaev.[31] According to Tishkov, voting took place in only 70 of the republic's 360 electoral districts, with a turnout of only 10–12 percent, but Dudaev did emerge as the winner among three candidates and declared himself president.[32] One of his first acts was to issue a declaration of sovereignty of the Chechen Republic, thereby splitting it off from the autonomous republic that had included Ingushetiia.

On November 2, 1991, the Russian parliament (Congress of People's Deputies) pronounced the Chechen elections illegal, and five days later Yeltsin declared a state of emergency in the republic and dispatched 2,500 interior ministry troops. Dudaev responded by declaring martial law and mobilizing forces for the defense of Chechen sovereignty. Under threat of Russian invasion, most of Dudaev's erstwhile opponents rallied to his side, a phenomenon that was repeated under his successor when Russia invaded again in 1999. At this point, most of the military means to enforce a state of emergency in Chechnya were still nominally under the control of the USSR, not Russia, and personally subject to the decision of the Soviet president, Mikhail Gorbachev. Gorbachev's ambivalence about the use of violence and his rivalry with Yeltsin led him to hesitate. In the meantime the Russian parliament rescinded Yeltsin's order to use force, reflecting the emerging political competition between its chair, Khasbulatov, and the Russian president. As historian Fiona Hill described, "Soviet television subsequently showed several hundred Russian troops leaving Grozny in tourist buses, as Chechen national guardsmen fired automatic weapons in the air in celebration."[33]

Not for the last time, threatening but indecisive Russian actions gave Dudaev a welcome boost. As one opposition critic complained, "before 9 November Dudaev was zero. Afterwards he became a national hero."[34] One could easily imagine other circumstances that would have hindered his success in consolidating power and driving out the former legal authorities. The constitutional crisis in the USSR itself, as Yeltsin's Russia led the way to the breakup of the Soviet Union, had an evident impact. As one observer put it, "the Yeltsin-Gorbachev rivalry, which was about to come to a head, paralyzed the activity of the Center and indirectly contributed to promoting Chechen separatism."[35] In broader terms, however, the series of events that led the fifteen constituent republics of the USSR to become independent countries also had a psychological impact on the leaders and followers of the Chechen nationalist movement. Actions that were literally unthinkable a year earlier became plausible, if not fully realistic by the end of 1991.

Independent Chechnya

In December 1991 Boris Yeltsin consolidated his victory over Mikhail Gorbachev by collaborating with the leaders of Ukraine and Belarus to remove the Slavic core from the Soviet Union, triggering its disintegration into fifteen newly independent states. In Chechnya, General Dudaev took advantage of Yeltsin's distraction to consolidate his position and prepare for any future challenges to Chechen sovereignty. He gave priority to accumulating weapons and to ridding Chechen territory of Russian military forces, two interrelated goals, as it turned out.

Emerging out of the disintegrating Soviet Union, Chechnya suffered an unemployment rate of some 40 percent. Lack of work was a particularly serious problem for village dwellers.[36] Its main source of wealth—oil—saw a steady decline from peak production of 21 million tons in 1971 to a low of 4 million in 1991, with projections of further decline to 1.5–2.0 million tons by the year 2000.[37] Three-fourths of the goods produced in Chechnya, including oil products, were dependent on deliveries from Russia and other countries of the former Soviet Union.[38] In focusing on what he knew best—war—Dudaev neglected everything else that Chechnya would need to become a viable political and economic entity, including good relations with Russia.

Arming the Chechen Revolution

Dudaev achieved the task of creating an arsenal of weapons with remarkable ease. Starting with at most a couple of thousand armed fighters—his "national guard"—he managed to intimidate the already demoralized remnants of the Soviet army stationed in Grozny. By February 1992 Dudaev's armed supporters had "moved into military settlements and began to control the activity of the Russian troops." In Grozny, General P. A. Sokolov, the last commander of the 173d Training Center of the North Caucasus Military District, had frequent encounters with Shamil' Basaev, the soon-to-be infamous guerrilla leader: He "was constantly sitting in my office, a real bandit who kept asking me to give him a machine gun."[39] The Chechens soon got a lot more than that.

On May 28, 1992, after months of intimidation by Chechen fighters, Russia's new defense minister, General Pavel Grachev, formally agreed to leave to Chechnya half of the weapons that had belonged to the Soviet armed forces.[40] According to some sources, "It was actually an attempt at a dignified cover-up of the fact that almost all the weapons had been lost," many of them apparently sold to Dudaev's representatives by retreating Russian soldiers and officers.[41] In fact, at least one press report implicated General Sokolov himself in the sale of weapons.[42] Others suggest that Dudaev paid bribes to key figures in the Yeltsin administration in return for access to arms.[43] In any case, Dudaev's forces inherited a sizable arsenal: 40,000 automatic weapons and machine guns, 153 cannons and mortars, 42 tanks, 18 Grad multiple rocket launchers, 55 armored personnel carriers, several training aircraft and helicopters, and 130,000 grenades.[44]

Because Chechnya did not possess a formal army, many of the weapons were dispersed throughout the population. They ended up in the hands of rival gangs, many of them oriented more toward crime than national defense. As the criminal activity spread beyond the borders of Chechnya into other parts of Russia, the Moscow authorities became increasingly determined to crush the Dudaev regime. In some respects, this very formulation—implying that Chechen-linked crimes originated in Chechnya—is misleading, since most Chechen gangs were originally part of networks based in Moscow and dominated by Russians. As journalist David Remnick put it, "there was no more criminal city in Russia than Moscow itself (and presumably the air force would not be called out to level the Kremlin). Moscow was lousy with hit men and racketeers, millionaires who made their money out of protection scams, thugs who evicted old ladies from the apartments to 'hasten privatization.' There was a Chechen mob in Moscow, but it was one clan of many that had turned the capital into a kind of criminal bazaar."[45] Another writer, after tracing the origins of post-Soviet organized crime to Moscow and describing the mob wars there in the early 1990s, turned his attention to Chechnya: "The two conflicts were related," he argued. "The Chechen War was a gangster turf war writ large."[46] But after Dudaev came to power and Soviet Army weapons became widely dispersed, some Chechen groups sought deliberately to spread violence beyond Chechnya's borders. They helped discredit Dudaev's government and gave Russia a pretext to intervene on Chechen territory.

In fact there was no shortage of pretexts. Even though the Russian army withdrew from Chechnya in summer 1992, it soon resumed military pressure on the republic and nearly invaded in November. The division of Checheno-Ingushetiia had exacerbated conflicts between Ingush and Ossets over the Prigorodnyi district, as even Central Committee officials in Moscow had anticipated a year earlier. The conflict had already claimed hundreds of victims and had involved direct participation by the Ossetian National Guard. Ostensibly to prevent Chechen intervention in the conflict, the Russian army moved to the still undemarcated border between Chechnya and Ingushetiia. Viewing Russia's actions as a thinly disguised pretext for invasion, Chechnya mobilized its armed forces and received offers of up to 500,000 volunteers from elsewhere in the Caucasus. Moscow backed down and withdrew its troops.[47] Over the next two years, even as negotiations were conducted between the federal government and the breakaway republic, Moscow never abandoned its efforts to overthrow Dudaev's regime by force.

Negotiations, with and without Dudaev

In 1992 General Pavel Grachev, newly appointed minister of defense, put forward a proposal for resolving interethnic conflicts in the republics, one very different from the approach he adopted to deal with the Chechen crisis:

> It's necessary to meet more often. It's necessary to come, sit around the table and talk, discuss, to dig down to the root of the conflict and find a generally acceptable variant, a compromise. There's no other

Map 2-1. *Southern Russia and the Caucasus*

way. Bayonets and machine guns are not going to fix the economy or the political situation. I'm saying this—a person who has spent his whole life with weapons. It's surprising that people who consider themselves professional politicians don't understand this.[48]

President Yeltsin failed to heed Grachev's advice. According to Colonel Viktor Baranets, a former adviser to the chief of the General Staff and later head of the Defense Ministry's press service, Yeltsin visited the Caucasus at least five times in the period 1992–94. "He went swimming in the sea, went hunting, went wine-tasting, played tennis. The only thing he didn't find the time for was to sit at a table with Dudaev and come to an agreement."[49]

The professional politicians in Moscow did undertake negotiations with representatives of Dudaev's government throughout the period from 1992 and even into the war.[50] Groups of "experts" from both sides met and came close to agreement on a number of issues. It did not seem implausible that Chechnya could have worked out a modus vivendi with the federal government along the lines of what Tatarstan eventually achieved. Many idiosyncratic factors undoubtedly influenced the course of the negotiations and prevented such a hopeful outcome. The key factor, however, was General Dudaev and the Russian government's attitude toward him. Even while carrying out negotiations, the Yeltsin regime seemed to prefer a forceful solution. Whenever it could support an internal armed opposition to the Chechen president it would do so, no matter how near to resolution the ongoing negotiations appeared. Dudaev, in turn, would withdraw support from his negotiating team as he felt increasingly under threat by Moscow-supported oppositionists.

The main manifestation of Moscow's attitude toward Dudaev was a refusal to invite him to meet President Yeltsin personally. Historian John Dunlop attributes this policy primarily to Sergei Shakhrai, Yeltsin's minister of nationalities, whose own ethnic background as a Terek Cossack meant that he had "internalized that community's historic animus against the Chechens." Whatever the explanation, "the cornerstone of the Yeltsin-Shakhrai strategy for managing the Chechen crisis was to avoid all personal contact with Dudaev."[51]

Colonel Baranets placed more of the blame on Nikolai Egorov, Shakhrai's successor as minister of nationalities. "If one attentively follows the whole chain of Egorov's actions in the Chechen tragedy, one can find out without difficulty that he was one of the most powerful generators of the idea of a forceful solution to the conflict." The "change of power" that would be brought about with the violent overthrow of the Dudaev regime was "for him a vitally important principle."[52]

Ruslan Khasbulatov also deserves some responsibility for hindering efforts to arrange a face-to-face meeting between Yeltsin and Dudaev. After having helped bolster Dudaev's position during the autumn of 1991, Khasbulatov turned against him. But the former Yeltsin ally—and, as speaker of the parliament, a powerful political figure himself—had by 1992 turned against the Russian president as well. According to one analysis, Khasbulatov "regarded Chechnya as his own fiefdom and blocked attempts by others to negotiate with Dudaev." When Galina Starovoitova, the liberal Russian lawmaker, attempted to arrange for Dudaev to come to St. Petersburg to meet with Russian government officials, Khasbulatov objected. When Starovoitova next tried to phone Dudaev, who had reacted favorably to her initial proposals, she found the phone lines from the parliament building to Grozny cut, presumably with Khasbulatov's blessing.[53]

Whether one prefers to blame Khasbulatov, Shakhrai, Egorov, Grachev, or any of the other hawks on Yeltsin's team, the ultimate responsibility for the invasion of Chechnya clearly rests with the Russian president himself. As I mentioned at the outset of this chapter, Yeltsin acknowledged as much in one of his several autobiographies. He also justified his refusal to meet with Dudaev: the Chechen leader had "threatened Russia, blackmailing it with terrorist acts and explosions at military bases and nuclear plants. On principle, a person who proclaims such things should not and cannot be negotiated with."[54]

Dudaev said many provocative things, and even his supporters acknowledge that they contributed to turning Yeltsin against him.[55] Yet Dudaev also made conciliatory remarks, including ones that would suggest the basis for a peaceful resolution of the conflict. In autumn 1993, for example, he stated: "We consider at the current moment all the necessary conditions are at last in place for the renewal and successful conducting of negotiations with the government of Russia on a whole package of problems which concern our relations on the basis of principles of multilateral cooperation, friendship, and mutual help. Moreover we do not see strategically a place for the Chechen Republic outside the single economic, political and legal space which covers the current Commonwealth of Independent States."[56]

Unfortunately, Dudaev made these conciliatory remarks at an inauspicious time. In autumn 1993 Yeltsin was distracted by the conflict with his opposition, led by Khasbulatov, in the parliament (Supreme Soviet). He ultimately resolved it by deploying force, disbanding the legislature, and ordering tanks to fire upon the parliament building, known as the White House. Ironically, Dudaev's conflict with his legislative opposition followed similar lines, as each side became more intransigent and violent. One account describes "an uncanny parallel between events in Chechnya and Russia. Just as Yeltsin did, Dudaev fell out with a once-friendly Parliament and used violence to suppress his opposition."[57]

The parallel was not lost on Dudaev himself. In April 1993, when Yeltsin held a referendum to bolster his position vis-à-vis the Russian parliament, Dudaev made an extraordinary announcement on Russian radio. He promised that his government would "not obstruct citizens of Chechnya who have not lost their Russian citizenship who want to take part in the referendum on 25 April. I too am ready to cast one vote. I have not yet lost my Russian citizenship." Two weeks before the referendum, Dudaev sent Yeltsin a personal telegram advising him to choose the "lesser of two evils—the dissolution of the Supreme Soviet and the calling of elections to Parliament with the simultaneous holding of a referendum on the adoption of a new Constitution." As it turned out, "Yeltsin, knowingly or not, followed Dudaev's advice almost to the letter."[58] Dudaev's expressions of solidarity earned him few points with Yeltsin. Indeed, if Yeltsin had acknowledged Dudaev's support, it would have rendered more difficult and even hypocritical the Russian president's efforts to criticize the illegitimate and undemocratic nature of the Chechen regime. In using force against political opponents, Yeltsin was acting much the same way as Dudaev.

Despite Yeltsin's personal animus toward Dudaev, it seemed obvious to most observers that a personal meeting between the two held the only real hope for peaceful resolution of the conflict. Yet, as Baranets writes, "it was as if a secret and evil force separated Yeltsin and Dudaev every time the idea of a meeting between them was floated."[59] Another source suggests that certain Yeltsin advisers were demanding hefty bribes from Dudaev in order to set up a meeting with Yeltsin but that the Chechen president refused to hand over any more money to them.[60] Dudaev later claimed that he needed only "half an hour with Yeltsin" to resolve the conflict between Chechnya and Russia. In December 1993, Ruslan Aushev, president of Ingushetiia, tried to arrange such a meeting and was confident that Dudaev would come to Moscow to attend it. But he was thwarted by hawkish members of Yeltsin's inner circle.[61] Evidently the opponents of peaceful resolution of the crisis shared the view that a personal meeting between the two presidents might resolve it.

The hawks increasingly gained the upper hand from the late summer of 1994. Evidently Yeltsin's more moderate advisers had lost his favor following an unrelated incident in Berlin, where Yeltsin had traveled to mark the withdrawal of Russian troops from Germany. The apparently drunk Russian president attempted to conduct the German orchestra, then "grabbed a microphone and began loudly and tunelessly to sing the Russian folk song 'Kalinka.'" When several of his liberal advisers later wrote to warn Yeltsin about such behavior, he responded by cutting them out of his inner circle and leaving them home on the next foreign trip—to the United States. On the return from that trip, Yeltsin was so drunk on the planned stopover at Shannon Airport in Ireland that he failed to get out of the plane to meet the waiting Irish prime minister.[62]

Yeltsin's advisers suggest that the contingent of hawks who favored a forceful solution to the Chechen crisis deserves the blame for pushing the president in that direction. Yet even before they managed to offend Yeltsin with their criticisms of his drunken performances, the more moderate members of the president's team were ineffectual and missed several key opportunities to forestall a violent outcome. Sergei Kovalev, a human rights activist who served for a time as an adviser to the Russian government, gives an interpretation of the role of the moderates that rings true: "If he is dealing with the Chechen issue, of course [an adviser] thinks about solving it, but the main thing for him is not that problem at all. The main thing is to coincide with the opinion of the boss."[63] If Kovalev is right, then one should not be surprised that the liberal economic advisers and the professional diplomats on Yeltsin's team did little to try to settle the conflict with Chechnya peacefully.

There were several apparent missed opportunities to avoid full-scale war in Chechnya. First of all, as even many Yeltsin partisans acknowledge, Dudaev was his own worst enemy and could well have been overthrown without Russian interference. Dudaev's regime faced serious opposition in the early 1990s, which, many of Yeltsin's advisers believed, might "itself be able to deal with the 'Dudaev problem.'"[64]

Dudaev made a number of proposals for renewing economic cooperation between Russia and Chechnya as a prelude to improvement in political relations. In a letter to Yeltsin in July 1992, for example, Dudaev proposed that Moscow grant Chechnya control of its oil exports in return for Chechen payment of transit fees to the Russian government for use of its pipelines. Yeltsin ordered his staff to study the offer, which his advisers dubbed the "Buy Chechnya" proposal, but nothing came of it.[65]

In June 1993 Dudaev traveled to Vienna with his economic advisers to discuss proposals with representatives of the United Nations Industrial Development Organization (UNIDO) to lure foreign investment to Chechnya. As one participant describes, "The prospects, developed in the course of the discussions, noticeably encouraged Dudaev—to such a degree that at the dinner party organized in his honor in one of the ancient castles of the Austrian capital he astounded those present with the declaration that he was ready to consider himself a citizen of Russia." The Russian government's representative to UNIDO responded by proposing "a toast to the new eminent citizen of his country." Despite the apparent concession on Dudaev's part, nothing came of the UNIDO proposals, which apparently required endorsement from the central government in

Moscow. At that point, Dudaev seems to have abandoned any hope of economic cooperation with Yeltsin's Russia. "The dog's barking, the caravan's leaving," he explained to his economics minister Abubakarov, employing a favorite saying.[66]

Another effort at improving relations came in the autumn of 1993, when Yeltsin was facing considerable opposition from his parliament and could have used a successful breakthrough in center-regional relations. This time he was thwarted not by the hawks but by the officials of his foreign ministry, the specialists in diplomacy. On September 2 Yeltsin ordered the government to establish a program for conducting negotiations with Chechnya aimed at resolving their differences. The last line of the order read: "I propose that this should be done by the foreign ministry along with other ministries." In response, First Deputy Foreign Minister Anatolii Adamishin undermined the very basis of Yeltsin's initiative. He pointed out that "the designation of the foreign ministry of the Russian Federation as the basic coordinator of the negotiating process with Chechnya would signify that the Russian side acknowledges the republic's status as a foreign state, just what the Chechen leadership has been intensively striving for."[67] Adamishin was presumably reflecting the views of his boss, Foreign Minister Andrei Kozyrev. By his own admission, Kozyrev later supported the invasion, anticipating that it would be "quick, decisive, and limited." He promised, reliably, as it turned out, "that the international community would treat the use of force in Chechnya as a strictly domestic Russian affair."[68] In dealings with other ethnic republics, most notably Tatarstan, Yeltsin had been willing to take a flexible response—flattering the republican leadership's pretensions to independence in the interest of maintaining the integrity of the federation. With Chechnya, on the advice of his diplomatic advisers, he was unwilling to do so.

On the Chechen side as well, the officials of Dudaev's Foreign Ministry did little to promote the cause of a diplomatic solution to the conflict with Moscow. According to Taimaz Abubakarov, on both sides "negotiations were carried out not in search of compromise but as the latest demonstration of the uncompromising nature of the sides' positions. Thus, the pauses between negotiations were filled with destructive political activities that led ultimately to war." Part of the blame, Abubakarov argues, lies with the Chechen Foreign Ministry, which failed to achieve either of its two main tasks: "recognition by the international community of the republic's sovereignty or the overall guarantee of its security." He points out that none of the Chechen negotiating teams was led by foreign ministry officials. Dudaev's first foreign minister, Shamil' Beno, was disqualified, according to Abubakarov, because of his "liberal views" and resigned after five months in office. Beno's successor, Shamsudin Iusef, was more straightforwardly unqualified: "He knew little of Russia, and, most importantly, didn't want to know." In Abubakarov's view, Iusef deliberately tried to poison relations with the Russian government. At one point in February 1993 while a Chechen delegation was negotiating in Moscow, Iusef sent a telegram to the Russian leaders disavowing its positions.[69]

Dudaev himself would have been far from an ideal negotiating partner, even if things had gotten that far. When he suspended the Chechen parliament's activities in April 1993 and imposed direct presidential rule, he conveyed the image of standard-variety military dictator. To be sure, he would not have been the first dictator—within the former Soviet territories or outside—with whom Boris Yeltsin had dealt. But the undemocratic nature of Dudaev's regime gave Yeltsin an easy excuse not to deal with it, even if Yeltsin was soon mimicking much of Dudaev's behavior vis-à-vis his own parliament. To make matters worse, Dudaev apparently lacked an important attribute of genuine dictators—the ability to impose his preferred policies. As Abubakarov described, "It wasn't hard to notice that however authoritarian [Dudaev's] power seemed, it appeared so only in its formal features. One got the impression that presidential rule had force only within the boundaries of the famous Presidential Palace in the center of Grozny. Beyond the garish external attributes hid an unauthoritarian, not to say purely nominal, power." As a negotiator, Dudaev had poor democratic credentials, which made it difficult for him to function as a genuine representative of the views of his republic's citizens. Nor, as an ineffective dictator, could he credibly commit to enforcing agreements that might be unpopular. Indeed, according to Abubakarov, ordinary people "blamed him not for his dictatorship at all but for his inability to construct an iron order."[70] His account accords with sociologist Georgi Derluguian's description of Chechnya under Dudaev as "a working anarchy ruled by an unsuccessful dictatorship."[71]

In May 1994, after two years of fruitless negotiations with the Chechen government, Yeltsin's regime made a surprising about-face. It indicated to the press that it had erred in trying to isolate Dudaev. Yeltsin's press secretary Viacheslav Kostikov suggested that Moscow was now "inclined to recognize Dudaev as the legal president of Chechnya and to conduct negotiations precisely with him."[72] Two days later, Sergei Filatov, Yeltsin's chief of administration, reported that Shakhrai would be removed from his position as minister of nationalities "in part because of the need to improve relations with Chechnya."[73]

On May 27, 1994, five days after the remarkable announcements by Kostikov and Filatov, Dudaev was nearly assassinated. A sophisticated remote-control car bomb had exploded, killing Dudaev's interior minister and deputy, both of whom were traveling in the same cortege with the Chechen president. Following the failed assassination attempt, the Yeltsin administration lost interest in a face-to-face meeting with Dudaev. Dunlop suspects, reasonably, that the press campaign associated with Shakhrai's removal was part of a ploy to lull Dudaev into letting down his guard. In fact, "Shakhrai reemerged from the shadows and, once again, de facto took over supervision of Russian nationality and regional affairs (although Nikolai Egorov, a militant Cossack from a Cossack village in Krasnodar krai, southern Russia, remained as titular minister of nationality affairs)."[74]

Was there any real interest on Yeltsin's part in negotiating seriously with Dudaev, or were Kostikov and Filatov just contributing to a ruse intended to make Dudaev let down his guard? Kostikov, unfortunately, missed an opportunity to set the record straight. In the year 2001 he and eight other former advisers to Yeltsin published a large tome on the "Yeltsin epoch." Yet in more than 800 pages, including seven chapters devoted to the war and its aftermath, they found no opportunity to address this event or even the general question of whether the Yeltsin administration's search for a negotiated solution was ever sincere.[75]

As Yeltsin stressed in his memoirs, Dudaev certainly said many provocative things. Moreover, in making weapons widely available in what was already a traditionally martial culture, the Chechen leader also bears some responsibility for the criminal violence that accompanied mobilization for national defense. Most threatening to the Russian government and citizenry were acts committed outside Chechnya. Hijackings and kidnappings in the regions bordering the country caused particular alarm, especially an incident in late July 1994, when four hijackers seized a bus near the resort town of Mineral'nye Vody (see map 2-1).[76] For Anatol Lieven, author of a major book on the Chechen War, these hijackings "were of critical importance in acting as the catalyst for new Russian moves against Dudaev." He offers two possible explanations for the hijackings: "They may have been a symptom of Dudaev's inability to control Chechen criminality, or they may have been deliberately planned by Russian agents to provide an excuse for intervention." "No verdict on this question is possible," he avers, "but still, these events absolutely have to be mentioned and discussed in any book about the origins of the war."[77] In Lieven's own book, he writes that "the timing of the Russian administration's decision to turn against Dudaev was a direct result of the last [July 1994] hijacking."[78]

To what extent should the hijackings be considered a catalyst? Or does it make more sense to consider them a pretext? The Russian authorities were clearly ready to take advantage of the hijacking to demonize Dudaev's government. As one account describes, "The official media began a propaganda blitz on the evils of the Chechen regime. A police official showed a photograph of the three severed heads of [Chechen gangster Ruslan] Labazonov's gang exhibited in the Grozny square in June—except that he said they were the heads of Russian police officers." Lieven points out that Dudaev's government cooperated in helping arrest the perpetrators of the first three hijackings. In the July 1994 incident, however, the Chechen president "refused to let either the hijackers or the Russian special forces into Chechnya, fearing with some reason that Russia would use this as an excuse to occupy part at least of Chechnya."[79]

Yelstin sought to allay such fears in August 1994, when he stated that "armed intervention is impermissible and must not be done." But he suggested that the internal opposition to Dudaev was growing and that it reflected Moscow's influence.[80]

Moscow had indeed decided to intervene actively on the side of Dudaev's opponents—and, at first, with considerable success. On November 26, 1994, the opposition forces seized control of Grozny, but they were soon routed by troops loyal to Dudaev. Among those taken prisoner were some seventy Russians, including army officers and soldiers. On November 28 Dudaev threatened to execute them if Moscow refused to acknowledge its participation on the side of the opposition. The next day Yeltsin issued an ultimatum for all the Chechen forces to cease fire, lay down their weapons, disband their units, and release all prisoners. According to his advisers, Yeltsin did not expect his terms to be met: "Inside he had already decided on a forceful, military solution."[81]

Yeltsin convened his Security Council on November 29 to discuss the Chechen crisis. The council, an advisory body to the president, was made up of the leading officials of the Russian government, including the prime minister, foreign, defense, interior, and justice ministers, parliamentary leaders, heads of intelligence agencies, and others.[82] The secret meeting was convened not to debate possible options but rather to endorse a decision Yeltsin had already made. As Iurii Kalmykov, then justice minister, reported, "When the official Security Council session was held, all the documents had already been prepared, and the Security Council members only had to vote—either to adopt or reject the 'force option.' This very much surprised me. I said let's discuss things first, I want to speak. But I was told that we would vote first. I again tried to put forward my view. The president said again, let's vote on it. I had to agree. . . . And I voted in favor. So did everyone. And then we started discussing it."[83] Besides Kalmykov only two other officials voiced objections to the invasion: intelligence chief Evgenii Primakov and Vladimir Shumeiko, chair of the Federation Council that represented Russia's regions. The rest, including Prime Minister Viktor Chernomyrdin and Foreign Minister Andrei Kozyrev, supported military action—assured by the "power ministers" that the invasion would be quick and effective. Kalmykov resigned in protest, one of the few civilian officials to do so. Formally, Yeltsin took the decision for war on November 30, 1994, when he issued secret decree no. 2137s, sanctioning the use of direct military force.[84]

During the next two weeks, as Russian forces from the Interior and Defense Ministries deployed along the border with Chechnya, Yeltsin authorized a series of negotiations with Dudaev's government but continued to refuse to meet directly with Dudaev himself. He designated Pavel Grachev, the hard-line Russian defense minister, as his main representative—an inauspicious choice for a peaceful compromise. Grachev announced in advance that "negotiations with the Chechen leader will take place only on condition that Dudaev appears at them in his capacity as representative of a subject of the Russian Federation." Although Dudaev made no such concession, the two did meet, as Grachev later reported on Russian television. The defense minister addressed the Chechen leader insultingly and threatened, "Dzhokhar, this is your last chance. . . . Do you really think you're going to fight against us? In any case, I'll crush you [ia tebia razob'iu]." Dudaev refused to back down. "Then it's war," vowed Grachev. "Yes, war!" agreed Dudaev.[85] Grachev, who had initially argued against an invasion at a Security Council meeting on December 7, now reversed position, caught up in the logic of his own ultimatum.[86]

One more Russian general met with Dudaev two days before the Russian army launched its invasion: General Aleksei Mitiukhin, commander of the North Caucasus military district, which formally included Chechnya. Mitiukhin's mission was to secure the release of six Russian soldiers captured by the Chechens in the failed "storm" of Grozny on November 26. Dudaev readily agreed, without any expectation that his gesture would forestall the war. "It's already late," he explained. If the Chechen leader made the concessions necessary to conciliate Russia, "the people won't understand."

Mitiukhin reported Dudaev's frustration in being unable to meet Yeltsin to work out their differences, echoing what many other participants had described. Dudaev complained that "he waited a long time to be invited to the Kremlin like a normal person [*po-liudski*]." "As late as the 29th or 30th [of November 1994], if they had only spoken with me as a human being [*po-chelovecheski*], everything could have been completely different. But all I heard was 'bandit, criminal, dictator, thief, leader of a criminal regime!' That didn't offend just me, but my entire people."[87]

In the next few days, the Chechen side made a number of initiatives intended to forestall an attack. Talks between Russian officials and Aslan Maskhadov, then chief of the Chechen general staff, led to the release of the Russian prisoners of war. At the last moment, on December 10, Chechen propaganda minister Movladi Udugov communicated that Dudaev would accept an official invitation, if it were made, to come to Moscow for negotiations. That same day, Yeltsin celebrated a national holiday, Constitution Day, at the Kremlin. On the official list of well-wishers was the name Dzhokhar Dudaev, president of the Chechen Republic. According to protocol, Dudaev, in turn, would have received a pro forma thank-you message from Yeltsin, were it not for the air and land blockade Russia had imposed in anticipation of the invasion. As his aides put it in their memoir, on the eve of the Russian attack, "Yeltsin's compliments would have gone out to the mutinous general, if a bewildered communications officer hadn't come in to a group of speechwriters and asked how to get a letter to Grozny."[88]

The War

The path to war was cleared by Yeltsin's hawkish advisers, who presented one-sided views of the Chechen conflict, and by the diffidence and ambivalence of the more moderate members of his team, who refused to take a stand in favor of a peaceful resolution. Once the invasion began, however, a number of the skeptics began to voice their reservations, at least among themselves.

Hawks Ascendant

On December 27, 1994, the Expert-Analytical Council of the President of the Russian Federation ("Analytical Center") met to discuss the political consequences of the Chechen invasion. Their discussion was tape-recorded by the presidential security services, headed by Yeltsin's personal bodyguard Aleksandr Korzhakov. Korzhakov sent Yeltsin a summary of the discussion, which the president's advisers later published.

Korzhakov was keen to present the Analytical Center's members as disloyal to the president, but their criticisms seem well founded, especially in retrospect. General Dmitrii Volkogonov expressed concern that the conflict would spread into other regions and advocated an immediate meeting between Yeltsin and Dudaev. Emil' Pain claimed that the Russian invasion of Chechnya had "saved Dudaev politically" when his power was "hanging by a thread." Mark Urnov worried that the situation in Chechnya was deepening the political crisis in Russia and damaging the president politically. Leonid Smirniagin argued that the entry of troops into Chechnya would only be justified if they could carry out a successful blitzkrieg. But he thought that the violent overthrow of Dudaev by Russian forces would be "a disgrace for Russia," and he favored new attempts at negotiation.[89]

Thus, by Korzhakov's report—which Yeltsin's liberal advisers reproduce in their memoir without questioning its authenticity—members of the Analytical Center expressed many doubts about the invasion and about the administration's overall policy toward Chechnya. Korzhakov summarizes their views, suggesting that the president's advisers "by no means share his political views in relationship to the Chechen problem and are not inclined to show solidarity with him in resolving this question by the methods that are now being used [armed invasion]. On the contrary, their point of view is closer to that of the parliamentary, and even non-parliamentary opposition." Korzhakov points out that except for Oleg Lobov (secretary of the Security Council) and Sergei Filatov (chief of the president's administration), "all the rest of the speakers had practically nothing to say about the violation of human rights by Dudaev's armed detachments, about the criminalization of the republic, the arms trade and the narcotics business, both flourishing in Chechnya, or even about how Chechnya is an integral part of the Russian Federation to which all federal laws and presidential decrees extend." Korzhakov concludes his memo with the veiled recommendation that all the doubters be fired ("It is necessary to resolve the question of strengthening the leadership cadres of the President's Analytical Center and its reorganization").[90]

The incident of the advisers' meeting is one of the best-documented cases of the hawks attempting to discredit the more moderate elements of Yeltsin's retinue. But Yeltsin himself was well aware at the time, and has acknowledged since, that the president's bodyguard (and drinking buddy) routinely prevented Yeltsin from receiving advice and information from the more liberal members of his team. As he (or, rather, his ghostwriter) put it, Korzhakov "was jealous of these 'rotten intellectuals' [and] tried to vigilantly block their 'access to the body,'" that is, to prevent them from meeting personally with Yeltsin.[91] Instead, those advisers had to put their views in writing, as Georgii Satarov did in late December 1994, with a lengthy letter expressing his doubts about Yeltsin's Chechen policy and the pernicious effect of hawks such as Egorov. But Satarov never sent his letter, so his heartfelt criticisms are only of historical interest—as evidence of the ineffectiveness and indecisiveness of the opponents of the "party of war." If, as his memoirs attest, Yeltsin was aware that he was not receiving the full range of possible views, because of Korzhakov's own prejudices, he bears ultimate responsibility for the poor decisions that resulted.

There is some evidence that Yeltsin's liberal advisers presented their behavior as more principled in retrospect than it actually was at the time. Nikolai Petrov, a geographer and political analyst who worked on the staff of the Analytic Center, remembers a more opportunistic approach: "There are no doubts that Baturin-Satarov-Pain-Urnov-Smirniagin et al. didn't participate in the real decision-making. Nevertheless they played a very negative role." He accuses them of supporting Yeltsin's confrontational approach by "doing the work of the propaganda department of the CPSU Central Committee and not doing any real analytical work."[92]

One gets a sense of the propagandistic nature of the moderates' work even from the memoir that, presumably, puts their contribution to the Yeltsin administration in its best light (why else would Satarov reproduce verbatim a 1,200-word letter that he never sent?). The authors of the memoir constantly refer to the most sensational of the charges against Dudaev. They quote, for example, his remarks reportedly made to a Turkish journalist during the war that Russia was attacking Chechnya with atomic bombs, and that he personally would fly a bomber to Moscow to retaliate; they quote his threats to kill Russian prisoners of war captured as they sought unsuccessfully to support the violent uprising of Dudaev's opponents in November 1994 (he released them instead); they present as incriminating evidence that Dudaev's defense plans, prepared in March 1992, identified the Russian armed forces as the "potential opponent" and insinuated that Chechnya intended to attack strategic targets in Russia. Finally, they charge that "Islamic fundamentalists, criminal groups, and terrorist centers" were all in the service of Dudaev's government.[93]

No one claims that in Dudaev Chechnya was blessed with the most sober and reasonable leader possible. Even his closest collaborators have attested to the Chechen president's suspicious nature, bordering at times on paranoia.[94] Yet Dudaev was the proverbial paranoid with real enemies. Nor does anyone doubt that Chechnya received support from foreign governments and Islamic groups sympathetic to its plight. Yet, in their memoir, Yeltsin's moderates fail to make an important distinction that comes through clearly, for example, even in the reporting of the Russian defense ministry's former press chief. Writing of support from Islamic countries, Baranets points out that it was not a cause but a consequence of Russia's attack: "Having begun the war in December 1994 against a single Chechnya, already by winter 1995 Russia was fighting against a coalition of Muslim countries." Baranets compares militant Islam to "a tiger in a Moscow zoo, obediently dozing in the iron cage of Soviet power." It was "released into Chechnya, set free and enraged by Moscow" when Yeltsin unleashed the war.[95]

The point is not that Yeltsin's liberal advisers presented outright falsehoods about Dudaev's regime. Instead, they appeared to be trying to justify their inaction and ineffectiveness in preventing Yeltsin from pursuing a course that they genuinely seem to believe was mistaken. But they tended to highlight irrelevant factors. Dudaev might have been as much the dangerous nut case they portray, yet the best solution—and they knew it at least in retrospect—was not an ill-conceived and unprepared use of armed force. Their focus on Dudaev's faults obscures the basic fact that Yeltsin's advisers did not choose to pay enough attention to the situation in Chechnya so as to be able to give the president good advice. As Petrov recalls, "I can remember Mark Urnov, at that time head of the Analytical Center, looking for a map of Chechnya several days after the war had been started, or Emil' Pain asking me about the ethnic composition of Chechnya by *raions* [districts] at the same time. For a short while I was making analyses of the reaction to the war in regions of Russia for the Center's daily reports for Yeltsin, all the time this section [of the report] was severely edited by the Center leadership in order to make the picture more positive."[96]

Not only did Yeltsin's "experts" allow themselves to remain ignorant of the situation in Chechnya. In some cases they deliberately hindered the dissemination of accurate information and analysis. In December 1994, for example, Leonid Smirniagin, Petrov's boss in the branch of the Analytic Center that focused on the regions, refused to allow publication of a critical analysis of Moscow's approach to Chechnya, drafted under Petrov's editorship. It was soon leaked to the Russian press, which published extensive excerpts.[97] This example is only one of many that reinforce Kovalev's judgment about Yeltsin's advisers: "Intelligent from one side and cynical from the other, they were used by the regime, and they themselves were eager to be used."[98] Petrov, an evident exception to this rule, resigned his position on the first working day of the new year, January 5, 1995, and was thereafter treated by many of his former colleagues as a traitor—even barred by guards from retrieving his personal effects from his office.

Military Misgivings

The failure of the liberals is especially striking given that their views on the Chechen situation were not particularly radical. If Yeltsin's administration was dominated by hawks, within the uniformed military there were a number of, if not doves, then critics who were highly skeptical about the idea of using military force in Chechnya. In fact, a cautious and sensible approach seems to have been fairly widespread at the Defense Ministry and in the General Staff. Yet the decisionmaking process there resembled that of the Kremlin, as proponents of war systematically excluded skeptics. Colonel Viktor Baranets reports that several of Grachev's deputy ministers of defense—Generals Boris Gromov, Valerii Mironov, and Georgii Kondrat'ev—were not invited to key meetings to plan the military operations because they were expected to object. "In the General Staff it was hardly a secret for anyone that Gromov, for example, from the beginning was categorically against any forceful solution to the Chechen problem."[99]

Serious doubts emerged within the General Staff about the wisdom of the invasion, first, and, more specifically, about the adequacy of planning if an invasion were nevertheless decided. Gromov in retrospect criticized Grachev for agreeing to have the army participate at all in military action in Chechnya. Moreover, he faulted Grachev for his unrealistic predictions of a successful completion of operations in a couple of weeks. If forced to accept the mission of invading Chechnya, Gromov suggested that Grachev should have responded by demanding more time. "He should have said: deeply respected supreme commander-in-chief, a minimum of six months is required for preparation."[100] Delaying the invasion to provide more time to prepare would also have avoided launching the attack in December— "the worst time for the beginning of an operation: practically constant cloud cover leaves no possibility for effective use of aviation."[101] But the invasion was not delayed in order to provide more time for preparation. It was already late November when the main operations division of the General Staff first began to study maps of invasion routes into Chechnya. General Mitiukhin, commander of the North Caucasus military district, was given only two weeks' notice that a major operation would be staged from his bases.[102]

What kind of evidence did Yeltsin receive about the likely duration of a war against Chechnya? Oleg Lobov, secretary of Yeltsin's Security Council, anticipated a brief one. Indeed, in November 1994 he reportedly advocated a "short, victorious war to raise the President's ratings" in the face of Yeltsin's flagging popularity. He had in mind the U.S. operation against

Haiti in September to overthrow the military regime there and its apparent effect in boosting President Bill Clinton's approval rate.[103] Defense minister Grachev's best-known claim was that a single Russian airborne regiment could have resolved the Chechen crisis in two hours. In private discussions with Yeltsin and his advisers, Grachev exhibited less bravado, but his estimate was still unrealistic: he promised that the operation would succeed within twelve days.[104]

Military opposition to the invasion from Grachev's subordinates was not long in coming. Colonel General Eduard Vorob'ev refused Grachev's order to lead what he considered an ill-prepared invasion. As he told David Remnick, "I am no pacifist. Had the preparations for war been adequate, I would have executed those plans without thinking twice." But he did think twice. "I began to think through the errors: our underestimation of the Chechen passion; the lack of military surprise; the dependency on air power in bad weather; the dependency on a phony opposition movement; the utter lack of preparation. My God, our tank troops went into battle without maps of the city!" Some tanks and armored personnel carriers entered Grozny without functioning guns. Attacked by snipers, they became instant burning coffins. On December 22, Vorob'ev refused the defense minister's order to lead such an ill-prepared invasion and submitted his resignation.[105]

He was not the only one. As Lieven reports, "In all, some 557 officers of all ranks are believed to have been disciplined, sacked or to have left the army voluntarily in protest against the intervention."[106] Initially the protests focused on the poor preparation. A week into the invasion, for example, the General Staff for the first time requested that the Defense Ministry's Institute of Military History provide information on earlier Russian campaigns in the Caucasus.[107]

Within days of the invasion another source of protest appeared. Russian troops sent into Chechnya met widespread resistance from ordinary, unarmed civilians. Many officers responded by questioning their orders. One captain, a medical doctor, complained to journalists: "We are not doing anything good by being here." Since "we are fighting civilians, it would be better if we left." He added that "almost all the officers think the way I do."[108] Indeed, Major General Ivan Babichev reacted much the same way when the tank column he was commanding came face to face with a crowd of angry civilians. "We are not going to shoot. We're not going to use tanks against the people. . . . If they give us such an order I would treat it as a criminal order. The military must execute only legitimate orders and the order to crush villages with tanks is not a legitimate order."[109]

Finally, officers and soldiers resented the fact that they were sent into a war that probably could have been avoided. At least they saw no evidence that Yeltsin had tried to avoid it. Colonel Baranets reports several conversations on this theme. He quotes one captain he met in Grozny: "You know, he says, what I thought most about when our tanks and armored personnel carriers were moving into Chechnya? About why our president couldn't, or for some reasons didn't want to, negotiate with Dudaev so that there wouldn't be a war." A paratrooper told him "if I had seen Yeltsin getting blisters on his tongue from trying to talk peace with Dudaev, I wouldn't be fighting with one eye looking over my shoulder."[110]

The War of Deceit

The soldiers' distrust of Yeltsin was widely shared by most citizens of Russia. Rather than boost Yeltsin's popularity as Lobov promised, the invasion saw confidence in the president plummet—and for good reason. Yeltsin lied about the war from start to finish, and his lies were often quite transparent. On the evening of December 27, 1994, he gave a televised address in which he claimed that "the Gordian knot of the Chechen crisis can be cut. But at too high a price—the price of the life of Russian citizens. For the sake of preserving people's lives I have given an order to exclude any bombing strikes that could lead to victims among the peaceful population of Grozny."[111]

Yeltsin was lying. The day before he had received a report from Sergei Kovalev, his human-rights adviser who had led a delegation of parliamentarians to Grozny. The bombs were already raining down on the Chechen capital when Kovalev wrote to Yeltsin, addressing him in the third person: "Why was the President quiet for three years" about the situation in Chechnya "and then sent bombers?" He urged that Yeltsin find out and reveal who took the decision to bomb population centers and "take measures so that the peaceful population is not destroyed." After all, Kovalev reminded Yeltsin, it was the president himself who had said "the right to life is a basic right."[112] As Yeltsin spoke to the television cameras, Kovalev and his team had already counted forty-two bodies—victims of air attack—in the city center. Moreover the bombs had destroyed the electricity and water systems, leading indirectly to further civilian deaths.[113]

After promising not to bomb the peaceful population of Grozny, Yeltsin concluded his speech by claiming that "the path to political resolution of the conflict, as previously, is open." And, as previously, he named three of his most obstinate, hawkish officials—Egorov, Stepashin, and Kvashnin—as his representatives.[114]

Bloody Endgame

In some respects Russia could have won the war in Chechnya. Its armed forces destroyed Grozny and gained nominal control of all the other major population centers. The Chechen troops were forced to retreat to the mountains and conduct a guerrilla campaign. If Moscow had used economic aid to win over the civilian population, it might have employed police methods to deal with the remaining rebel forces. Instead the Russian forces treated the residents of Chechnya, including thousands of ethnic Russians who lived in Grozny, indiscriminately as enemies. The occupying Russian army—with drunken and drugged soldiers robbing, harassing, and otherwise maltreating Chechen civilians—did little to try to win over hearts and minds.

The Chechen resistance forces turned the tide of the war and ultimately put an end to the Russian occupation by becoming what Moscow had always branded them: terrorists. Two events stand out as major turning points. In June 1995, Shamil' Basaev led a raid on the Russian town of Budennovsk (see map 2-1, p. 23). He justified the action as a response to the Russian army's massacre at the village of Samashki two months earlier.[115] Basaev's forces apparently intended originally to attack a military target of some sort, but when that mission failed they seized a hospital and took more than a thousand hostages. After several days of fruitless negotiations, during which Basaev demanded safe passage for his troops, the Russian forces unsuccessfully tried to storm the hospital as medical workers begged them to hold their fire. More than a hundred Russian civilians died.

With Boris Yeltsin at a summit meeting in Halifax, Nova Scotia, Prime Minister Viktor Chernomyrdin handled the situation from Moscow. He asked Sergei Kovalev to meet with Basaev and work out an agreement. Basaev demanded an immediate cease-fire in Chechnya and the opening of peace talks. Meanwhile Yeltsin in Halifax criticized the "barbaric" Chechen action and claimed that "the world community has finally understood whom the federal forces are fighting." The "criminals in black headbands" had to be "annihilated," he vowed. Instead Chernomyrdin, filmed on television negotiating by phone with Basaev, worked out a deal for the Chechens to escape across the border to Chechnya and release the hostages there. The Budennovsk events have been called "a pivotal episode of the war. Facing defeat, the Chechens had launched a ruthless raid that appeared suicidal both for themselves and their cause. Yet they emerged not only relatively unscathed but in a stronger position than before. They had won a much-needed ceasefire and forced Russia to be serious about peace talks."[116]

In January 1996 another prominent Chechen field commander led a raid on Kizliar, an old Russian fortress town on the Terek River in Dagestan. Salman Raduev's original target was apparently the Russian helicopter base outside town, but when his forces met unexpectedly strong resistance from the Russian side, they retreated into town. There they carried out a repeat of the Budennovsk action by capturing the town hospital. Raduev's troops went around town seizing additional hostages until they held some 2,000 or 3,000 of them. Russian forces quickly attacked the hospital but stopped when the Chechens began to execute the hostages. Local Dagestani officials then negotiated safe passage for the terrorists, on the Budennovsk model, but Russian forces reneged on the deal and attacked the Chechen convoy at the village of Pervomaiskoe, just as it was about to cross a bridge into Chechnya. The Chechens attacked a local police post and then retreated into the village with their hostages.

President Yeltsin responded to the new hostage crisis by flying to Paris to attend the funeral of French president François Mitterrand. He vowed to punish the "bandits," without harming the hostages and claimed that "we have thirty-eight snipers posted around the village to catch the terrorists." Meanwhile another armed group—Turkish citizens of Abkhaz and Chechen origin—hijacked a passenger ferry in Turkey's Black Sea port of Trabzon, demanding that the Russian army free their "Chechen brethren" in Pervomaiskoe (see map 2-1). Instead the Russian troops bombed the village with Grad rockets. Many of Raduev's troops managed to escape, taking eighty hostages with them. They were later released to Dagestani authorities at a press conference that highlighted the humiliating failure of the Russian special forces. The Russian attack had left, by official count, sixty-nine dead, including twenty-eight civilians.[117] With its army in shambles and its citizens thoroughly demoralized, the Russian government finally began to take seriously the need to end the war.

Several additional factors contributed to the Russian decision to pursue peace. In April 1996 the Russian army assassinated Dzhokhar Dudaev. The Chechen president was talking by satellite phone to Konstantin Borovoi, a Russian member of parliament who was trying to arrange negotiations between Dudaev and Tatarstan's president Mintimir Shaimiev, as a first step toward direct negotiations with Yeltsin or Chernomyrdin. Nearby Russian forces used the satellite signal to target Dudaev with a guided missile that killed the Chechen president and two of his aides.[118]

The assassination of Dudaev removed an unpredictable and unreliable negotiating partner. He was succeeded by his "acting" vice president Zelimkhan Iandarbiev and by Aslan Maskhadov as commander of the armed forces. With competent Chechen leaders in place, there still remained an unpredictable and unreliable negotiating partner on the Russian side, namely, Boris Yeltsin. But the Russian president was motivated to change—at least in appearances. Popular opposition to the war was widespread. The Committee of Soldiers' Mothers was especially active, supporting efforts of parents to travel to Chechnya and rescue their sons from the army or at least find out how they died and recover their bodies. Founded originally during the years of *perestroika,* to promote military reform and an end to the brutal practice of hazing (*dedovshchina*) conscripts, the committee, with branches throughout the country, kept the war's human costs in the public eye.[119]

The presidential election campaign also played an important role, as Yeltsin openly acknowledged that he could not be reelected if he did not make a convincing effort to end the war. Particularly important was the influence of retired General Aleksandr Lebed'. First as a presidential candidate who openly criticized the war, Lebed' threatened to draw enough votes from Yeltsin to throw the election to his communist rival, Gennadii Ziuganov. Then, after having been co-opted by the Yeltsin team, Lebed' served as the broker who negotiated the final peace agreement and withdrawal of Russian forces.[120]

The endgame of the first Chechen War was as complicated and violent as the beginning. First of all, the Yeltsin government remained reluctant to negotiate with representatives of the Chechen government, even after Dudaev's death. In October 1995 Moscow had installed, of all people, Doku Zavgaev—the former first party secretary from Soviet times—as puppet head of the Chechen Republic, staging his bogus election to the presidency in Russian-controlled zones of Chechnya in December of that year.[121] Following Dudaev's death, V. A. Kovalev, the Russian minister of justice who took over after Iurii Kalmykov's resignation, insisted that there was no longer any doubt as to the legitimacy of Zavgaev as Chechnya's leader. Few in Chechnya took that claim seriously. Moscow eventually recognized the futility of its position; in May 1997 Zavgaev was appointed Russian ambassador to Tanzania.[122]

Once Russian officials acknowledged the necessity of negotiating with Dudaev's successors, they carried out the negotiations with the same cynicism and bad faith as they had exhibited throughout the crisis. Yeltsin's handlers sought to portray the president as genuinely interested in restoring peace and withdrawing Russian troops, even as the army sought to impose its violent solution to the Chechen problem up to the last minute. They were particularly worried that the war would undermine Yeltsin's reelection campaign. On May 23, 1996, with less than a month to go before the election, Yeltsin expressed a willingness to meet with Iandarbiev. The announcement came from Tim Guldimann, the Swiss diplomat who headed the Grozny mission of the Organization for Security and Cooperation in Europe (OSCE). The Chechen delegation arrived in Moscow a few days later and met with Yeltsin on May 27. The next morning, as his negotiators continued meeting with the visiting Chechen officials, Yeltsin took a surprise trip to Chechnya. He met at an airport with Russian troops and congratulated them on their "victory" in the Chechen War.[123]

This publicity stunt was followed by a resumption of Russian ground and air attacks, despite the cease-fire signed with Iandarbiev. Nevertheless, further negotiations yielded a tightly sequenced and promising proposal for Russian withdrawal and Chechen disarmament: Russia would reliquish its military posts along Chechen roads (*blok-posty*) by July 7, at which point the Chechen side would begin disarming its fighters, completing the process by August 7. The Russian army would then begin its withdrawal from Chechnya and be out of the country by the end of the month.[124]

With the promise of peace in the air, and the threat of a communist presidential victory as a further incentive, Russian voters gave Yeltsin a first-place finish in the June 16 elections, but far from the majority necessary to avoid a runoff. At that point, Yeltsin invited the third-place challenger, retired General Aleksandr Lebed', to join his administration as the president's national security adviser and secretary of the Security Council, an offer made and accepted with such alacrity that few doubted it had been negotiated in advance. On June 25 Yeltsin announced that troops from the Leningrad, Moscow, Volga, and Urals military districts—key electoral constituencies—would be brought home from Chechnya by September 1. The following week he was reelected in the second round.

His reelection secured, Yeltsin immediately reneged on the agreements he had made to stop the war. On July 7, the deadline for dismantling the Russian *blok-posty*, Moscow announced that it would not carry out its commitment. On July 9 and 10 Russian forces blockaded and attacked the mountain villages of Gekhi and Makhkety. They were hoping to destroy the headquarters of Iandarbiev and catch the Chechen officials who were meeting in Makhkety. Many civilians were killed, including some children hiding in a cellar, but every Chechen leader escaped unharmed. The next day a bomb exploded in a Moscow subway station, killing four people and hospitalizing another dozen. A month later two more bombs went off on Moscow trolleys, wounding over thirty people between them. Moscow mayor Iurii Luzhkov blamed Chechens and ordered his police officials to take "retaliatory actions" against the city's Chechen diaspora.[125] Some observers have argued that Russian secret service operatives, acting on behalf of the "party of war," deliberately set off the explosions to thwart the peace process.[126] On July 29, after a full resumption of Russian military activity, an unsuccessful attempt was made to kill Aslan Maskhadov. Moscow and its puppet Zavgaev blamed Maskhadov's domestic enemies, but the pattern since Yeltsin's reelection seemed unmistakable: renewal of full-scale war, accompanied by efforts to liquidate the top Chechen leaders.

Throughout these events General Lebed' found himself in an unusual position. On the one hand, his efforts at negotiating an end to the war seemed rather futile in the face of renewed Russian military operations. Indeed, one of the general's envoys was nearly killed while meeting with Maskhadov when the Russians attacked Makhkety. On the other hand, the army's apparent successes might have helped Lebed' in his talks with the Chechens by strengthening his bargaining position. Some observers have argued that Lebed' himself initially supported the attacks on Makhkety and Gekhi, with hopes of achieving a "blitzkrieg victory." Only when they failed did he opt for a "blitzkrieg defeat," accepting a humiliating peace agreement and total withdrawal of the Russian forces.[127]

In any case, the Russian army's position was not as strong as it appeared. On August 6, 1996, some 1,500 Chechen fighters, led by Maskhadov, stormed Grozny and pinned down the nearly 12,000 Russian troops supposedly defending it. The Russian command reacted with typical brutality and deceit. On August 20 General Konstantin Pulikovskii, commander of the Russian forces, issued an ultimatum: all Chechen fighters must leave Grozny or he would order an air and missile attack on their positions. The general gave the civilian population forty-eight hours to leave the city but waited barely a day before launching a devastating attack. As for negotiations, Pulikovskii announced that "there was no longer anything to talk about" with Maskhadov. Pulikovskii's optimism was misplaced. The August assault cost the Russian army some 494 dead, 1,407 wounded, and 182 missing in action. Estimates of civilian deaths were around 2,000, and more than 220,000 refugees fled the carnage.[128]

Yeltsin finally faced reality and gave Lebed' authority to negotiate the Russian withdrawal. On August 31 Lebed', Maskhadov, and their associates, in the presence of the OSCE's Guldimann, signed an agreement on "principles for the determination of the basis of relations between the Russian Federation and the Chechen Republic." It became known as the Khasaviurt Accord, after the town where it was negotiated. The document formally left the status of Chechnya's relationship to Russia undecided until December 31, 2001, and, therefore, subject to further negotiations.[129]

The origins of Russia's 1994–96 war in Chechnya defy easy summary. Undoubtedly most of the factors that previous studies have identified played some role: the legacy of Soviet ethnically defined political institutions; Chechnya's historical grievances amplified by power-hungry politicians; the strategic location of Chechnya, astride major oil and transportation routes; and Moscow's concern that Chechnya's successful bid for independence would lead to the breakup of the Russian Federation. This last factor I find relatively less persuasive. The Yeltsin administration had dealt with similar bids for autonomy from strategically more important regions, such as Tatarstan and Bashkortostan, and had worked out a modus vivendi by negotiation and conciliation, as I describe in chapter 5. Yeltsin would not have found in Chechen president Dzhokhar Dudaev as reasonable a negotiating partner as he found in other regions. But Yeltsin deliberately chose not to deal with Dudaev as someone deserving of any respect. He seemed determined to settle the Chechen situation by force rather than by making concessions. Yeltsin's advisers pushed for a "short, victorious war" to boost the president's sagging popularity, and those who had doubts kept silent or were forced out. The first Chechen War had many contributing causes, but a more responsible and competent leadership in Moscow could have prevented it.

3

No War, No Peace

Undoubtedly, we [that is, Russian leaders] are guilty for the fact that the war began, we destroyed Chechen homes. We need to rebuild them, we need to feed people. Let's at least set right what we're responsible for. We need to get rid of the illusion that hungry young people, having gone through a war, will just sit quietly.

—Magomedsalikh Gusaev, Dagestan's minister of nationality affairs and external relations, May 1998

Between the withdrawal of Russian forces in late 1996 and the outbreak of renewed warfare in August 1999, the situation in the Chechen Republic of Ichkeria (as it now chose to be called) continued to deteriorate. The end of the war allowed Chechen citizens to go about their daily lives without fear of Russian air attack or arrest and internment in "filtration camps," but people were far from secure. Kidnappings reached epidemic proportions. Some of them seemed crude money-making operations, pursued with no political purposes whatsoever. Yet they had an evident political impact in demonstrating the weakness of the Chechen government. And some of the kidnappings, judging by their timing, had direct political motives as well.[1]

The influence of radical Islamic movements, such as Wahhabism, increased in the wake of the war and the physical and economic devastation that it wrought. Indeed, the precipitating cause of the second war was an August 1999 invasion of Dagestan by Chechen and Dagestani fighters, marching under the banner of Islam and unconstrained by the central government in Grozny. The invasion was led by the Chechen field commander Shamil' Basaev and Habib Abd al-Rahman, better known as Khattab, a guerrilla fighter from Saudi Arabia or Jordan. The incursion was readily halted thanks, in part, to opposition from local Dagestani villagers who welcomed Russian military support.

Emboldened by their success in thwarting the attacks, Russian leaders chose to escalate the conflict with aerial bombardment of Chechen territory and ultimately a full-scale invasion. Unlike the previous war, this one received widespread support from the public, owing to a spate of terrorist bombings in Moscow and other Russian cities that were attributed to Chechens. There is considerable suspicion, however, that those bombings were not the work of Chechen terrorists but of the Russian secret services. Moreover, some observers have linked the events surrounding the invasion of Dagestan to power politics in Moscow, particularly Boris Yeltsin's attempt to protect himself and his family by choosing a successor— Vladimir Putin—who could defeat his political rivals.

In the face of such contending explanations, the immediate origins of the second Chechen War remain in dispute. One prominent chronicler of the Chechen conflicts has even suggested it might be necessary "for a contemporary historian to write an 800-page book devoted to the tangled and sanguinary events of the autumn of 1999" before they could be fully understood.[2] Other specialists have predicted that "the complex interplay of financial, political, military, loyalty-related, nationalist, religious, and other motivations" involved in the war's origins "will occupy political analysts and historians for decades to come."[3] Chapter 4 represents my attempt to make sense of the outbreak of the second war (although in considerably fewer than 800 pages), but before doing so I review here the events of the "interwar" period. Whatever political machinations in Moscow contributed to the renewed warfare, circumstances in Chechnya itself played an important role, particularly the devastated economy, the breakdown of political authority, and the rash of violent crimes, including widespread kidnapping. This chapter sets the scene for the second Chechen War by exploring the complicated landscape of Chechen politics following the signing of the Khasaviurt Accord.

The Maskhadov Administration and Its Opponents

Even as Moscow conducted the withdrawal of the Russian army from Chechnya, some groups sought to undermine the situation. On December 14, 1996, forces under the command of Salman Raduev kidnapped twenty-two Russian Interior Ministry troops and initially refused to release them, despite receiving a "tough warning" from interim Chechen prime minister Aslan Maskhadov. Raduev was the notorious commander responsible for the hostage raid on Kizliar and Pervomaiskoe the previous January.[4] Two days after the kidnapping of the Interior Ministry troops, a government delegation from North Ossetiia was abducted on the way to Grozny for talks with Chechen officials. On the night of December 16–17, six medical personnel working for the International Committee of the Red Cross in a town south of Grozny were shot dead, and the next night six Russian civilians were murdered in Grozny itself. Yeltsin's press secretary described the killings as a provocation directed against the peace process. Boris Berezovskii, the financial "oligarch" then serving as deputy secretary of the Russian Security Council, flew to Grozny to consult with First Deputy Prime Minister Movladi Udugov and field commander Shamil' Basaev to seek the release of Raduev's hostages. They were freed on December 18 in just one of many instances in which Berezovskii played a key role in a Chechen hostage crisis.[5]

In an attempt to reestablish political normality, Chechnya conducted elections in January 1997. General Aslan Maskhadov, the hero of the war and the peace, handily won against his opponents. Maskhadov took 59.3 percent of the vote, followed by Shamil' Basaev with 23.5 percent, and acting president Zelimkhan Iandarbiev with 10.1 percent.[6] International observers declared the elections "legitimate and democratic." Tim Guldimann, head of the OSCE mission to Chechnya, characterized them as "exemplary and free."[7] Boris Yeltsin's spokesperson reported the Russian president "satisfied" with the vote. He added that Yeltsin believed Maskhadov's election "provides a serious chance" for successful talks resulting in "mutually acceptable decisions on Chechnya's status within the Russian Federation."[8]

Signs of trouble persisted despite Maskhadov's election. The rogue commander Raduev refused to recognize the results. He insisted that Chechen president Dzhokhar Dudaev was still alive and that only Dudaev could order him to cease fighting against Russia. Raduev threatened to "burn to cinders" at least three Russian cities if Moscow did not acknowledge Chechnya's independence. Basaev and Iandarbiev meanwhile declined suggestions that they join Maskhadov's new administration. Basaev vowed to return to his pre-war career selling computers, while Iandarbiev, a well-known writer, announced that he would resume his literary pursuits.[9] Chechnya's fate might have been very different, had they kept their promises.

One of Iandarbiev's final acts before handing over the presidency to Maskhadov was to have his Foreign Ministry declare OSCE mission head Guldimann persona non grata. Maskhadov later reversed the decision when he invited the Swiss diplomat who had played such an important role in ending the war in Chechnya to his inauguration. In mid-February 1997 Iandarbiev had his 300-member presidential guard stage a demonstration against Maskhadov's plans to combine his office of the presidency with that of prime minister.[10] In early March Iandarbiev spoke at a rally organized by Raduev to proclaim the anniversary of the Kizliar-Pervomaiskoe hostage raids as a "day of historic Chechen combat glory." Two hundred of Raduev's armed supporters paraded through central Grozny and attracted a crowd of some 3,000 people.[11]

Despite such provocations, Maskhadov attempted to fashion a broadly representative government. It included two members of the Dudaev-Iandarbiev cabinet and even two officials who had served under the pro-Moscow regime of Doku Zavgaev. He appointed Movladi Udugov as his chief negotiator with Russia, and in April 1997 nominated Shamil' Basaev to the post of first deputy prime minister.[12] Basaev was put in charge of industrial affairs, where he would share responsibility for oil production with First Deputy Premier Khozh-Ahmed Iarikhanov, director of the Southern Oil Company (Iunko). Basaev's new post gave him opportunities for personal enrichment in a highly corrupt sector of the economy, but perhaps more important, it provided potential jobs for his armed followers. A priority of the Maskhadov government was to secure the flow of Caspian Sea oil from Baku in Azerbaijan through a pipeline connecting Grozny to the Russian Black Sea port of Novorossiisk, something Basaev promised he could do (see map 3-1, p. 54).[13]

Basaev's appointment followed a late March visit to Grozny by Boris Berezovskii, in his capacity as deputy secretary of Yeltsin's Security Council. Given Berezovskii's long-standing involvement in Chechnya and investments in the oil industry, the appointment might have seemed to Maskhadov a way to get on good terms with the Yeltsin government. Some Russian politicians disagreed with Maskhadov's choice. Given that Basaev was still under investigation by the federal prosecutor's office for his role in the Budennovsk hostage-taking, his appointment was considered by some "a slap in the face for Moscow."[14]

Maskhadov lived to regret his overtures to Basaev and Udugov, as well as his association with Berezovskii.[15] He came to blame Berezovskii for contributing to the strength of his opponents. "For Chechnya," he told a journalist from *Der Spiegel*, just after the start of the second war, Berezovskii "is very bad. He is hatching plots and linking up with opposition officials such as Basaev and Udugov. He pays for their television, Internet access, and their satellite telephones. His negotiators have been involved in all major extortion jobs." But Maskhadov, like everyone else, seemed at a loss to explain Berezovskii's motives: "Maybe he has orders to weaken Russia's position in the Caucasus. Maybe he has his own oil interests here. The fact is that his intriguing is highly dangerous for the entire region."[16]

Competing Visions of Chechnya's Future

Much of the kidnapping carried out by Chechen gangs—with victims in the hundreds—seemed driven mainly by the prospect of ransom money. Yet some of the kidnappings appeared to have a political purpose, as an instrument in the struggle against Maskhadov by his many opponents. One particularly plausible analysis relates the kidnappings during the first two years of Maskhadov's presidency to the conflict over the nature and future of Chechnya. On the one side was Maskhadov, portrayed as a moderate figure interested in asserting Chechnya's nominal independence and sovereignty, but within the framework of economic and political cooperation with Russia. The foundation for such cooperation—and the key to the revival of the Chechen economy—was integration into the regional system of oil production and transport. Such integration required coordination not only with Moscow, but also with regional neighbors such as Azerbaijan.

The competing vision of Chechnya's future was based on the dream of an Islamic state encompassing Chechnya and Dagestan and perhaps other Muslim peoples of the North Caucasus. The proponents of such a future did not seek peace with Russia—even on the favorable terms, entailing unilateral withdrawal of the Russian army, negotiated by Maskhadov with Aleksandr Lebed'. Only a continuation of the war beyond Chechen territory would make the union with Dagestan possible, providing an outlet for landlocked Chechnya to the Caspian Sea in the east. If such military action provoked a Russian reaction, all the better. The other Muslim peoples of the North Caucasus would rise up in response to Russian repression, and the whole region would become independent. At that point, the "Islamic Nation" (as one of the Chechen nationalist groups was named) would gain access to the Black Sea to the west, as well as the Caspian to the east, and Chechnya's viability and survival would be assured.[17]

Oil also played a role in this scheme, because control of the Dagestan coast would provide access to two-thirds of the Caspian shelf.[18] This was a utopian vision for sure, and one that depended on many faulty assumptions, including at a minimum the desire of the peoples of Dagestan to join with Chechnya in an Islamic state. The analysis also neglected the cruder motives of personal greed and power that undoubtedly drove many of the leading Chechen oppositionists. But the basic political goals espoused by the various Chechen opposition groups amounted to an outright rejection of a Russian presence in the North Caucasus in favor of some kind of Islamic confederation. Such goals would not have been served by the policy of rapprochement pursued by Maskhadov.

Indeed, Maskhadov's leading opponents all held top positions in the main Islamic organizations. For example, the "Caucasus Confederation" promoted nationalist movements in Dagestan, Kabardino-Balkariia, and Karachaevo-Cherkesiia against the "Russian occupation." Iandarbiev and Raduev were its main leaders. In January 1998 they issued a statement condemning the policies of the Maskhadov government as "insufficiently tough." They were particularly critical of the unproductive and "humiliating" meetings between Maskhadov's representatives and the Russian "leaders of the former empire." Maskhadov's opponents also criticized his commitment to Islam and to Chechen independence, as when Raduev ridiculed the Chechen president because he had used his Russian passport to travel to Mecca for the *hadj* (Saudi Arabia, like every other country, did not recognize the Chechen passport as legitimate).[19]

Another major opposition group, the Congress of Peoples of Ichkeria and Dagestan, was convened under the leadership of Basaev and Udugov. Both had served in Maskhadov's government, with Basaev justifying his participation as being useful to monitor the Chechen president and "correct him in the case of attempts to deviate from the course of independence." Although not formally affiliated with the Wahhabi movement, the congress supported efforts of the Wahhabis in Dagestan in their struggles against the traditional Muslim institutions there and in their attempt to "liberate" Dagestan from Russian control.[20]

Strategic Industries: Oil and Kidnapping

Maskhadov's vision of a nominally independent Chechnya working in close economic and political cooperation with Russia appeared within reach in the first months of his administration. A number of agreements between the Russian and Chechen governments, signed in May 1997, seemed a promising start. In the early days of May, Maskhadov had made numerous efforts to improve the atmosphere for cooperation by seeking to crack down on criminal activities. He gave senior interior ministry officials a deadline of one month to improve their performance or be fired. He had his vice president issue a warrant to detain Salman Raduev after the maverick commander claimed credit for recent bomb attacks in Russia.[21] Maskhadov sought the release of Russian journalists from NTV whose capture had received wide attention and reflected poorly on his new government.

Boris Berezovskii sought to bolster the prospects for the Russo-Chechen agreements by promoting them to Russian television audiences a week before they were actually signed on May 12, 1997. As an incentive to further economic cooperation, Ivan Rybkin, the Security Council secretary, suggested "offering Grozny a share of tariffs from oil exports via Chechnya"—essentially the "Buy Chechnya" proposal that Dzhokhar Dudaev had floated to an unresponsive Yeltsin administration in 1992.[22] The May agreements seemed to bear fruit, at least as far as the oil factor was concerned, on July 3, 1997, when Geidar Aliev, the president of Azerbaijan, signed an agreement in Moscow endorsing the shipment of Caspian oil through Chechnya. Western support for the proposal came in the form of partnership with British Petroleum (BP).

The day after the oil agreement was signed, Jon James and Camilla Carr, two British volunteers at a home for troubled children, were kidnapped at gunpoint in Grozny.[23] A number of observers have suggested that the kidnapping of British citizens was intended to wreck the BP-Azerbaijan deal and thwart Chechnya's integration into the international oil market. In response to the kidnapping, President Maskhadov ordered an antiterrorist brigade to storm the headquarters of warlord Arbi Baraev in Urus-Martan, where he suspected the captives were being held. The operation failed, owing to unanticipated resistance from forces loyal to Raduev.[24] On August 18, 1997, however, the three NTV journalists abducted in Chechnya in mid-May were freed through the efforts of Berezovskii. He and NTV director Igor' Malashenko acknowledged that the captives were ransomed for "a seven-figure dollar sum."[25]

In May 1997, when the oil deal seemed close, Raduev was interviewed by a Russian newspaper and made a prescient threat: "Now they think they've won the oil contract. They're mistaken. They've lost. Only for that reason, knowing my influence, they're now looking for the possibility to begin separate negotiations with me."[26] He also gave a strong indication of the role Berezovskii would play: "He has a personal interest in this oil. I often meet with him personally. We don't have close relations, but I respect him. He is a very courageous and businesslike person. Whenever the need arises for me to have an intermediary in negotiations with Russia, I call Berezovskii. He's an honorable person."[27]

During the summer of 1997, kidnapping and general insecurity were not the only barriers to Russian-Chechen economic cooperation. Plans for transshipment of oil across Chechnya foundered over disagreements about the transit fees that Moscow would pay and whether material support for maintaining the pipelines would be forthcoming. Apparently as a bargaining ploy, Russian officials began hinting that Moscow would seek alternative routes for oil transshipment and bypass Chechnya altogether. On August 6, 1997, for example, Sergei Kirienko, then first deputy minister of fuel and energy, told journalists in Moscow that talks on the transit of Azerbaijan's Caspian oil via Chechnya to Novorossiisk were "deadlocked" because of Chechnya's "impossible" tariff demands.[28] On August 21, *Nezavisimaia gazeta*, a newspaper with financial ties to Berezovskii, quoted his charge that the Russian finance ministry was sabotaging the oil pipeline deal by not transferring the necessary funds to Chechnya. The charge was repeated a few days later when Chechen vice president Vakha Arsanov met in Baku with Azerbaijani president Aliev. The Chechens also objected to the wording of the agreement with Moscow, which appeared to smuggle in "politically charged" references to "Chechnya as a member of the Russian Federation."[29]

As the time approached for the first shipment of "early" oil from Baku, Moscow again threatened to bypass Chechnya and transport the oil by barge to Astrakhan and Volgograd for refining. Grozny in turn vowed to build a pipeline to Georgia and leave Russia out of its Azerbaijani oil deal altogether.[30] On September 5, 1997, however, Boris Nemtsov, Russia's fuel and energy minister, made a conciliatory gesture by suggesting that Russia sign an agreement with Chechnya on repairing the Chechen sector of the pipeline, even while disagreements on tariffs were still being negotiated. Despite threats from Raduev to disrupt the flow of oil if Russia did not officially recognize Chechnya's independence, the agreement was signed on September 9. It immediately came into question, though, as Chechen terrorists bombed a truck carrying Russian workers to a repair site and as Russian prime minister Viktor Chernomyrdin was accused of refusing to transfer the funds required by the agreement. Finally, on September 15, Nemtsov announced Moscow's decision to construct a 283-kilometer pipeline across Dagestan to North Ossetiia, thereby cutting Chechnya completely out of Russia's Caspian oil affairs.[31]

Map 3-1. *Caspian Oil Routes*

In order to salvage his plan to integrate Chechnya into the international oil market, Maskhadov sought further support from Western backers. He relied on a fellow Chechen with broad international contacts, Khozh-Akhmet Nukhaev. Nukhaev, the reputed "father of the Chechen mafia," had served as chief of counterintelligence in the Dudaev government before moving to Azerbaijan to represent that country's oil interests in negotiations with Chechnya and Western companies.[32] He founded an organization called Caucasian Common Market, which boasted an impressive list of advisers, including Jacques Attali, former head of the European Bank for Reconstruction and Development. In October 1997 Maskhadov and Nukhaev signed a protocol of intent with Lord McAlpine to set up an investment trust to restore the Chechen oil complex. In March 1998 Maskhadov traveled to London where he met former British prime minister Margaret Thatcher, an adviser to both British Petroleum and the Caucasian Common Market. By April 1998, with British endorsement,

Maskhadov had secured the support of leaders of the North Caucasus republics and the representatives of Georgia and Azerbaijan for the common market project, in which the transport of oil across Chechnya would play a key role.[33]

Again the opponents of Chechen economic integration disrupted Maskhadov's plans with violence. On May 1, 1998, they kidnapped Valentin Vlasov, Yeltsin's envoy to Grozny. Vlasov met and was held in the same location as the two British captives, Carr and James—evidence that the kidnappings were part of a coordinated plan.[34] The British couple was released on September 20, 1998, after fourteen months in captivity, thanks to a deal worked out between Berezovskii and Raduev. Berezovksii reported that he had secured their release by donating computers and medical aid to Raduev, but most observers consider these a euphemism for a substantial ransom. Leaders of republics neighboring Chechnya criticized Berezovskii, suggesting that Raduev now had "more computers than some Russian intelligence services possess." Taped telephone intercepts of conversations between Berezovskii and Movladi Udugov suggest that Berezovskii was indeed involved in sending money to ransom some victims of Chechen kidnappings.[35]

In this case, Berezovskii flew Jon James and Camilla Carr back to London on his private jet. But his efforts were not an act of individual altruism. In addition to conducting his business affairs, Berezovskii was at that time also serving as a government official in the Commonwealth of Independent States (CIS), the organization that brought together most of the countries that had made up the Soviet Union. In fact, in an interview with Russian media, Raduev made clear that "Berezovskii was dealing with us not as a politician-businessman, but as the executive secretary of the CIS." As such, one of Berezovskii's goals was to further economic cooperation in the Caucasus region, including collaboration in the shipment of Azerbaijani oil across Chechnya to Novorosiisk.[36]

Neither Moscow nor Western governments were, however, satisfied that the situation in Chechnya was adequately secure to proceed. Two weeks after the release of James and Carr, four engineers (three British citizens and one New Zealander), employed by a British telecommunications company, were kidnapped in Grozny. President Yeltsin's personal envoy Vlasov was still held captive. He was released on November 13, 1998, presumably with Berezovskii's intervention. On the same day kidnappers captured Herbert Gregg, an American teacher at an orphanage in Dagestan's capital of Makhachkala.[37] He was eventually released, but the four engineers were not so lucky. They fell victim to a botched rescue operation by

Maskhadov's government.[38] Their captors executed them and left their severed heads by the roadside; the bodies were found a week later. In early December a senior official of the Grozneft oil company was kidnapped in Grozny and the chief of the Chechen antikidnapping unit was assassinated.[39] With such grisly determination, Maskhadov's opponents made it clear that they were not giving up their attempts to thwart his plans to use the oil pipeline as a means of improving relations with Russia.

Moscow Lets Maskhadov Lose

Maskhadov's domestic opponents availed themselves of other means besides kidnapping to undermine the Chechen president. Maskhadov had been under increasing pressure, for example, to adopt Islamic Shariah law and thereby reduce his own power. At first Maskhadov's concession to Islam seemed to serve him well as Chechnya's Supreme Shariah court on November 4, 1998, sentenced Salman Raduev in absentia to four years in prison for attempting to overthrow the president. But on December 24 the court ruled against Maskhadov himself and called on the president to dissolve the Chechen parliament, arguing that its legislative activities contravened Islamic law.[40]

Maskhadov was not getting much help from Moscow either, despite claims by Sergei Stepashin, the interior minister, that "Maskhadov is supported by Russia and other countries" and should be able "to consolidate his authority." According to Stepashin, Prime Minister Evgenii Primakov had assured him at a meeting in early November 1998 that funds had been allocated from the federal budget to improve social conditions in Chechnya. Primakov had made a similar pledge the previous month, but there was little to show for it. Charges of widespread embezzlement of funds intended for Chechen reconstruction and social welfare seem well founded. Stepashin nevertheless expressed confidence that the receipt of the money—payments of pensions, in particular—"would enhance Maskhadov's prestige."[41]

But other initiatives emanating from Moscow seemed designed to undermine the Chechen leader's prestige. In early December 1998, for example, the Russian press reported that President Yeltsin had annulled his directive of September 1997 to negotiate a treaty with Chechnya on the mutual delegation of powers, along the lines of the one that had led to a modus vivendi with Tatarstan. Yeltsin's policy reversal seemed an ill-timed slap in the face to Maskhadov, who in an interview on December 2 had expressed his readiness for "any dialogue" with the Russian government that would lead to the signing of "a full-fledged treaty" between Moscow and Grozny. Alluding apparently to the oil issue, Maskhadov had also declared himself ready to assume "a certain responsibility for defending the strategic interests of the Russian Federation in the Caucasus."[42]

Despite Moscow's rebuff, Maskhadov continued the struggle against his terrorist opponents. Faced with a rash of kidnappings, he had nevertheless managed to score a few successes against terrorism—and not always with Berezovskii's dubious intervention. In early November 1998 a spokesperson for Anatolii Chubais acknowledged that Chechen intelligence had helped prevent a planned assassination of the then first deputy prime minister a year earlier.[43] On December 11 the Chechen interior ministry arrested a suspect in the beheading of the four Western hostages. Moreover, Deputy Premier Iusup Soslambekov made a commitment, unfortunately never fulfilled, to expel "an Arab terrorist group led by Khattab." Soslambekov said that his government did not want Chechnya converted into a "terrorist morass."[44] Ironically, what was left of the democratic aspects of Chechnya's political system in some respects hindered the government's attempt to deal with terrorism. In mid-December, for example, when President Maskhadov called up army reservists to help police the country's territory, his opponents declared the move unconstitutional.[45]

In early 1999 a number of Russian observers became alarmed at the deteriorating situation in Chechnya and the Yeltsin administration's apparent complacency. In mid-January Aleksandr Lebed', the retired general and former Security Council secretary who brokered the agreement that ended the war, issued a warning to the press. He predicted another war if Moscow failed to take action to bolster Maskhadov. Forces opposed to the Chechen president, argued Lebed', are "ready to start an armed insurgency at any moment." As one report described, "Lebed also blamed Moscow for not having taken advantage of the opportunity offered by the peace agreement that he and Maskhadov signed in late August 1996 to stabilize the political and economic situation in Chechnya and the neighboring North Caucasus republics."[46] A few days later, Valentin Vlasov, the presidential envoy to Chechnya who had survived more than six months in captivity there, issued a similar judgment. He faulted the Yeltsin government for not having provided more economic and political support to Maskhadov in accordance with the May 1997 agreements. He specifically criticized the Russian president for inadequately monitoring his government's implementation of the agreements.[47]

By February 1999 Maskhadov seemed to have conceded defeat. Under pressure from field commanders led by Shamil' Basaev, he suspended the

Chechen parliament and ordered the immediate transition to Shariah law throughout Chechnya. Russian observers, such as former Security Council secretary Ivan Rybkin, recognized Maskhadov's move as a desperate attempt to prevent an open split with the opposition. But Rybkin also noted—accurately, if unhelpfully—that Maskhadov's decree violated the Chechen Constitution. That constitution, adopted under Dudaev, established Chechnya as a secular republic with freedom of religion for all. It did not grant the president power to dissolve the parliament or impose universal Islamic law.[48] Within days of Maskhadov's decree, the rebel field commanders formed an alternative governing body—a council called the Shura—and elected Basaev as its head. The Shura demanded the immediate implementation of Shariah, the resignation of the president and the parliament, and the drafting of a new constitution.

Maskhadov's concessions only seemed to embolden his enemies. On February 22 the Supreme Shariah Court demanded that Maskhadov dismiss the prosecutor general because of his service in the Russian police force during the first Chechen War, and the president complied.[49] The next day Maskhadov's adviser on matters related to Chechnya's Russian-speaking population was kidnapped on his way to work in Grozny. Meanwhile Basaev publicly criticized Maskhadov for his allegedly pro-Russian orientation and suggested, with some reason, that the president had adopted Shariah reluctantly, under pressure from the opposition.[50]

A turning point came on March 5, 1999, when Major-General Gennadii Shpigun of the Russian Interior Ministry was abducted in Grozny. Interior Minister Stepashin vowed that if Shpigun were not released soon Moscow would pursue "extremely rigorous measures to ensure law, order, and security in the North Caucasus region." He criticized the Maskhadov government's unsuccessful efforts to crack down on terrorism. "In effect," Stepashin said, "several thousand armed scoundrels dictate their will to Chechen society, driving it into medievalism and obscurantism." He threatened that further "terrorist acts" would prompt Russia to intervene and destroy the "criminal formations' bases," albeit "in conformity with international practice."[51] Maskhadov's press secretary responded to Stepashin's criticisms by blaming Russian authorities for circumventing the Chechen president and dealing directly with his rivals—the practice established by Boris Berezovskii right at the outset of the Maskhadov administration. He suggested that Russian intelligence services had conspired with Basaev to abduct Shpigun.[52]

Basaev, for his part, denied responsibility for the kidnapping but urged whoever had abducted the general to turn him over to the Shura as a "war criminal." On March 9 Basaev's ally Movladi Udugov threatened reprisals against individual Russian politicians if Moscow should attack Chechnya.[53] Trying to calm the situation, Maskhadov went on Chechen television and vowed, "I am doing my best to prevent war." He offered a $200,000 reward for information on Shpigun's whereabouts and claimed that some twenty separate groups were investigating his disappearance, despite a lack of cooperation from Russian authorities.[54]

Stepashin responded the next day by insisting that Moscow "has been supporting and will support the legitimate Chechen president." Valentin Vlasov, Yeltsin's special envoy to Chechnya, and Oleg Sysuev, first deputy chief of the presidential administration, both ruled out Moscow's use of force in Chechnya.[55] In fact, as Stepashin later acknowledged, this was precisely the time when planning for a new, limited invasion of Chechnya was begun.[56]

By the end of March Russian helicopter gunships had encroached on Chechen airspace and President Maskhadov responded with orders to shoot down all unauthorized aircraft flying over the country. This was not the first time that the Chechen government had warned Moscow about such aerial intrusions. On August 13, 1997, Russian fighter aircraft staged simulated attacks on Grozny's airport and central market, according to Chechen officials, in an apparent attempt to disrupt a forthcoming meeting between Maskhadov and Yeltsin. The Chechen government made similar claims as recently as January 1999, at a particularly tense time in Chechen domestic politics, but Russian air force officials denied the charge.[57] Given the warlike atmosphere in March, the claims seemed quite plausible this time.

On March 29 Maskhadov's government attempted to use its last bit of leverage. Blaming Moscow's failure to pay for adequate security—payments of 100 million rubles ($4.13 million) were in arrears for the past six months—it halted the shipment of Azerbaijani oil through the Chechen sector of the Baku-Grozny-Novorossiisk pipeline.[58]

Along the Path to War

The next few months witnessed a series of border skirmishes between Chechen and Russian troops. Most of the reports came from Stepashin's Interior Ministry, which was already planning a new invasion of Chechnya, so their reliability cannot be assumed. But there was obviously an escalation of conflict in the border areas. In April 1999 several kidnappings and killings in the Stavropol' region bordering Chechnya prompted

Stepashin to close the frontier. It "will be closed for gangsters, not for civilians," he said. But, he added, "this will effectively be a war zone," patrolled by helicopter gunships.[59] On July 19 the Interior Ministry reported an attack by Chechens on the Stavropol' border posts, killing two Russian soldiers and wounding five. Russian helicopters retaliated by launching some forty missiles.[60]

On May 27, 1999, the Interior Ministry reported an attack on a Russian border post between Chechnya and Dagestan. The next day Stepashin's ministry sent helicopters to attack what it claimed was a terrorist base on a small island in the Terek River. Chechen security minister Turpal Atgeriev denied that Chechens were responsible for the border attack, which he blamed on residents of Dagestan. He said the Russian air attacks were intended to provoke a new conflict with Chechnya.[61] Stepashin meanwhile met with two Russian priests who had just been released from captivity in Chechnya. He promised that criminals who "kidnap and kill people" must be "eliminated." The next day officials from Chechnya and North Ossetiia met to draft measures to cooperate in eradicating kidnappings for ransom.[62] The gesture was, unfortunately, too little and too late.

In July Russian troops arrested Atgeriev but were obliged to release him after prosecutors announced that they had inadequate evidence against him. Nevertheless, the Chechen government responded by closing, first, the offices of all of its regional representatives in the Russian Federation, and then even its "embassy" in Moscow.[63] During the night of July 25–26 fighting broke out along the Dagestan-Chechen border, but no casualties were reported.[64]

Amid all the bad news, it was hardly noticed that U.S teacher and missionary Herbert Gregg, who had been kidnapped in Dagestan the previous November, was finally released on June 29, 1999. General Shpigun, much dearer to his boss Sergei Stepashin, remained a captive.[65]

On July 27 President Maskhadov, conforming to a now familiar pattern, made conciliatory gestures simultaneously to his domestic opposition and to Moscow. He named Ruslan Gelaev—a comrade-in-arms of Basaev and Khattab—first deputy premier with responsibility for law enforcement. Maskhadov told his cabinet that he expected Gelaev's appointment to lead to a reduction in kidnapping, theft of oil, and other crimes. To placate Moscow, and Western oil interests, Maskhadov dispatched his national guard and presidential guard to protect the section of the Baku-Novorossiisk pipeline between Grozny and the Dagestani border. His presidential spokesperson explained that Chechnya wanted to demonstrate an ability to adhere to the 1997 export agreement it had made with the oil industries of Russia and Azerbaijan.[66]

Again, in a familiar pattern, Maskhadov failed to satisfy either his domestic opponents or the Russian government. Basaev and Khattab were on the verge of plunging Chechnya into war—a war that Moscow had also been planning for nearly five months.

It is now known that the Russian authorities had been planning to resume the war against Chechnya long before the attack on Dagestan and the apartment bombings. This information was revealed already in early 2000 by Sergei Stepashin, an active proponent of the first war who had been Yeltsin's prime minister from late April 1999 until August 1999. Yeltsin fired him on August 9, two days after the first Chechen incursion into Dagestan. In a newspaper interview, Stepashin stated:

> In relation to Chechnya I can say the following. The plan for active operations in this republic was worked out starting in March [1999]. And we planned to move to the Terek in August-September. So this would have happened even if there had not been explosions in Moscow. I actively conducted work on strengthening the borders with Chechnya, preparing for an active offensive. Thus Vladimir Putin did not discover anything new here. You can ask him himself about this. He was at that time the director of the FSB [Federal Security Service, the descendant of the KGB] and had all of the information.

Stepashin implies that the original planning for the war did not necessarily include a full invasion and attempt to recapture Grozny and control all of Chechnen territory: "I was always a supporter of a strong and tough policy in Chechnya. But I would have thought well about whether it was worth crossing the Terek and going further to the south."[67]

As this chapter has shown, the situation in Chechnya following the withdrawal of Russian troops was dangerous and unstable. Moscow's unwillingness or inability to fulfill the terms of the agreement that ended the first war—particularly in the provision of economic aid and reconstruction—certainly contributed to making independent Chechnya an unviable proposition. Yet the sources of Chechnya's failure are also found in its internal politics, the rivalry among political factions with competing visions of Chechnya's future, and the greed for oil and ransom money.

But did Chechnya's instability require another military invasion and occupation? Would, as Stepashin suggested, a more limited effort to secure the border area have been less costly and more effective? Chapter 4 explores the origins of the second Chechen War and seeks to explain why Vladimir Putin chose the course of all-out war to resolve the Chechen situation.

4

Putin's War

I had already decided that my career might be over, but that my mission, my historical mission—and this will sound lofty, but it's true—consisted of resolving the situation in the North Caucasus. . . . I have a little time—two, three, maybe four months—to bang the hell out of those bandits. Then they can get rid of me.

—Vladimir Putin, March 2000

The second round of Moscow's war with Chechnya began with an attack from across the Chechen border into Dagestan during the first few days of August 1999. Reports ranged from some 300 troops to over 2,000. The force consisted of Dagestani Wahhabis, Chechens, and various other Muslim soldiers, including some from Central Asia and the Middle East. They were led by field commanders Shamil' Basaev and Khattab, an Arab fighter married to a Dagestani woman. Responding to a request for assistance from the leadership of Dagestan, Moscow sent Interior Ministry troops to the Tsumadin and Botlikh districts on August 4.[1] Local Dagestani forces resisted the invasion as well—apparently to Moscow's surprise—and they were soon supported by regular Russian army troops.

This was not the first military action involving Wahhabis in Dagestan. In May 1997 a force of Dagestani fighters associated with the sect took control of several villages, including the one where Khattab's wife was born. In December 1997 a group of Chechen guerrillas joined the Wahhabi force to attack a Russian armored brigade near Buinaksk. The residents of the villages "liberated" by the

Wahhabis and Chechens declared their independence from Dagestan and established another "little Chechnya" within the Russian Federation.[2] The August incursion looked like another step on the path to creating a united Chechen-Dagestani Muslim state, the explicit goal of Basaev and his allies.

But the Dagestanis by and large resisted the Chechen incursion and spurned the Wahhabi fundamentalism that threatened to undermine their own Islamic traditions of governance.[3] Yet the Russians continued their military operations against Chechnya with massive aerial attacks in early September, followed by a ground invasion. At first it seemed that the Russian forces might stop at the Terek River and try to create a positive example in Chechnya's traditionally pro-Russian Nadterechnyi district. But they kept going all the way to Grozny. Unlike the first Chechen War—which very nearly led to Boris Yeltsin's impeachment—this one was popular.[4] Support for the war effort stemmed first from its apparent defensive origins and second from the fact that the defeat of the Chechen invaders coincided with a series of terrorist bombings on Russian territory. During the first two weeks of September, four apartment buildings were blown up in Dagestan, in Moscow, and in Volgodonsk. Suspicions naturally fell on Chechens.

Putin Chooses War

Vladimir Putin, appointed prime minister and heir apparent by Boris Yeltsin just days after the attack on Dagestan, seized on the opportunity to prosecute the war while it still enjoyed public support. If one can believe his "astonishingly frank self-portrait"—as a collection of Putin's interviews with Russian journalists was called—Putin did not expect the popular support to last. But after just four months of war Yeltsin decided to resign the presidency early, putting Putin in an excellent position to move from acting president to the real thing with elections in March 2000. Renewal of the war against Chechnya, supported by an increasingly docile and servile Russian press, secured Putin's victory.

The war itself dragged on for years. Even after most of Chechnya was bombed into rubble and thousands of its citizens killed, driven away, or "disappeared" into internment camps and mass graves, the country remained a dangerously insecure place, with frequent guerrilla attacks, assassinations, and abductions. Even the assassination of Khattab in March 2002—apparently killed by a poisoned letter prepared by the Russian secret services and delivered by a traitor within his circle—failed to stem the tide of terrorist acts.[5] Putin undoubtedly managed "to bang the hell out of those bandits," but he fell far short of fulfilling his "historical mission" of "resolving the situation in the North Caucasus."[6] If he managed to preserve the Russian Federation from further disintegration, it was despite rather than because of his policy in Chechnya. The causes of the second Chechen War are rooted in the unique characteristics of the Chechen situation and the political instincts of Vladimir Putin, both relevant for understanding the future of the Russian Federation.

Defending Dagestan

On August 10, 1999, newly appointed prime minister Putin reported that President Yeltsin had instructed him to "impose order and discipline" in Dagestan and that the Russian authorities would resolve the situation there in "one-and-a-half to two weeks."[7] On August 13 the Russian forces initiated two days of intense air and artillery bombardment of villages in the Botlikh district, creating a refugee crisis, but failing to dislodge the invaders.[8] Eventually the Russians drove the attacking forces back over the border. On August 25 Russian military aircraft attacked the Chechen villages of Vedeno and Urus Martan, where rebel forces retreating from Dagestan had fled. A Russian military official in Makhachkala confirmed the attacks, but the defense minister himself denied them.[9]

On August 27, Putin flew to the Botlikh district of Dagestan to present medals to Russian soldiers and Dagestani volunteers who had repulsed the invaders. At the same time he warned of further possible attacks. Indeed, two days later an attack was launched against the Dagestani village of Karamakhi. It came not from Chechnya, but from a combination of local Dagestani police forces and federal Russian troops. Karamakhi had been a hotbed of Wahhabism. Along with the neighboring village of Chabanmakhi, it had been run for the past year by the local Islamic *djamaat,* or council of elders, with little influence of the Dagestani or Russian governments. For reasons still hard to understand, this arrangement had the blessing of then Russian interior minister Sergei Stepashin, who visited the area on September 2, 1998, and subsequently arranged for substantial "humanitarian aid" to be delivered to the already relatively prosperous villages.[10] A prominent Chechen religious leader later described how "Stepashin—who is a non-Muslim and does not know what Islam is—visited these two villages and said about their residents: 'They are good Muslims. They are not hardliners and should be helped.'" He accused Stepashin of having sent two truckloads of weapons to the villages, under the guise of medical supplies.[11] A year later, the Russian authorities had a new perspective on Wahhabism, following the invasion of Basaev and Khattab, and decided to snuff it out.

Map 4-1. *Chechnya and Dagestan*

Although the government suppression of the Wahhabis received passive support from the local population, it triggered a further escalation of violence elsewhere. On August 31 a bomb exploded in a popular shopping complex off Red Square in Moscow, killing one person and wounding forty. Basaev later attributed the terrorist attack to his Wahhabi allies from Dagestan.[12] On the night of September 4, 1999, a bomb exploded in an apartment building in Buinaksk, Dagestan. Sixty-four people died and hundreds more were injured. On September 5 some 2,000 Chechen militants crossed the Dagestani border and attacked several villages in the Kazbek and Novolaksk districts.[13] Basaev's press service described the attacks as intended to divert federal forces from their punitive operations against the Wahhabis of Karamakhi and Chabanmakhi.[14]

In Moscow bombs destroyed two apartment complexes, one on September 9 and another on September 13. Three days later a truck bomb exploded near an apartment in Volgodonsk in Rostov *oblast'*. Between these three explosions and the earlier one in Buinaksk, some 300 people were killed. Although widely attributed to "Chechens," the crimes remain unsolved. Demolition experts quickly destroyed the remains of the first Moscow building that had been bombed, making observers wonder how, without physical evidence, an investigation could be conducted to find the perpetrators. In the case of the Buinaksk bombing, six suspects were arrested in September 2000 and put on trial in Dagestan two months later. All were Dagestani followers of Wahhabism. The Dagestani prosecutor charged that Basaev and Khattab had arranged the explosion.[15]

The apartment bombings had a traumatic and galvanizing effect on Russian public opinion, comparable to what happened in the United States after the attacks of September 11, 2001. They provoked widespread and uncritical support for expanding the war against Chechnya.

By mid-September 1999 Russian forces had defeated the Wahhabi militants of Karamakhi and Chabanmakhi and driven the Chechen invaders out of Dagestan. Unfortunately, their main method of air and artillery bombardment had destroyed several Dagestani villages in the course of liberating them. Russian defense minister Igor' Sergeev charged that several thousand rebels remained concentrated at three locations on the Chechen border. He vowed that the Russian army was "fully ready" to repel any new incursion.[16] Instead of waiting, the Russians launched their own air assault. Ostensibly intended to interdict invasion routes, the initial attacks across the border expanded by September 23 to include "ammunition depots, the [Grozny] airport, oil refineries, industries, and television and telephone facilities."[17]

Basaev: "Some Women Curse Me"

As Russian military activities intensified, newly installed prime minister Putin issued Chechen president Maskhadov an ultimatum: to arrest those responsible for the invasion of Dagestan or face further Russian attacks. Putin was undoubtedly buoyed by the widespread—and unexpected— support for his hard line from a Russian population unnerved by the terrorist bombings. Yet in retrospect it would have been more sensible to try to work with Maskhadov rather than threaten him. The Chechen president had attempted to discredit the supporters of the incursion into Dagestan. On August 29 Maskhadov issued a decree removing his extremist rival Movladi Udugov from Chechnya's National Security Council. He accused Udugov, an ally of Basaev and a longtime supporter of a combined Chechen-Dagestani Islamic state, of fomenting "a large-scale ideological sabotage operation against the Chechen state" and of having "pushed the traditional friendship between the Dagestani and Chechen peoples to [the] breaking point."

Moscow missed an opportunity to bolster Maskhadov at the expense of Basaev, Udugov, and Khattab. In an interview with a BBC reporter, Basaev acknowledged that in Chechnya "some women curse me" because his military activities in Dagestan had provoked a renewal of Russian bombing.[18] Indeed, few Chechens supported Basaev's continued military provocations, especially when they jeopardized Chechnya's hard-won independence and peace. Few were willing to support the holy war that he, his friend Khattab, and their "band of madmen" had promoted. Such a characterization was typical of the ordinary Chechens interviewed by reporter Anne Nivat. One woman referred to Basaev as "that criminal" who "should have been arrested a long time ago." A group of Chechen men who did not join the fight against the new Russian invasion insisted that "all of us here would willingly fight the Russians for our independence, but not as long as Shamil' is leading the troops."[19]

Maskhadov acknowledged Basaev's unpopular position, even if those in Moscow did not. He told an interviewer in late September 1999, "Basaev has forfeited much of his reputation here through these guerrilla actions. Our people are tired of war and condemn such acts of provocation." But when the interviewer asked why Maskhadov would not arrest Basaev, Raduev, and Khattab, "or at least strip them of their operational bases in the Chechen mountains," Maskhadov responded: "I cannot simply have Basaev arrested as a gangster; people here would not understand that. After all, we fought together for our country's independence."[20] Maskhadov often used the formula "people would not understand" as a way of avoiding admitting that he would be powerless to do something because his enemies still commanded considerable influence.

Yet much of Basaev's influence appeared to stem from his support from certain quarters in Moscow—especially from Berezovskii, who reportedly supplied him with telecommunications equipment, computers, and probably ransom money.[21] As Sergei Kovalev, a leading human-rights activist, described, "Berezovskii publicly said he gave Shamil' Basaev $2 million to build a cement factory and provide work for unemployed Chechens. I don't know how Basaev builds factories, but I do know how he buys weapons and wages wars. So why did Berezovskii choose Basaev? Everyone knows Basaev is a terrorist. His disputes with Maskhadov, his intrigues and adventurism are well known."[22]

Despite Berezovskii's support, by autumn 1999 the tide of Chechen public opinion seemed to be turning against Basaev. He was rescued by Vladimir Putin himself. As in 1994, when the unpopular leader Dzhokhar Dudaev was able to silence his critics and rally support in the face of a Russian invasion, this time too the rival Chechen leaders came together to meet the Russian challenge. As Basaev told the BBC, "In the current situation we are united and our unity is strengthened by Russia—and for that we are very grateful."[23]

Replaying War

On September 29, 1999, Putin expressed willingness to begin negotiations with the Chechen leadership, but only on condition that (1) Maskhadov condemn terrorism "clearly and firmly;" (2) he rid Chechen territory of armed bands; and (3) he be willing to extradite "criminals" to Moscow. Putin said that the Russian leadership "will never allow a replay" of the 1994–96 Chechen War, because it could lead to "unnecessary casualties among troops" (he did not mention Chechen or Russian civilians). But he added that he still did not exclude a ground attack to "solve the main task—destroy the bandits, their camps and infrastructure." The next day Russian tanks spearheaded a ground invasion into Chechen territory, while an air campaign targeted dams, oil wells, and bridges.[24]

With such actions, Putin left Maskhadov little alternative than to rely on Basaev and the other field commanders to help defend the country. On October 1, 1999, just two days after issuing the conditions of his ultimatum, the Russian premier declared that Russia no longer recognized the legitimacy of Maskhadov's rule in Chechnya. For him the "only legitimate organ of power in Chechnya" was the parliament elected under dubious conditions of Russian military occupation in 1996 and exiled to Moscow after the Chechen victory. Putin claimed that a flood of Chechen refugees, then estimated at more than 90,000 by Russian officials, proved the illegitimacy of Maskhadov's rule. "They are voting against the current regime with their feet by going to Russia," Putin said, as if acknowledging the Chechen position that Chechnya and Russia were two different countries. Putin neglected to add that most refugees were fleeing a Russian bombing campaign and sometimes even seemed themselves to be a target of the attacks. On October 21, for example, a Russian missile strike on a market in Grozny killed over 100 civilians. The pace of bombing accelerated to a rate of 150 air strikes a day by the end of the month, as the number of refugees in neighboring Ingushetiia alone exceeded 124,000.[25]

The Russian government's method of convincing Chechnya to remain part of the federation seemed somewhat counterintuitive, to say the least. Russian planes bombed Chechen cities and villages, sending tens of thousands of refugees fleeing to the "border." As they reached the border (which was not an international one, because Moscow did not recognize an independent Chechnya), the refugees were turned back by the Russian army and refused entry into what was, according to the Kremlin, another part of their own country, Russia. In the meantime, the army tried to create a cordon sanitaire to keep Chechens out of the rest of Russia—especially Dagestan.

With the new invasion of Chechnya in September 1999, a parallel process of refugee creation got under way in Moscow and other cities in Russia. While the Kremlin was insisting that Chechnya remain part of Russia, the proponents of "Operation Foreigner" were sending another message. The government of Moscow, for example, during the week of September 14–20, expelled at least 11,000 of its own Russian citizens, with their Russian passports, calling them "foreigners" because they happened to be of Chechen descent. A Chechen diaspora group in Moscow appealed to Muscovites and the mass media not "to put an equals sign between banditry and the Chechen people"—a lost cause, given the harsh rhetoric emanating from the Kremlin and the harsher reality of indiscriminate bombing of Chechnya itself.[26]

Why War?

As noted in chapter 2, the origins of the first Chechen War—or at least an important reason why the conflict was not resolved peacefully—lay in the idiosyncratic personalities and leadership styles of Boris Yeltsin and Dzhokhar Dudaev. Some analysts argue that the course of the second war also owes something to such personality factors. Its origins, as suggested in chapter 3, are tied to internal political conflicts over the nature of the Chechen state and competition, both internal and external, over the control of oil. Individuals are not irrelevant. Berezovskii's peculiar role, for example, should certainly not be disregarded, nor should the political motivations of Yeltsin and Putin. Before turning to the question of leadership and personalities, however, two other possible explanations merit consideration.

Religious Motivations?

If what seemed to motivate the fighters of Basaev and Khattab to invade Dagestan was the desire to create an Islamic state and spread the doctrine of Wahhabism, one needs to ask what role religion played in the second Chechen War.[27] However, the impact of religion should not be exaggerated. Wahhabism in Dagestan was a minority belief, representing just a small percentage of the population before the Chechen Wars broke out. It was not a major force in Chechnya either. Khattab evidently practiced Wahhabism, the dominant form of Islam in Saudi Arabia. But Basaev himself has called into question the religious motivations for Khattab's actions. When a reporter asked Basaev if his radical friend Khattab was a "Wahhabite," he said, "No, he is a Khattabite."[28] It was a revealing, if somewhat coy, answer. Khattab and Basaev seemed less interested in religion or in fashioning an independent and viable Chechen state than in fighting for its own sake.

Raduev was the same. In one interview with a Russian magazine in May 1997, he waxed poetic about all of the wars he looked forward to fighting after driving the Russians out of Chechnya:

> I will create a powerful army of five thousand. It will liberate the Caucasus. First, I'll help the Balkars. Then with a powerful strike of three battalions, I'll wipe out Erevan. I can do it even now. I spoke about this to the courageous and patient president of Azerbaijan. Then I'll help Georgia. I'll destroy like trash the Shevardnadze regime. . . . I'm ready to help the Belarusian opposition, even though they're not Muslims. . . . Lukashenko's antidemocratic regime must be destroyed. . . . And then I'll bring Yeltsin to his knees. . . . I'll use chemical weapons against Russia. I'm not playing games here.

Confronted with such lunatic ravings, the interviewer could not resist mentioning to Raduev that some people thought he was "not quite right in the head." Raduev readily acknowledged that other Chechen political leaders were questioning his sanity. "Udugov said that I'm a medical case, Maskhadov announced that I'm a schizophrenic. . . . But I consider myself a student of the great Dzhokhar [Dudaev]," hardly a reassuring response, but a revealing one, nonetheless.[29]

Dudaev had come into power expecting to promote a secular republic, independent of Russia, which would respect Chechen traditions that had been stifled by the Soviet regime. His model was the independence movement of Estonia, where he had been stationed as a Soviet air force commander before being drawn into Chechen politics. Yet the more Moscow resisted making concessions to Chechnya's claims of sovereignty the more Dudaev fell back on Islamic forces—including some outside the country—for support. In the early months of the war, Dudaev could respond to an interviewer's question about the role of religious leaders in Chechen politics that they "do not play an essential role here. Religious and public figures, representatives of peoples and confessions place their trust in the legally elected president and the government."[30]

If such a claim about the lack of Islamic influence on Chechen politics had some plausibility at the beginning of the first war, it lacked any by the end. As Georgi Derluguian described, "Eventually, every powerful man in Chechnya, starting with President Aslan Maskhadov, scrambled to acquire a degree of Islamic discourse and representation—beards grew longer, prayers became conspicuous, women were expelled from the remaining offices."[31] Timur Muzaev, in his encyclopedic review of the evolution of Chechen political organizations, has highlighted a steady radicalization and Islamicization that he attributes mainly to Yeltsin's war against the Dudaev regime. Before the war there were several political parties and organizations of a pro-Russian orientation that favored Chechnya's membership in the Russian Federation. By the end of the war all political organizations promoted Chechen independence. They differed only over whether a sovereign Chechnya should cooperate with Moscow or seek to undermine Russia by interference in its internal affairs and by military intervention in the Muslim republics of the North Caucasus.[32] Clearly, one of the great missed opportunities of the Yeltsin administration was its failure to work out a modus vivendi with Chechnya before the republic fell victim to forces espousing radical Islam.

The base for radical Islam in Chechnya was the country's third-largest city, Urus-Martan, with a population of about 100,000 people. Starting in 1997, Arab fighters began arriving one by one, until they numbered about 500. According to Shervanik Iasuev, an administrator appointed by

Moscow to run the city, the new arrivals "were bearded, wore green or black shirts and long robes over their pants, and were armed with expensive pistols." They called themselves Wahhabis, although they came not only from Saudi Arabia but from throughout the Middle East. "They went to the market and they paid with dollars," said Iasuev. "There was no power here; there was disorder everywhere, and their influence was very strong." With unpromising economic prospects and an astronomical rate of unemployment, Chechnya seemed fertile ground for recruiting fighters to march under the banner of Islam. Young recruits were sent to a camp for three months of religious and military training at Serzhen-Iurt, about 40 kilometers from Urus-Martan. "The poor Chechen people were already suffering so much and our young guys simply couldn't think," Iasuev explained. "They were ready to accept any ideas." At Serzhen-Iurt the young Chechens met Khattab and joined his force of Wahhabis, the troops that would later link up with Basaev to invade Dagestan and set off the second Chechen War.[33]

Military Pressures?

As mentioned earlier, many Russian officers reacted skeptically to the prospect of a military resolution to the Chechen conflict already in 1994, before the first war began. As the war dragged on, opposition to it increased, even within the Defense Ministry. Colonel Viktor Baranets's conversation with "one wise and far-sighted General Staff general" was typical: "What are we going to do with Chechnya?" asked Baranets. "The general blurted out the answer instantly: 'Leave.' And I understood that this answer had been ready for a long time."[34] Despite widespread opposition to the first war, and the humiliating withdrawal in 1996, the Russian military high command tried its hand again at a military solution just three years later. One possible explanation for this surprising turn of events is that most or all of the officers who were opposed on principle to a renewed war in Chechnya had already resigned in protest against the first war. The remaining military leaders had learned different lessons from the first war.[35] They seemed eager for revenge.

Perhaps more significant is the fact that the initiative for renewal of the war seems to have come not from the Defense Ministry but from the Interior Ministry, as the revelations of Sergei Stepashin, reported in chapter 3, suggest. And it was the kidnapping of the Interior Ministry official General Shpigun that prompted Stepashin to get the plans under way. Ironically, Stepashin began his plans for a new war to regain Russian control over Chechnya just when the Russian public was least interested in such a campaign. Public opinion polls in March 1999 reported, for example, that barely a third of Russians considered Chechnya part of the Russian Federation, and few seemed to miss it.[36]

Putin's Personality

Why did the war escalate from the fairly limited operation that Stepashin had in mind? How did the second war become so popular, given that its prospects for long-term success seemed hardly better than in the previous one? Here it worth considering what role the personality and ambitions of Vladimir Putin played. Russian journalist Andrei Piontkovskii has tried to relate Putin's approach to the war to his background in the KGB and even to his difficult childhood. Piontkovskii focuses especially on Putin's easy use of *fenia*, the slang of the criminal world, which became increasingly popular among Russian politicians as they abandoned the artificiality of Soviet-era political speech. "But none of the politicians resort to this underworld jargon as abundantly and naturally as Putin," argued Piontkovskii.

> "Wipe out in the shit house," "a control shot in the head," "whoever offends us won't live 3 days,"—this is clearly not the work of image-makers, but something very personal and rooted in experience. This kind of language isn't typical for the KGB, and even less for its foreign intelligence officers who always stood out for their polished education and well-schooled manners.[37]

Echoing similar analyses of Yeltsin and his intensely personal reactions to Dudaev's inflammatory language, Piontkovskii sought sources in Putin's childhood to understand his policy toward Chechnya.

> When British Prime Minister Tony Blair, who came to Petersburg to express his respect for the future ruler of Russia ahead of time, timidly reproached Putin for annihilating Grozny, Putin replied sincerely and with conviction. His lips even trembled in indignation. It turns out that one of the Chechen rebels called him a "kozyol"— something close to "bastard." In the St. Petersburg courtyard of his childhood, such insults were never forgiven. Turning Grozny into Dresden or Hiroshima is, in Putin's understanding, a perfectly suitable response to being called a bastard.[38]

Lest the reference to Dresden and Hiroshima be dismissed as journalistic hyperbole, Piontkovskii had earlier described to his readers the widespread sentiment in Russia that weapons of mass destruction should be used against Chechnya in response to the invasion of Dagestan and the apartment bombings. Among those who advocated such means were professional politicians who, in a seminar held in the Duma building, "were discussing in all seriousness the question of using thermonuclear weapons in Chechnya." They also included fellow journalists:

> Returning home, I opened up the latest edition of the most popular Russian paper. On the first page, the writer argued: "It is necessary to put the question before Chechnya—either they cease all military activity on Russian territory or face the physical destruction of the whole republic with air raids, bacterial weapons, psychotropic nerve gas, Napalm, everything that our once-strong army has at its disposal."[39]

Finally, some members of the Russian public as well advocated whosesale destruction of Chechen society. In the early days of the war, when it seemed that the Russian forces might stop at the Terek River, the online edition of the Russian newspaper *Vesti* asked its readers whether they favored crossing the Terek and carrying out a large-scale invasion. By a ratio of 5 to 2, respondents favored the invasion. Particularly striking was the rationale of some of those who opposed an invasion—they were not necessarily doves: "We don't need to cross the Terek. Let them die from hunger and bombing," one of the opponents of invasion wrote. "I don't understand why they don't use chemical or nuclear tactical weapons!"[40] This was by no means a representative sample of the Russian population, because computer and Internet users were still relatively rare. If anything, it oversampled the middle classes and intelligentsiia and perhaps called into question one politician's claim that "Internet users are the most progressive class of the Russian society."[41]

These reactions from Russian politicians, journalists, and the public suggest that Putin's emotional response to the Chechen crisis is one widely shared—or at least widely propagated. In any case, one needs more than Putin's boyhood humiliations in a Leningrad courtyard to understand the origins and course of the second Russian war against Chechnya.

Some Russian journalists have made further inferences about the origins of the war by building on the information that the Defense Ministry was already planning a second invasion, even of limited scope, and that Stepashin himself visited the North Caucasus militay district to oversee preparations for the attack. Pavel Fel'gengauer, for example, suggests that the invasion of Dagestan by the forces of Basaev and Khattab may not have been simple "unprovoked aggression." It might be seen "as a clever preventive strike which thwarted Russian military plans and postponed the inevitable invasion for two critical months." Alternatively, he suggests the possibility "that Russian secret services actually lured Basaev into Dagestan to create a pretext for the coming Russian invasion."

> Troops that had been set to invade Chechnya from the north were tied up for several weeks in Dagestan and the rebels decimated several units. Stepashin says that the initial plan was to reach the Terek River in August or early September, but it took the Russians until October to achieve this goal. Russian troops encountered heavy resistance from rebels in Dagestan, so when the delayed invasion of Chechnya began, they advanced step by step, in constant fear of ambushes. The end result: Grozny was surrounded only by December and the Russian command managed to organize a serious assault on the city only this week—in the middle of January (2000)—the worst possible time of year to fight in Chechnya.[42]

Neither of Fel'gengauer's inferences is without problems. As to the likelihood of a "clever preventive strike" on the part of Basaev and Khattab, it assumes that they were acting on behalf of Chechnya or the Chechen government to defend their country's territory. But at the time of the incursion into Dagestan, Basaev and Khattab considered Maskhadov their opponent and would not have been in a position to coordinate with him a plan for preventive defense. The inference that Basaev and Khattab were somehow drawn into Dagestan—perhaps by some expectation that it would be an easy victory—is more plausible. As he flew to Dagestan to try to quell the fighting there, Sergei Stepashin, in his last act as prime minister, vowed that "Russia will not repeat its mistakes in the north Caucasus. No more Russian soldiers will die there."[43] It is also clear, as undoubtedly Basaev and Khattab knew as well, that Stepashin had supported the Wahhabi *djamaat* in Dagestan a year earlier. Might the Chechens have concluded that the prime minister would accept further Wahhabi inroads into Dagestan with equanimity? If Stepashin was indeed planning an invasion of Chechnya since the previous March, then his promise not to send any more Russian troops there to die was a blatant lie. But perhaps he did intend to encourage the Chechens to get entangled in Dagestan, as a pretext for subsequent Russian military actions.

Putin's Putative Political Ploys

Much debate has focused on the relationship between the second war against Chechnya and Putin's political ambitions. The Chechen attacks against Dagestan coincided with Yeltsin's replacement of Sergei Stepashin as prime minister with Putin. Putin at the time was a political nonentity, known for his loyalty to the president, but not for much else. He received broad approval for his conduct of the war, essentially escalating it. And his crude determination, expressed in crude language, to eliminate "terrorists" and "bandits" further boosted his popularity.

The links between the war and Putin's rising political fortunes are mainly circumstantial. The account in Yeltsin's memoir alludes to the relationship between Putin's appointment and the situation in Chechnya, but only obliquely. Yeltsin claims that he had wanted Putin to serve as prime minister as early as 1998 when he became dissatisfied with the incumbent, Evgenii Primakov. Yeltsin did not, however, think the time was right to appoint Putin, "so Stepashin was inserted temporarily." Indeed, he lasted barely three months in the job.

On August 5, 1999, Yeltsin summoned Putin to explain to him "the state of affairs" and tell him that he wanted him to take over the government, even as "a fierce battle loomed ahead." Elections were coming up. "It would not be easy to keep the entire country under control. The northern Caucasus was very troubled. Some political provocations were possible in Moscow." To some extent those last two factors, with their seeming allusion both to the Chechen invasion of Dagestan and the apartment bombings in Moscow, probably loom larger in retrospect than in the actual discussion Yeltsin conducted with Putin. Only the former president and his ghostwriter know for sure.

Was Basaev's Invasion a Setup?

In any case, Chechen forces led by Basaev and Khattab invaded Dagestan two days after Yeltsin appointed Putin. Unlike Yeltsin, who at the outbreak of the first Chechen War had disappeared for days to have an operation on his nose, Putin visibly and publicly took control. As Yeltsin rhapsodized, "within a matter of weeks, he had transformed the situation within our power ministries. Each day he would bring together the heads of each ministry or agency into his office. He forced them to gather all their resources into one united fist."[44] What is most surprising is that Yeltsin, whose career had nearly collapsed in the wake of the disastrous first war in Chechnya, would decide that the best instrument for dealing with the North Caucasus three years later was a "united fist." But equally surprising is the fact that the Russian public seemed to agree. Three months into the war, pollsters found that 77 percent of respondents in St. Petersburg and Moscow approved of the invasion. Even in the provinces the approval rate averaged 64 percent, despite the fact that the regional media often portrayed the local impact of the war—deaths of hometown police and soldiers, for example—more truthfully than those in the capitals. Along with support for the war itself, Putin's personal approval rating soared, from 35 percent when Yeltsin appointed him in August to 65 percent in October, as he escalated the war. As one Russian journalist explained, "The secret of this popularity is in the single forceful expression which Putin used about Chechnya—'We will wipe them out.'"[45]

Russian observers raised suspicions about Putin's motives in escalating the war and about the origins of the first attacks by Basaev's forces into Dagestan in August 1999. They pointed out that Basaev met little resistance from Russian forces, which were evidently withdrawn from the border area just before the Wahhabi incursion, and suggested that Basaev might have been drawn in to create a pretext for a full-scale Russian invasion. Suspicions fell particularly on Boris Berezovskii because of his close ties to Basaev. Vitalii Tretiakov, editor of *Nezavisimaia gazeta,* claimed unequivocally that "the Chechens were lured into Dagestan and allowed to get involved there so as to have a legal pretext to restore federal authority in the republic and begin the active phase of the fight against terrorists gathered in Chechnya." He insisted that "this was clearly an operation planned by the Russian secret services" and that it "was approved at the very top."[46] Another Russian commentator suggested that Tretiakov's revelations were mainly an attempt to defend Berezovskii, the primary financial backer of his newspaper, or, in his more colorful language, "The whole thrust of the article is to prove that oligarch B., who is spiritually close to Tretiakov, has less shit on his snow-white suit than his competitors."[47] Regardless of motives, there remains for many a lingering suspicion—apparently shared by Basaev himself—that the Chechen commander was lured into attacking Dagestan in early August 1999.

Robert Bruce Ware, a leading specialist on Dagestan, has stressed that key developments in the region go back a bit earlier than August. Already at the end of June 1999 Wahhabi militants began infiltrating villages of Dagestan's Tsumadin and Botlikh districts from Chechen bases. "They entered the villages in small numbers and made their presence felt as their numbers gradually grew. Generally, they were courteous to the locals, paid for everything they required, and harassed no one, except in so far as they forbade alcohol. They did not confront local law enforcers, who would have drawn upon their families for support and revenge." According to Ware, military conflict did not begin with an invasion by Basaev and Khattab, but with a local skirmish on August 2, "when Dagestani police forces were dispatched from Buinaksk and Makhachkala to reestablish administrative authority in the region." Basaev and Khattab used the police action as a pretext to carry out an invasion in support of the goal they had explicitly advocated since the April 1999 Congress of the Peoples of Ichkeria and Dagestan: "the creation of an independent Islamic state." Dagestani and then Russian federal forces, apparently surprised at the success of Basaev's incursion, responded by seeking to dislodge the invaders.[48]

Rather than validating the notion of a scheme "approved at the very top," Ware offers two explanations for why the border was so poorly defended. One is that Basaev bribed "Russian officers near the Dagestani border to permit him access by retracting their troops just prior to his advance and later permitting his escape," a tried and true method from the previous war. A second is that Russian officers in the area, confident in the local Dagestanis' commitment to resist the Wahhabi invaders, pulled back their troops in order to set a trap for Basaev.[49] Ware suggests that Russia was not seeking a pretext to invade Chechnya, and that on the surface Stepashin's revelation of an invasion plan dating to April 1999 appears to be "trivial," indicating only normal contingency planning to cope with a dangerous situation. Against the various conspiracy theories, Ware offers another plausible explanation: "Basaev became over-confident as a consequence of surrounding himself with representatives of that small minority of Dagestanis who supported him, and who appear to have misled him concerning the support he was likely to receive from the broader Dagestani population."[50]

The most intriguing evidence that Basaev was lured into invading Dagestan comes apparently from French intelligence sources, via the Russian press.[51] They revealed that in the summer of 1999 Basaev met, at the estate in southern France of the arms dealer Adnan Khashoggi, with Aleksandr Voloshin, chief of staff for then-president Yelstin (and later Putin), and Anton Surikov, a former Soviet military intelligence officer. Surikov had worked with Basaev some years earlier when the Chechen commander was leading military forces of the Abkhaz separatist movement in Georgia, with Moscow's blessing. Voloshin is claimed to have provided $10 million to Basaev in order to fund the invasion of Dagestan. Furthermore, Russian military intelligence officers who later observed the forces of Basaev and Khattab crossing the Chechen-Dagestani border were reportedly ordered not to respond.

In this account, the main objective of the invasion, instigated by Yelstin's administration, was to undermine the political prospects of an emerging coalition between Moscow mayor Iurii Luzhkov and former prime minister Primakov.[52] If Basaev and Khattab had succeeded in seizing the Dagestani capital of Makhachkala and delaring an Islamic republic, Yeltsin would have gained a pretext for imposing emergency rule and postponing the parliamentary elections scheduled for December 1999. The Luzhkov-Primakov movement would have lost momentum, and Yeltsin's political fortunes would have had a chance to revive. In the event, the fierce resistance of local Dagestani villagers thwarted the plans of Basaev and Khattab, as well as those of Yeltsin and Voloshin—if indeed they harbored any.

The fact that Yeltsin did not find adequate justification to declare emergency rule in autumn 1999 does not, however, mean that he did not put the invasion of Dagestan to some other political use. Here most speculation focuses on Yeltsin's promotion of Vladimir Putin. One need not accept that Putin deliberately engineered the second war, counting on his newfound popularity to propel him into the presidency as Yeltsin's successor. Yeltsin's own pronouncement on this matter is unequivocal: "Putin's sudden popularity in the face of the Chechen War was not remotely predictable."[53] That may be so, but once it was clear that fighting Chechen kidnappers and terrorists played well at home, Putin abandoned the limited objectives that Stepashin claimed lay behind the original plan to renew the war. As one Russian analyst put it, "Basaev's raid on Dagestan and the bombings in Moscow both served to reinforce in the public opinion a single, simple chain of conditioned reflexes—Chechens—terrorists—liquidate, wipe out in the toilet." [54]

Did Putin also seize the opportunity to promote his political prospects by escalating the conflict? Some observers believe so. According to Aleksandr Iskandarian, director of Moscow's Caucasus Studies Center, for example, "This was a war fought on TV screens to boost the popularity of the president" and ensure his election.[55] The renewal of warfare in Chechnya served as well to undermine the political standing of retired General Aleksandr Lebed', the only potential challenger who could have campaigned on the platform of law and order that Putin used so successfully. Having brokered the failed peace accord with the Chechens, Lebed' was now made to look naïve and impotent—hardly presidential material.

The Riazan' Connection

One issue surrounding the renewal of war in Chechnya has caused more suspicion than perhaps any other: who bears responsibility for the bombings of apartment buildings in Russian cities in September 1999? The leading suspects, including Basaev and Raduev, have denied responsibility, even though the latter was occasionally prone to take credit for other terrorist acts regardless of his actual participation. The apartment bombings appear to account for most of the support for this second war from ordinary Russians, who had opposed the first war in large numbers. In Russia, a country particularly susceptible to both consiracy theories and genuine conspiracies, many observers began to wonder if the federal security forces had arranged the explosions. At least two candidate theories have been proposed.

The first is linked to Yeltsin's purported campaign to undermine his political rival, Moscow mayor Luzhkov. What better way to discredit the popular Lukhkov than to demonstrate that he could not keep his own residents safe from terrorist attacks? The second theory suggests a deliberate effort to provoke a "rally 'round the flag" effect on the Russian populace to solidify the rule of Yeltsin and his designated successor. Russian journalists once asked Putin himself about such theories. He reacted with characteristic bluster: "What? We blew up our own houses? Nonsense! Total rubbish! There are no people in the Russian secret services who would commit such a crime against their own people. The very suggestion is amoral and fundamentally nothing more than part of an information war against Russia."[56]

Putin's denials failed to allay suspicions about the apartment bombings. In fact, the most suspicious apartment bomb was one that did not go off at all. On September 22, 1999, in the provincial city of Riazan', residents prevented a possible explosion of their apartment complex on Novoselov Street after seeing three people—two men and a woman—carrying several big sacks from their car into the basement of the building.[57] The car's license plate indicated that it was registered in Moscow, but a piece of paper had been taped over it to suggest, by replacing the last two digits, that it was local. The residents phoned the city police, whose experts found that the sacks contained the explosive hexogen and were set with a timer to detonate early the next morning, the pattern that had characterized explosions earlier that month in working-class flats of Moscow and Volgodonsk. An alert went out, and road blocks were set up to capture the terrorists, whom Moscow would soon describe as Chechens, although witnesses said the woman was blonde and the men looked Slavic.

As the search for the terrorists got under way, Nadezhda Iukhanova, an operator at a local telephone bureau, overheard a suspicious call to Moscow. The voice instructed the caller in Riazan' to "get away separately, there are road blocks [*perekhvaty*] everywhere." Iukhanova reported the conversation to authorities at the Riazan' branch of the Federal Security Service (FSB). They were convinced that they had found the terrorists and they managed to trace the call—to "one of the official premises of the metropolitan FSB," their parent organization in Moscow.[58]

The next day, September 23, the press service of the Russian Ministry of the Interior confirmed the presence of hexogen in the sacks found in the Riazan' basement. They were sent to Moscow to the central FSB headquarters for further tests. Major General Aleksandr Sergeev, head of the local branch of the FSB, congratulated Riazan' residents on surviving such a close call.[59] That same day Russian airplanes began bombing Grozny. Prime Minister Putin made a terse announcement of the attack and added that "the bandits will be pursued wherever they are found"—implying perhaps that Chechens were responsible for the attempted terrorist act in Riazan'.[60]

Also on September 23, FSB general Aleksandr Zhdanovich appeared, as scheduled well before the Riazan' incident, on the NTV television program *Hero of the Day*. He presented the government line of the moment that citizens of Riazan' had thwarted an attempted terrorist bombing.[61] The next day, however, the FSB in Moscow offered a different story. It reported that the sacks found in the basement of the Riazan' apartment building were not explosives after all, but ordinary sugar. Still attempting to conform to the previous line, a police spokesperson told the *Moscow Times* that terrorists frequently plant a few dummies before laying real bombs—but this story was now at odds with the one coming out of the FSB headquarters. FSB director Nikolai Patrushev announced that the placement of sacks with timers and detonators was part of a *training exercise*.[62] The local Riazan' authorities resisted this conclusion. "It was a live bomb," insisted Lieutenant Iurii Tkachenko, an officer of the bomb squad who had done the original inspection. He and his colleague, Petr Zhitnikov, later received official recognition and monetary awards for their bravery in dismantling the bombs, as did telephone operator Iukhanova for her contribution to apprehending the terrorists. Nevertheless, Patrushev ordered his subordinates at the Riazan' bureau to release the Moscow-based FSB agents, who had so successfully posed as terrorists.[63] The Russian minister of the interior, Vladimir Rushailo, having congratulated his officers for thwarting the terrorists, was put in a bit of an awkward position.[64]

Because Patrushev took two days to announce that the Riazan' bomb scare was a training exercise, the local media had plenty of time to record the contrary impressions of Riazan' officials. V. N. Liubimov, the governor of the Riazan' *oblast'*, indicated that he was unaware of any exercise. Neither was the head of the local FSB, General Sergeev, informed about it. Following Patrushev's announcement, he sent his agents back to the apartment block to apologize to the residents for unnecessarily creating such a panic. He later visited there himself, urged the residents not to file a lawsuit, and managed to arrange some improvements for the complex—such as a more secure entryway.[65]

Moscow later tried to justify the exercise and the delay in revealing it after the bombs had been discovered. Even the local Riazan' FSB spokesperson, Lieutenant Colonel Iurii Bludov, insisted that the episode was a useful test of the citizens' responses. But, as one journalist wondered, "if it was a training exercise, who was being trained? Why, after the residents had practised evacuation procedures, were they not reassured and allowed to go home?"[66] Instead many of them felt lucky to be able to spend the night in a bus, as one of the residents who had first discovered the bombs was a local busdriver. As another account summarized the official position, it looked a bit feeble: "Residents may have had to spend the night in the cold, and they may have lived for two days thinking they had been the target of a terrorist attack that almost succeeded, but the lessons learned were valuable."[67]

Aleksandr Litvinenko and Iurii Fel'shtinkskii, authors of the most thoroughly investigated account of the Riazan' incident, raise serious doubts about the official story belatedly offered by Patrushev and endorsed by Bludov. They wonder, in particular, how to account for the delay in announcing that the bomb scare was in fact a training exercise. "Let's propose just for a minute that in Riazan' exercises were actually being carried out," they write. "Is it possible to suppose that for the entire 23rd of September, while the world was shouting about the prevention of a terrorist act, the FSB kept silent? No, it's impossible to imagine that. Can we assume that information about the 'exercises' was not made known to the prime minister of Russia, a former director of the FSB, who, moreover, had close personal ties to Patrushev?"[68]

In summarizing the Riazan' affair, one U.S. journalist suggests that there were two competing versions of reality at issue: "Either the authorities tried to kill a couple of hundred Russian residents, or they simply tried to scare the daylights out of them and spread panic through a city for two days to see what would happen."[69] A third version of reality is the political reality that Vladimir Putin fashioned from the incident. One need not accept the darkest interpretation of the Riazan' incident—that the security forces planned to blow up an apartment building and deliberately kill hundreds of Russian citizens—in order to draw some conclusions about Putin's political machinations. It certainly would have been easier for him to justify the bombing of Grozny on September 23, if "terrorists" had destroyed yet another Russian apartment complex the day before. If, however, there was no deliberate intention to blow up the apartment complex on Novoselov Street, Russian authorities nevertheless took advantage of twenty-four hours of panic and confusion to pin the attempted terrorism on Chechens and escalate the war.

Some of the survivors of the Riazan' exercise remained skeptical of the government's position. Aleksei Kartofelnikov, the first to spot the FSB agents on the night of September 22, was well aware of the link to the Chechen War. "The government started bombing Chechnya the next day," he remembered. But he was reluctant to accept Chechen responsibility for the apartment bombings. "I know Chechens. I served with them in the army. They are good people. How can one suspect them of such a thing? How can one suspect it of anybody?" Another resident, Ivan Kirilin, "a scrappy 67-year-old who talks through a cigarette," was more cynical. "Whom should I believe—what the government says or what was in the basement?" he asked. "I don't think the Chechens would blow up a residential house. You have to ask—who is responsible for the war? Who needed the war? The government, of course." As Maura Reynolds, who interviewed many of the residents, concludes: In Riazan' "the government's assertions have made little headway against residents' suspicions. There are too many details that don't fit. And there's the undeniable fact that the bombings led to the war, and the war fed the rise of Vladimir V. Putin." [70]

Putin's war against Chechnya was not a matter of the "two, three, maybe four months" that he anticipated. In late January 2000, after five months of fighting in Dagestan and Chechnya, the Russian Defense and Interior Ministries reported nearly 1,200 deaths among the Russian forces.[71] By March 2000, the figures had reached 1,991 dead and 5,925 wounded on the Russian side—very close to the figures for the first seven months of the previous war.[72] In June 2000 a respected military journal suggested that the army was still sustaining up to 50 deaths a week, or 200 a month.[73] By the end of the year 2001, nearly 4,000 Russian soldiers had been killed and as many as 13,000 wounded.[74] The toll of military casualties is remarkably close to what the Soviet Union sustained during its ten-year war in Afghanistan.[75] The difference is that this time the civilian victims—some tens of thousands of whom perished during the two Chechen Wars—were nearly all Russian citizens.[76]

Russia had gained control of most Chechen territory, except for the impenetrable mountain strongholds that would indefinitely shelter the tenacious guerrilla fighters. As in any classic guerrilla war, the central authorities controlled the peripheral territory at best by day. The guerrillas were in charge at night. As one observer put it, "Before 5 p.m. Grozny is in the hands of the federal troops; after that the checkpoints close down and start defending themselves."[77]

With any national liberation movement as advanced as the Chechen one—and, after all, the country's independence was tacitly recognized with the August 1996 agreement to withdraw Russia's army—it was hard for Moscow to find reliable local representatives. In June 2000 Putin signed an order establishing an interim civilian administration in Chechnya that would report directly to the Kremlin. He appointed the Chechen mufti, Akhmad-Hadji Kadyrov. Unfortunately for Moscow, Kadyrov's appointment led to the immediate resignation of several local Chechen administrators who had been working with the Russian government.[78]

Many observers, especially among the Chechens themselves, blamed the resumption of war in 1999 on the Russian government's failure to fulfill the more than fifty agreements it signed with Chechnya in the wake of the 1996 peace accord. The agreements were supposed to provide for reconstruction of the devastated country. Perhaps it never intended to do so. In May 1997 Presidents Yeltsin and Maskhadov signed the Treaty on Peace and the Principles of Relations between the Russian Federation and the Chechen Republic of Ichkeria. The first principle on which the two sides agreed was "forever to repudiate the use and the threat to use military force to resolve whatever disputes may arise." The status of Chechnya was supposed to be decided peacefully through diplomacy by the year 2001. Evidently someone in Moscow wanted to give war another chance—and many of Maskhadov's enemies in Chechnya were more than willing to oblige.

5

Regions at Risk?

The general position was unanimous: We cannot stand idly by while a
piece of Russia breaks off, because that would be the beginning of the
collapse of the country.

—Boris Yeltsin, on the decision to launch
the first war against Chechnya, Autumn 1994

What's the situation in the Northern Caucasus and in Chechnya today?
It's a continuation of the collapse of the USSR.

—Vladimir Putin, on the decision to launch
the second war against Chechnya, Autumn 1999

The worst-case scenario for Boris Yeltsin and Vladimir
Putin was a breakup of the Russian Federation along
the lines of what happened to the Soviet Union. That
country was also nominally a federation, consisting of fifteen so-called union republics, and when it collapsed each
one of them became an independent country. The Russian
Federation is far more complicated and its disintegration
would be far messier.

As a federation, Russia consists of eighty-nine "subjects," in a wide diversity of sizes and political designations.
They include twenty-one ethnically defined republics, two
cities (Moscow and St. Petersburg), forty-nine provinces
(*oblasti*), six territories (*kraia*), and eleven ethnically
defined autonomous districts (*okruga*) and provinces
located within Russian-majority *kraia* or *oblasti*.[1] Some of
the "subjects" of the federation are certainly large enough
to be independent countries. Tatarstan and Bashkortostan,
for example, have populations greater than seventy mem-

ber states of the United Nations, including such countries as Panama, Ireland, and New Zealand.[2]

Unlike the Soviet Union, however, where barely half the population was Russian, some 80 percent of the Russian Federation's citizens consist of ethnic Russians. An additional large number, perhaps another 8 or 9 percent, identify themselves culturally as Russian, with Russian as their first or only language. Political scientist David Laitin captured the picture well with the Russian ditty, "Mama tatarka, otets grek, a ia russkii chelovek"— "Mom's a Tatar, Father's a Greek, yet I'm a Russian."[3] Given the predominance of Russians and Russian-speakers throughout the federation, those concerned about separatism have focused mainly on the twenty-one republics, even though they constitute just 28.6 percent of the country's territory and 15.2 percent of its population.[4] For the pessimists, Chechnya's declaration of independence in 1991 sounded the tocsin of the federation's demise.

This chapter begins by exploring the impact of the first Russian invasion on other Russian regions. It was not the Chechen independence movement but rather the Russian military reaction that posed the gravest threat to the country's territorial integrity—especially in the volatile North Caucasus, where Chechnya's neighbors took a strong stand against Moscow's intervention. Yet neither these regions, nor any others in the Russian Federation, chose to secede. Clearly, the fears of Boris Yeltsin and Vladmir Putin were overblown, if indeed they were genuine at all. To explain where Russian leaders went wrong in their understanding of the sources of their country's cohesion, I devote the rest of the chapter to an analysis of four cases typically considered "at risk" for secession, the ones many observers claimed were most likely to follow the Chechen example: Dagestan, Tatarstan, Bashkortostan, and the regions of the Far East. I argue that their circumstances differed considerably from Chechnya's. Their movements for autonomy did not pose any serious threat of secession that could not be handled by peaceful negotiations, elite-level bargaining, and concessions—the same recipe that could have avoided the wars in Chechnya as well.

The Chechen Brushfire

Boris Yeltsin explained the 1994 invasion of Chechnya as being necessary to maintain the territorial integrity of the Russian Federation and prevent further secessions. Vladmir Putin made the same case to justify renewal of the war in 1999. Yet when Russian army forces began attacking Chechnya in December 1994, they seemed more likely to precipitate further loss of much of the Russian North Caucasus rather than the reintegration of Chechnya.

Opposition to Moscow's invasion was immediate and widespread throughout Russian society, but particularly along the invasion route and even within the armed forces themselves. As the Russian armored columns advanced through Ingushetiia and Dagestan, they were constantly blocked by crowds of civilians, including women and children. Snipers shot at Russian tanks and armored personnel carriers and were in turn attacked by Russian helicopters. In retaliation for the deaths of several civilians, residents along the Dagestani border with Chechnya captured some fifty-nine Russian soldiers, including four officers.[5]

Leaders of neighboring Ingushetiia opposed the transit of Russian armed forces through its territory, because, as then president Ruslan Aushev put it, "the Chechens are our brothers" and any use of force against Chechnya would result in "massive bloodshed" and guerrilla war. The Ingush vice president, retired Russian General Boris Agapov, warned that the Russian invasion "may compel people to take up arms" in Ingushetiia as well. The Ingush were predisposed to criticize the Russian military action. Only two years earlier, Moscow had backed the Ossetian side in a conflict over the disputed Prigorodnyi district. As Aushev explained to a Moscow television station, his people could not forget how the same Russian armored columns "and the same defense minister" assisted in the destruction of Ingush settlements and the expulsion of Ingush population from North Ossetiia in 1992.[6]

Chechen representatives sought to amplify any expressions of solidarity from Russia's Caucasian minorities. The Chechen People's Congress in Grozny called for a regional alliance "from the Caspian to the Black Sea" to oppose Russian military intervention. In a practice that would become widespread during the second Chechen War, unverified news reports circulated back and forth from Russian and Chechen media sources. The Russian agency ITAR-TASS, for example reported that detachments of armed volunteers were forming among various ethnic groups in Dagestan, under the slogan, "Chechnya and Dagestan are one." The report originated with the "Chechenpress" agency and was obviously intended to create the impression of widespread regional support for the Chechen struggle. Certainly, there was extensive opposition to Russia's military actions throughout the North Caucasus region of Russia, as well as some efforts at recruiting volunteers to fight on the Chechen side.[7]

Expressions of support for Chechnya, or at least criticisms of Moscow's resort to force, were not limited to the North Caucasus, however, or even the Russian Federation itself. In January 1995 leaders of several republics of the Volga-Urals region met in Cheboksary, the capital of the Republic of Chuvashiia, to condemn the Russian invasion.[8] In Georgia, the former Soviet republic bordering Chechnya, separatists from the Abkhazia region backed the Chechen independence drive. Chechens had in 1993 fought in the Abkhazian revolt against the Georgian government—ironically, alongside Russian troops and with Moscow's blessing. From Azerbaijan, the Grey Wolves opposition party sent 270 fighters to Chechnya in mid-December. In the Crimea region of Ukraine, members of the Crimean Islamic Party and the Organization of the Crimean Tatar National Movement began recruiting volunteers. A group of armed Ukrainian nationalists also sought to travel to Chechnya to join the fight but was detained en route in Russia.[9]

The widespread, sometimes violent opposition to the Russian invasion of Chechnya led many observers—politicians, military leaders, and scholars—to make dire predictions about the future integrity of the Russian Federation. Galina Starovoitova, leader of the Democratic Russia party and a former adviser to Yeltsin on ethnic affairs, predicted that Russia's resort to force would "produce mistrust of the center's policy and centrifugal tendencies in Tatarstan, Bashkortostan, Yakutia, Karelia," and other parts of the Russian Federation. Colonel General Eduard Vorob'ev, a Russian army officer who resigned his command in December 1994 rather than lead the ill-prepared invasion of Chechnya, also offered a gloomy prognosis: "Russia has lost in every respect in Chechnya: politically, militarily, morally. Russia has more than a hundred ethnic groups. Will it resolve all disputes through force?" A Russian scholar summarized a common view, that Chechen secession could set a dangerous precedent: "the 'brushfire' of drives for independence may pick up elsewhere across Russia, leading to the eventual destruction of Russian territorial integrity."[10]

But the brushfire of drives for independence did not spread in the aftermath of the first Chechen War, despite the damage Russia inflicted upon itself by the brutal, and ultimately futile, use of military force to prevent Chechnya's secession. An important account of Moscow's first war against Chechnya was aptly called *Chechnya: Tombstone of Russian Power*. Publishing his book after the peace agreement brokered by General Aleksandr Lebed', but before the renewal of fighting in August 1999, Anatol Lieven depicted the war in Chechnya as signaling not only the demise of Russian military power but heralding a systemic crisis in Russian politics, society, and economics. He did not, however, anticipate the further disintegration of the Russian Federation as other regions sought to follow the Chechen example.

President Aushev of Ingushetiia, a retired general and veteran of the war in Afghanistan, had tried to act as mediator of the conflict between Moscow and Chechnya's separatist regime. The hawks in the military, such as Generals Anatolii Kvashnin, commanding the troops of the North Caucasus military district (and later Yeltsin's chief of the general staff), and Anatolii Kulikov, leading the Chechen operation (and later interior minister), were particularly inclined to invoke the domino effect: if Moscow "gave Chechnya independence all their neighbors would want it too." Aushev, whose republic borders on Chechnya and was in fact united with it for many years, disagreed. "I told them, Comrade Kulikov, Comrade Kvashnin, you give them independence and I promise that we will never ask for independence."[11]

Representatives of the other regions typically considered most "at risk" for secession shared Aushev's view that Chechnya's example would not be widely followed. In the wake of nearly two years of devastating warfare and wholesale destruction of Grozny and many other villages and towns, one could understand why leaders of Russia's regions might deem the cost of Chechnya's seeming independence too high. As an official from Tatarstan told me in November 1998, the "lessons of Chechnya should be a warning to everybody"—"to radicals in Tatarstan or any other republic, to radicals in Russia, governmental or nongovernmental radicals"—that military conflict between the center and the regions "should not be repeated in any form." He maintained that "too big a price was paid in Chechnya" on both sides.[12] Yet even without the negative example of Chechnya's destruction in the first war and the fact that Russia reneged on its subsequent commitment to peaceful negotiation of the republic's future, the prospects for a "brushfire" of independence movements was never great.

Dagestan

Dagestan was the republic most immediately affected by the catastrophic events associated with the wars in Chechnya. Out of a population of about 1.8 million, some 58,000 Chechens lived in Dagestan in the 1990s and an estimated 130,000 refugees fled there in the wake of the first war.[13] As the situation in Chechnya seemed increasingly hopeless to Russian authorities, diminishing the prospects for maintaining transportation links and oil transshipment across the republic, they turned to Dagestan as a possible alternative. Plans were developed for a new oil pipeline and a new rail line, both intended to bypass Chechnya.

Dagestan in the late 1990s was also one of the few Russian regions perceived by Moscow to have a genuine fundamentalist Islamic presence in the form of Wahhabi Muslims, organized and armed to promote an Islamic republic on the territory of Chechnya and Dagestan. If, as some argued, the first Russian war against Chechnya was the product mainly of ethnically charged strategic interests—including concern about protecting oil resources and defending against an "Islamic threat"—then Dagestan seemed to present a similar set of conditions.

To what extent was it reasonable for Russian policymakers to perceive Dagestan as "another Chechnya" and anticipate that it might follow its neighbor in a cascade of falling dominoes? The mountain republics of Dagestan and Chechnya do resemble each other a great deal, both in their histories and in their present situations. The ancestors of Chechens and Dagestanis have lived in the same region for some six millennia. Both peoples were converted to Islam over the course of several hundred years, starting around the eighth century. Many Muslims in Dagestan and Chechnya adhere to the mystical Sufi movement, in contrast to the modernist Jadidism practiced elsewhere in the former Soviet Union and tolerated (and somewhat co-opted) by the communist government back then. The Sufi influence seems to account for why, according to survey data, religious belief and practice are far higher in Dagestan and Chechnya than in any other of Russia's Muslim republics, such as Tatarstan and Bashkortostan.[14] The higher the level of religious practice, the more Islam can serve as a mobilizing force for resistance to Russian dominance, as it has done throughout the history of both Dagestan and Chechnya. Indeed, two of the legendary Islamic heroes of the Chechen resistance to tsarist rule—Imam Shamil' and Kazi Mullah—were actually ethnic Avars from Dagestan.

In addition to religion, the peoples of the two mountain republics share many customs, such as a reputation for generous hospitality, a martial tradition and widespread expertise with weapons, and the practice of the blood feud. Both societies are loosely organized, around extended clans (*teips*) in Chechnya and groupings of villages (*djamaats*) in Dagestan.

Among the present-day shared characteristics of Dagestan and Chechnya the most significant is probably their extreme poverty. Of the eighty-nine subjects of the Russian Federation, these two republics are the poorest. Dagestan ranks eighty-eighth and Chechnya eighty-ninth in level of wealth, and their official rates of unemployment are many times the national average.[15] Dagestan's average per capita income is a third that of the rest of the federation. The influx of refugees has worsened the prospects for employment. In the late 1990s in Russia as a whole there were on average 7.8 unemployed persons for every job vacancy. In Dagestan there were 115. Unemployment was particularly severe for women and youth. More than 62 percent of women seeking employment could not find jobs. For young people from eighteen to twenty-eight years of age, the unemployment rate was 60 percent.[16] Unemployment among young men, especially in Chechnya, undoubtedly contributed to the appeal of joining armed bands and engaging in organized crime.

Most observers would understand Dagestan's poverty as a deterrent to secession from Russia. On economic grounds, the republic would be worse off without Russia, as it would lose the redistributed resources, however inadequate, that it received from the center. The role of such economic dependency in keeping Dagestan within the Russian Federation was readily acknowledged to me in an interview in November 1998 with Mamai Mamaev, Dagestan's plenipotentiary representative to Moscow, as he sat at his desk wearing a Rolex watch and chain-smoking Western cigarettes.[17] A region's economic situation is not an entirely objective matter, however.[18] One would have predicted, for example, that Chechnya's economic dependence on Moscow would have muted its separatist demands, if not for Dudaev's grandiose misconceptions that his republic's oil resources could turn it into another Kuwait.[19]

The differences between Dagestan and Chechnya turned out to be far more important than the similarities when it came to assessing the prospects for further disintegration of the Russian Federation. Dagestan lacks Chechnya's relatively homogeneous population and strong tradition of opposition to Moscow. Its nearly 2 million residents live in 700 villages, comprise some thirty-four ethnic groups and speak nearly as many languages, making it the most ethnically and linguistically diverse of all the regions of the Russian Federation. Dagestanis (except for Akka-Chechens, living at the border with Chechnya) did not suffer the mass deportation that Stalin inflicted on the Chechens in 1944. That action, intended to destroy the Chechen nation, instead contributed to its sense of identity, its attachment to its homeland, and its long smoldering grievances against the Russians. Dagestanis, by contrast, do not generally express the intense anti-Russian sentiments of many Chechens, and indeed the republic still reflects much of Soviet "internationalist" ideology. Robert Chenciner, in his anthropological study of Dagestan, calls it "a microcosm of the ethnic mosaic of the Soviet Union."[20]

Although Moscow's political leaders seemed oblivious, many specialists viewed Dagestan as an island of relative peace in a sea of ethnic strife. Despite extreme economic deprivation, exacerbated by massive inflows of refugees from neighboring conflicts, Dagestan managed to avoid outright civil war—even when provoked by the incursion of Basaev and Khattab. Some analysts have described the delicate ethnic balancing act of Dagestan's political system as a form of "consociationalism"—the arrangement that has preserved functioning democracies in ethnically divided countries such as Belgium. Pessimists were more inclined to note a resemblance to aspects of the system that prevailed in Yugoslavia from the 1974 constitution until the country tore itself apart. "Dagestan might have been expected to turn into a dozen miniature Yugoslavias," wrote one observer. "Paradoxically, however, the complexity of the ethnic map actually long helped prevent a crisis."[21]

Differences in social organization between Dagestan and Chechnya appear to account for both the relative stability of the two societies and their propensity to get along with Moscow. Kisriev and Ware develop this argument in some detail. On one hand, the Chechen *teip* "functions like a Sicilian family in terms of its cohesion and loyalty." At times of great external threat, *teips* can cooperate to defend the interests of the entire Chechen people, but even then the basic loyalties lie within the *teip* structure. Thus "a member of one *teip* is loathe to place himself under a commander from another *teip*, and conversely all Chechen field commanders became aldermen of their *teips*." After the first war, "this peculiarity became the major obstacle for the formation of the national political institutions and state discipline" in Chechnya.[22]

Chechnya's dependence on clan allegiances should not, however, be overstated. Former Chechen finance minister Taimaz Abubakarov pointed out in his memoir of the Dudaev years, for example, that the Chechen president did not seem aware of the *teip* membership of "at least half of his ministers." By contrast, when Abubakarov proposed streamlining and "downsizing" the government apparatus by 40 percent during 1993, Dudaev took matters into his own hands and produced a secret list of suspected political enemies who were the first to lose their jobs. Dudaev's suspicions were not obviously based on the *teip* membership of his supposed opponents.[23]

On the other hand, the key political unit of Dagestan is the *djamaat*, "a village or a coherent group of villages that transcends blood relations and operates more or less like an ancient city-state." Under Soviet power, when the mountain peoples of the region were organized into the Republic of

Dagestan, they retained the essence of their traditional social structures. During the Soviet era,

> the traditions of the *djamaat* became the basis for a political organization that transcended not only blood, but ethno-linguistic barriers. Unlike the Chechens, who never accepted Russian rule, the Dagestanis developed a trans-ethnic national identity and settled fairly comfortably within the Soviet federal system, which was, for them, in some respects, the *djamaat* writ large. Today, many Dagestanis are nostalgic for that system, which brought them pavement, plumbing, electricity, education, sexual equality, and security.[24]

Such nostalgia for Soviet rule came through clearly in my discussions with Mamai Mamaev, Dagestan's representative to Moscow, as he pointed out his republic on an old map of the USSR tacked on the wall behind his desk. Yearning for the stability of Soviet rule is hardly surprising. The first Chechen War wrought havoc on Dagestan, where some 130,000 refugees fled from the destruction of Grozny and surrounding villages. In the capital city of Makhachkala competing political factions commanded their own armed militias and threatened civil war in the autumn of 1998.[25] Mamaev played down the violence, inviting me to visit the capital and insisting that only the border area with Chechnya posed any risks. The day after my interview, the American teacher Herbert Gregg was kidnapped in Makhachkala in broad daylight. Within the year, the border conflicts erupted into full-scale war, as Russian troops used the incursion by forces of Basaev and Khattab and the apartment bombings to justify a full-scale invasion of Chechnya.

To what extent does religion influence the political situation in Dagestan?[26] In May 1998 Dagestan's minister of nationalities responded to a journalist's question about "the danger of religious extremism in Dagestan"—an obvious reference to Wahhabism—by making a distinction between religious belief and political activity: "Surely among the Wahhabis are normal people who consider that this religious theory suits them." But, he continued, "if today you explain to them that their leaders are determined to change the constitutional order of Dagestan by armed means then they would come out against this and not support those who plan to come to power with weapons in hand."[27] His comments reflected a confidence about the Dagestanis' allegiance to the current political system and to Russia, regardless of their religious beliefs, and—in light of the widespread resistance to the Wahhabi attacks from Chechnya in autumn

1999—were well founded. In the same interview, the minister also addressed the question of how to deal with Chechnya in the wake of the 1996 peace accords, and again his views were prescient. He urged that Moscow follow through with a program of economic aid, which, he implied, could reasonably be considered reparations for the damage that Russian military forces inflicted, a characterization that Chechen president Aslan Maskhadov had also advanced. The key point is that religious belief by itself is not enough to destabilize a country like Dagestan or Chechnya, without additional conditions—in particular, the desperation and humiliation that come from hunger, unemployment, and lack of hope for the future, and political organizations able to mobilize to exploit grievances.[28]

In the wake of renewed warfare in Chechnya, one might have expected the situation in Dagestan to become unstable, given the republic's poor economic prospects and the growth of Wahhabism. At least in the short term, however, the opposite seems to have occurred. Encouraged by the Dagestani villagers' resistance to the Wahhabi attacks, and seeking to buy their loyalty to Moscow, Russian officials provided long-overdue economic aid. Four months into the war, then prime minister Vladimir Putin himself traveled to Dagestan to celebrate New Year's Eve 2000 and express his appreciation. He was there when Boris Yeltsin announced his surprise resignation of the Russian presidency in favor of Putin. It was said to be "auspicious for Putin, perhaps intentionally so, that, in this moment of highest drama, he was seated, not at Yeltsin's feet, but at the table of a people previously conceived as potential antagonists."[29]

The economic aid promised by Moscow was substantial indeed: for the year 2000, an increase of 2.7 times over the previous year. State employees, including teachers and doctors, received salary increases of 50 percent, and pensions were being paid regularly "for the first time in recent memory."[30] The aid did little, however, to address a crucial problem of economic disparity within Dagestani society: "There is no other place in Russia where the difference in income between a narrow circle of wealthy families and the rest of the population is so significant." Some 200 "families," or about 6,500 people, control most of the republic's wealth. They represent just 0.3 percent of the population.[31] Despite the vast disparities in wealth, the war against the Wahhabi and Chechen militants fostered—at least temporarily—a new sense of unity. It enhanced support for both the government in Makhachkala and the federal authorities, including the Russian army. Finally, the war gave some justification for the Dagestani government to crack down on Wahhabi organizations in the republic, something that it had been reluctant to do previously.[32]

Although Dagestan was hardly an island of stability, neither was it ever a leading candidate for a Chechen-style independence movement. Nor did the Chechen and Dagestani rebels who favored uniting their countries into an Islamic republic ever stand a chance of succeeding. The fears and pretexts of Russian officials from Yeltsin and Putin on down find little support in the case of Dagestan. That is not to say that long-term stability in Dagestan is by any means guaranteed. Politics there is a delicate balancing act, based largely on dividing up political offices and economic spoils among the leading ethnic groups. Political-economic assassinations seem to be one of the key methods of "recalibrating" the balance when things go awry.

Tatarstan

In the wake of the first Chechen War, the "Tatarstan model" was frequently invoked as a peaceful alternative to what happened in Chechnya.[33] Both republics were the only ones of eighty-nine Russian regions to have refused to sign the Federative Treaty that Boris Yeltsin proposed in 1992 as a basis for a renewed Russian Federation. Yet Tatarstan subsequently negotiated a bilateral "treaty" with Moscow that helped mute the demands of radical Tatar nationalists for full independence, while at the same time reassuring the federal authorities that Tatarstan would not secede.[34]

It is not surprising that the Moscow government should be concerned about the fate of Tatarstan. After Russians, Tatars are the largest ethnic group in the Russian Federation, numbering 5.5 million (3.8 percent) in 1989 out of a total Russian Soviet Federated Socialist Republic (RSFSR) population of 147 million. Nearly 5 million lived in the European part of the country, with about 51,000 in the North Caucasus. Some 157,000 Tatars lived in Moscow and 44,000 in Leningrad (St. Petersburg). More than a million more Tatars lived outside Russia in other republics of the Soviet Union. Of those within Russia, only 1.7 million lived in the Tatar Autonomous Soviet Socialist Republic (32 percent of the Russian total), with more than a million more living in neighboring Bashkir ASSR. Within Tatarstan, ethnic Tatars are the largest group at 48.6 percent of the population, with Russians a close second at 43 percent.[35]

The Republic of Tatarstan is a highly industrialized economic powerhouse. Its extensive industries include petrochemicals, various forms of military technology, timber, pulp and paper-processing, and the largest truck manufacturing complex of the former Soviet Union. With proven oil reserves of some 700–800 million tons, its annual production is about 12 million tons (roughly 7 percent of Russia's output in 1994). Tatarstan also boasts significant reserves of natural gas and coal, as well as an extensive system of oil and gas pipelines.[36]

The Tatar nationalist movement emerged during the *perestroika* era of Mikhail Gorbachev's reforms. As in much of the rest of the Soviet Union, a number of groups, known as *neformaly*, emerged during 1987 and 1988 to support such issues as environmentalism and preservation of the indigenous culture and language.[37] In June 1988 some faculty and graduate students of Kazan' University and the Institute of Language, Literature, and History formed the Tatarskii Obshchestvennyi Tsentr, the Tatar Public Center, or TOTs, as it became known after its founding congress in February 1989. The center worked closely with republican authorities and came to represent the dominant force for asserting Tatarstan's economic and political sovereignty.[38]

Unlike the leadership in Chechnya, that of Tatarstan did not engage in what some analysts have called "ethnic out-bidding" in order to gain support—or at least what efforts there were proved unsuccessful.[39] In April 1990, for example, the Tatar writer Fauziia Bairamova founded a party of Tatar national independence called Ittifak. Despite its name—which means agreement, unity, or harmony in Tatar—Ittifak threatened to divide the movement for Tatarstan's autonomy.[40] At one point a group of radical nationalists declared another prominent Tatar writer an "enemy of the Tatar people" because he opposed making Kazan' Tatar the sole official language of the republic. (Given that Tatars and Tatar-speakers were a minority in the Tatar ASSR, his position would not appear unreasonable.)[41] As political scientist Sergei Kondrashov describes, despite such provocations, "the political and economic elites did not split but retained their unity." Tatarstan's leaders engaged "in a battle with Moscow for power and resources," he argues, "but it was not ethnic nationalism at all that animated the republican ruling elite in their push to sovereignty. Far from jumping on the nationalists' bandwagon, the establishment fought, if at times half-heartedly, to contain nationalism. They worked out their own strategy as an alternative to the nationalist project."[42]

What about the role of religion? One of the main reasons Tatarstan has appeared on Russian officials' list of "regions at risk" is that it has a sizable Muslim population. Thus it is worth noting that an organized Islamic movement did not appear in Tatarstan until quite late in the process of Soviet reform. In March 1991 the Islamic Democratic Party of Tatarstan was formed to liberate the republic from the "colonial communist regime" and establish an independent Islamic state. During the following summer, an

All-[Soviet] Union Islamic Democratic Party was established, with branches in Bashkortostan, Dagestan, and elsewhere.[43] Yet for most residents of Tatarstan, religion was not a major factor serving to mobilize their support for national autonomy. First, Tatars represented less than half the population of the republic. Second, among Tatars in the early 1990s, 30 percent considered themselves atheists, 30 percent believed in but did not practice Islam, and barely a quarter both believed and practiced their religion.[44]

The main grievance on which both Russians and Tatars agreed was economic. In particular, residents complained that within the USSR the status of the Tatar ASSR—or Tatariia, as it was called—did not match its economic importance. In the late 1980s, for example, one Tatar scholar calculated the annual allocations from the central budget in Moscow to the various republics for socioeconomic needs as follows: Russia, more than 800 rubles per capita; Estonia, more than 1,300; the Tatar ASSR, only 212. The author highlighted the perceived injustice of the situation by pointing out that the value of the output of the Tatar ASSR's Kama Automobile Works alone exceeded that of the entire Estonian economy.[45] Total industrial output of the three Baltic republics of Estonia, Latvia, and Lithuania did not match that of Tatarstan in the late 1980s.[46]

Comparisons with the Baltic republics seemed particularly salient in the early years of the Tatar movement for autonomy.[47] The reasons are straightforward. Latvia, Lithuania, and Estonia held the status of a union republic—of which there were fifteen in the Soviet Union—whereas Tatariia was merely an autonomous republic within Russia (then known as the RSFSR). Concern about Tatariia's status was not merely a product of the *perestroika* period. As early as 1917, with the demise of the tsarist empire, proposals arose for an "Udel'-Ural Republic" within a federal Russia, *Udel'* being the Tatar word for the Volga River. In 1918 the Bolsheviks had suggested a combined Tatar-Bashkir Soviet Republic before deciding to establish Bashkiriia and Tatariia both as autonomous republics within the RSFSR, in 1919 and 1920, respectively.[48] Tatars had raised the issue of elevating their republic's status many times since then—in connection with adoption of the "Stalin" Constitution in 1936, then in 1951, 1954, 1964, and in 1977, as the "Brezhnev" Constitution was implemented.[49] For their efforts to secure a union republic under the 1936 constitution "the entire government of the Tatar republic was arrested, together with many intellectuals." Despite such setbacks, "the Tatars never lost sight of the goal of sovereignty," and in particular of becoming a union republic.[50]

The difference in status between a union republic and an autonomous republic was not trivial, as can be seen by comparing the Tatar ASSR with the union republic of Kirghiziia. With comparable populations (3.5 million versus just over 4 million, respectively), Tatariia's annual gross domestic product exceeded that of Kirghiziia (17 billion versus 11.5 billion rubles, respectively). "Nevertheless," as Shnirel'man points out, "Kirghiziia had three economic-research institutes with a total staff of about two hundred, while Tatarstan had a single department of economics with a staff of three. As a union republic Kirghiziia was permitted to withhold five percent of the revenue from the sales of its oil industry; Tatarstan had no such privilege, even though it was the locus of one of the main oil-extraction centers of the country." The Tatar republic's lower status also meant it had limited support for indigenous culture and language compared with the situation in the union republics.[51]

In 1989 the consensus among Tatar political activists was that their region should be "upgraded" to the level of union republic. Facing a recalcitrant Moscow, the Tatar leaders issued a unilateral declaration of republican "sovereignty" in August 1990. In the spring of 1991 the leaders of the radical Ittifak Party sought to undermine Tatarstan's relations with Russia as well as the Soviet Union. Fauziia Bairamova staged a two-week hunger strike in the central square of Kazan' in order to persuade the authorities not to hold elections in the republic for the presidency of Russia. The Tatarstan Supreme Soviet reversed its previous decision and chose not to sponsor the elections officially, but to assist anyone who wished to take part. The victory of the nationalists was, however, somewhat chimeric. They made a great effort to keep residents of the republic from participating in the election of Boris Yeltsin to the Russian presidency on June 12, 1991. But in the race for president of Tatarstan, held on the same day, the nationalists endorsed Mintimir Shaimiev, putting forward no alternative candidate of their own. Indeed, the nationalists' electoral weakness was striking, with opinion polls indicating that TOTs and Ittifak together (the main nationalist parties) received support from less than 14 percent of the population. Even the Communist Party did better at nearly 19 percent, with the Democratic Party of Russia—the vehicle of Moscow-based reformers and their Kazan' allies—coming in at almost 24 percent (more than 41 percent of those polled expressed no preference). Thus running unopposed, Mintimir Shaimiev, the moderate former communist leader, was elected to the presidency of Tatarstan, with 71 percent of the vote.[52]

Shaimiev performed a delicate balancing act between the nationalists and the conservative forces from the old Communist Party *apparat*. He nearly lost his balance in August 1991 when Mikhail Gorbachev's hard-line enemies staged a coup in Moscow. They opposed the Union Treaty that

Gorbachev had offered as a way of preserving the USSR in a looser confederal system. The coup was timed to disrupt the union-wide referendum expected to endorse the new treaty. In seeking to preserve the union—and not incidentally their own jobs—the coup plotters triggered the complete breakup of the country.[53] Shaimiev was put in a bind. He had succeeded in getting the grudging acquiescence of Gorbachev and Yeltsin, the presidents of the USSR and Russian republic, respectively, for Tatarstan to sign the Union Treaty independently of Russia, as if it were already a USSR union republic. But in fact, he was quite concerned about the economic implications of the treaty for Tatarstan. Nor, as an old communist *apparatchik*, did he seem to mind taking orders from the "emergency committee" that sought to depose Gorbachev.

Shaimiev was wary of Yeltsin, the figure who emerged as the main opponent of the putschists. When Tatarstan issued its declaration of sovereignty a year earlier, Yeltsin had given his blessing: "I repeat again what I said at the Congress of People's Deputies on my election: the formation of the share of power should go from the bottom to the top—from town to republic. Whatever kind of independence Tatariia chooses for itself we will welcome it."[54] But shrewd observers recognized what only later became apparent to many more. Yeltsin's support of republican independence movements was an opportunistic attempt to weaken Gorbachev rather than a genuine commitment to decentralization. Moreover, Shaimiev was reluctant to support the liberal economic reforms promoted by Yeltsin's advisers: "At this juncture they were too radical for the liking of the Tatarstan establishment, on which President Shaimiev relied."[55] So Shaimiev supported the coup.

His "blind obedience" to the orders of the Moscow coup plotters undermined Shaimiev's credentials as a supporter of Tatarstan's sovereignty, whereas his failure to rally behind Yeltsin left his commitment to democracy in doubt. When the coup attempt quickly failed, Shaimiev was "accused of betrayal by both the nationalists and the democrats in Tatarstan, who called for his immediate resignation." As Kondrashov described, "Yeltsin would not have been Yeltsin if he had not tried to use the moment simply for toppling Shaimiev on the grounds of his complicity in the failed coup." He sent Sergei Shakhrai "to engineer Shaimiev's dismissal." But cooler heads prevailed. When Shakhrai arrived in Kazan' in late August 1991, the Tatarstan establishment closed ranks behind Shaimiev, and even the nationalists supported the president "as a symbol of republican sovereignty in the face of Moscow's interference."[56]

At this point events could have gotten out of control. Beyond supporting Shaimiev against Moscow's interference, the Tatar Public Center took the opportunity to push for full independence for Tatarstan. More ominously, it announced the formation of a National Guard to defend Tatarstan militarily. The TOTs vice president, a retired army colonel, was made commander in chief and a call-up of fighters began—with some 3,000 reportedly recruited: "In effect the nationalists set about creating their private army."[57] Meanwhile, the leader of the Islamic Democratic Party declared the establishment of an "Islamic Democratic State of Bulgar-Tatar." Nationalist groups rallied thousands of supporters to demonstrate at the Supreme Soviet building, where confrontations with the police left several injured.[58]

Not surprisingly, many observers at the time believed that Tatarstan was about to embark on the same course of violent confrontation with Moscow as Chechnya was pursuing at precisely the same time. As a Tatarstan official later recalled, "It was an extremely difficult situation. It was absolutely close to Chechnya in terms of, I would say, the explosive character of it."[59] The nationalist radicals in Tatarstan, noted Kondrashov, "did not conceal the fact that their design was modeled on the Chechen Republic."[60]

In September 1991, under seemingly similar circumstances in Chechnya, the Yeltsin administration had sent Ruslan Khasbulatov to urge Doku Zavgaev and the communist-era officials to step down—a move that implicitly favored the nationalists led by Dzhokhar Dudaev. When Dudaev called a general military mobilization and used his National Guard to dominate his rivals, Moscow had second thoughts. Yeltsin declared a state of emergency in the republic and dispatched a force of 2,500 interior ministry troops, the first of many ill-fated military interventions.

Fortunately, Moscow—after the failure of the Shakhrai démarche—pursued a different course with Tatarstan. In September 1991 the Yeltsin administration sent Galina Starovoitova, the president's adviser on ethnic issues, to Kazan'. Starovoitova had a reputation as a defender of ethnic rights from her work with Armenians in the Nagorno-Karabagh enclave of Azerbaijan and her efforts to mediate various disputes in the North Caucasus and elsewhere. A professional ethnographer by training, she had actually studied the ethnic community of Tatars in her native Leningrad— an unusual and somewhat controversial topic for the time.[61] In any case, Starovoitova was a good choice for envoy because she was respected in Tatarstan. Her message, moveover, was a balanced one. On the one hand, she insisted that Kazan' not undermine the democratic reforms that Moscow intended to implement and warned that the federal center would use all means necessary to enforce its laws in Tatarstan. On the other hand, she did not rule out the possibility of an autonomous republic's secession from the Russian Federation, but only if three conditions were fulfilled: (1) the titular nationality should be indigenous to the territory, (2) it should constitute a majority of the population, and (3) the population must endorse secession in a referendum.[62] It is worth noting that Chechnya probably could have fulfilled those criteria, but Tatarstan would be a more difficult case. Tatars represented a relative rather than absolute majority of the population, and even if all of them favored secession, it is doubtful that the other groups would go along.

Perhaps more important than Moscow's approach to Tatarstan's drive for autonomy—which veered from attempts to overthrow the republic's elected president to willingness to work out a modus vivendi—was Shaimiev's skill as a politician. While General Dzhokhar Dudaev was working his way through the ranks to reach the pinnacle of his military career as a commander of an air force base in Estonia, Mintimir Shaimiev was learning the ropes of the Soviet political system from Brezhnev's *zastoi* (stagnation) through Gorbachev's *perestroika*. That experience apparently paid off. He was able to forge coalitions with nationalists and *apparatchiki*, keep his democratic opponents off balance, and prevent violence with Moscow. When Dudaev's popularity was flagging in autumn 1991, he sought to revive it by calling for a broad military mobilization. When trust in Shaimiev's leadership hit a low point (18 percent) at the same time, the Tatarstan president took a different course. In mid-October 1991 he banned all paramilitary organizations and prosecuted violations—arresting 673 people and confiscating 742 weapons.[63]

In any event, the people of Tatarstan seemed more interested in protecting their economic and political prerogatives in a time of rapid transition than in outright secession for its own sake. Even in Naberezhnye Chelny, the most nationalist of Tatarstan's cities, only 18 percent of Tatars supported complete independence, with the majority favoring some kind of economic autonomy within the USSR or RSFSR. Among Russians there, 45 percent advocated Tatarstan's economic autonomy within the Russian Federation.[64] By pursuing a course intended to maintain ethnic peace within Tatarstan while asserting the republic's rights vis-à-vis the central government, Shaimiev appeared to be following the general interest of his constituents.

After the breakup of the Soviet Union, a delegation from Tatarstan participated in the initial negotiations in Moscow to refashion the Russian Federation and produce a new Federative Treaty. One of the more contentious issues concerned the relative rights of republics, designated by their titular nationality, and other subjects of the federation. Representatives of the nonrepublican regions were resentful of the special rights that the republics sought. The Tatarstan representative proposed that all subjects be granted equal rights, with a leveling up to the rights of the republics rather than a leveling down. Ten of the republics reached a consensus on the proposal, even though it would have limited their relative advantages, but the government negotiators rejected the initiative. In protest, the Tatarstan delegation quit the constitutional convention and returned to Kazan'.[65] The government's position was widely supported, with only 23 percent of those polled claiming that Tatarstan should sign the Federative Treaty. Confidence in President Shaimiev climbed to 58 percent.[66]

As other subjects of the Russian Federation were signing the Federative Treaty, Tatarstan's leaders conducted a referendum on the republic's status. On March 21, 1992, voters were asked: "Do you agree that the Republic of Tatarstan is a sovereign state, a subject of international law, that builds its relations with the Russian Federation and other republics and states on the basis of equal treaties?" The wording was deliberately ambiguous, as it did not propose outright secession from Russia, but the reference to sovereignty and international law implied that Tatarstan would not automatically be subject to the Russian Constitution. Shaimiev's supporters in the Tatarstan parliament conducted negotiations with Moscow on the language of the referendum and issued a declaration to the effect that it "did not violate the state and territorial integrity of the Russian Federation, and that Tatarstan would delegate some functions to Moscow." The nationalist TOTs leaders were unhappy about this maneuver—as it seemed to undermine in advance the implications of a "yes" vote—but they did not believe they had any other choice than to urge their followers to support the referendum. Leaders of the democratic reform movement were, however, willing to promote a "no" vote out of concern that Shaimiev and the ruling *nomenklatura* would use an endorsement of sovereignty to isolate themselves from the political and economic reforms that the federal government was expected to pursue. In any event, the referendum received an overwhelming endorsement from Tatarstan voters. With a turnout of 81.6 percent, 61.4 percent voted for the sovereignty declaration and 37.2 percent against.[67]

The endorsement of Tatarstan's sovereignty gave the Shaimiev government a mandate to negotiate its relationship to the federal authorities, but the process itself was anything but smooth.[68] Eventually the two sides concluded a bilateral treaty, signed on February 15, 1994, and a series of subsequent agreements, but many disputes remained. Nevertheless, among both Tatars and Russians, support for the way Kazan' handled its relationship to Moscow remained strong. In a March 1997 survey of public opinion, respondents were asked their views on the original declaration of state sovereignty that Tatarstan issued in August 1990. A majority of both Russians and Tatars expressed either positive or ambivalent feelings toward the declaration (57.7 percent of Russians, 66.9 percent of Tatars), with a slight majority of Tatars (51.4 percent) giving an outright positive evaluation and agreeing that "it was the right decision." Support for Shaimiev was even higher. When asked, again in March 1997, what evaluation they would put on the president's activities over the previous two years, 86.9 percent answered "good" or "satisfactory" (40 percent and 46.9percent, respectively), with little difference between Tatars and Russians.[69] Support for a "high level of decentralization" in relations between the Russian Federation and Tatarstan was strong among both groups (66 percent of Tatars, 50.1 percent of Russians), compared with support for "strong centralization of the Russian government" (12.2 percent and 26.3 percent, respectively).[70]

Outside Tatarstan, opinions about Shaimiev and his policies were less sanguine. For some observers the signing of the bilateral treaty between Russia and Tatarstan raised concerns that Russia's "constitutional federation" would be replaced with an unstable "negotiated federation." One of the more outspoken critics of this process was Vladimir Lysenko, a parliamentary deputy and specialist on nationality issues. His subcommittee on federal and regional policy issued a report pointing out how the treaty of February 1994 violated various articles of the federal constitution and warning about the dangerous precedent it set for the future of Russia.[71] He predicted that the treaty between Moscow and Kazan' would set off a "chain reaction" as other ethnic republics, and even Russian-majority provinces, sought to negotiate bilateral arrangements.[72] Indeed, many regions followed Tatarstan's example until more than forty bilateral agreements were signed.

Ironically, even before the year was out, Lysenko appeared to have changed his mind about the merits of the Tatarstan model. As the conflict with Chechnya threatened to explode into full-scale war in December 1994, he drafted a statement on behalf of the small political party he headed, in which he wrote, "We think that a Treaty on the delimitation of authorities, similar to the Tatarstan one, should be concluded with Chechnya."[73] Lysenko's ambivalence about the merits of a "negotiated," asymmetric federation was widely shared in Moscow. By the end of the 1990s, with the Chechen conflict still unresolved, many of the center's leaders increasingly came to criticize the bilateral treaties. Vladimir Putin set as one of his first tasks to bring the wayward republics and other regions back into line.

But at some basic level the Tatarstan model must be considered a success. A number of observers have suggested that without the bilateral treaty, and the process of peaceful negotiation that led to it, Tatarstan's drive for autonomy could have provoked a violent response from Moscow and resulted in a Chechen-style conflict, as the events of autumn 1991 seemed to portend.[74]

How, then, did Tatarstan avoid violent conflict with Moscow? Chechnya's road to war presents, as Georgi Derluguian has put it, "an astonishingly overdetermined picture." Among the factors typically cited are "oil interests, resurgent Islam, imperial collapse, international terrorism, organized crime." "Superficially," argues Derluguian, "Chechnya shares most of these features with Tatarstan—another defiant republic of the Russian Federation which has oil, notorious gangsters, and a native population of Islamic heritage."[75] Presumably these were the features that made Russian leaders from Yeltsin to Putin fear that if Chechnya were allowed to secede, Tatarstan would be the next domino. Yet, as Derluguian and others point out, besides the formal Soviet institutional context, Tatarstan and Chechnya shared little in common, making it highly dubious that Tatarstan would be the "next Chechnya."

A first, important difference between Chechnya and Tatarstan relates to their geographic and geopolitical positions. Chechnya lay on the periphery of the Russian empire and was only subjugated in the second half of the nineteenth century—at great cost, especially to the Chechen side. The wars of resistance from 1785 to 1864 led to the deaths or emigration of half the Chechen population, many of whose descendants now live in Turkey and Jordan.

The Tatars, by contrast, were widely dispersed nomads and traders who lived throughout what is now Russia. The thirteenth-century Tatar principalities (khanates) dominated their Russian counterparts by controlling the main trade routes from northern Europe to the Orient. The core homeland of the Tatars was the Khanate of Kazan' in the Volga River basin. In 1553 Ivan the Terrible ended the Tatar domination by conquering Kazan', but despite occasional campaigns to convert the Tatars to Christianity, relations between the Muslim locals and the Russian immigrants were nowhere near as conflictual as in the North Caucasus two centuries later. As Derluguian describes, "The Volga region remained an open steppe frontier equally attracting Russian and Tatar peasant settlers." Tatars rarely rebelled against Russian rule, "and when they did, such as during the massive uprisings of Stepan Razin in 1667–1671 and of Pugachev in 1773, Tatars often fought against the imperial authorities alongside Russian peasants and Cossacks." In sharp contrast to Chechnya, "traumatic memories of ethnically-directed violence are all but absent in Tatarstan."[76] Thus in the last years of the Soviet Union, relations between Tatars and Russians were generally friendly, even if Tatars expressed concern about the preservation of their culture and language. As one author put it, "ethnic discord did not exist even among the notorious Kazan' juvenile gangs."[77]

Tatar populations, the fact that Tatar political organizations preceded Russian ones, and the early conquest by the Russian tsar mean that Tatars and Russians have been living together for a long time in what is now the Russian Federation. Some Tatar nationalists, such as Ittifak's Fauziia Bairamova, have sought to use this shared history to promote their cause. In October 1991 she argued that half of present-day Russian territory had once belonged to the Tatars: "It is a good time now for Tatarstan to lay claim to the old Tatar lands where Tatars still live—the lands of Simbirsk, Saratov, Samara, Astrakhan', and Orenburg, and the vast territories of Ufa and of all the Ural region." She called on Tatar historians to confirm that these lands belonged to the Tatar people.[78] If they had done so, they would have confirmed Eric Hobsbawm's aphorism that historians are to nationalist politicians what poppy growers are to heroin dealers.[79]

Instead, the majority of Tatars seem to accept the interpretation offered by Rafael' Khakimov, a historian himself, author of the founding program of the TOTs movement, director of the Institute of History of the Republic of Tatarstan, and adviser to President Shaimiev. Khakimov drew on the same evidence as Bairamova—the shared history of Tatars and Russians across the vast Eurasian continent—to make a contrary argument: that it seemed quite normal for present-day residents of Tatarstan, Tatars and Russians alike, to consider themselves part of Russia. "Suffice it to say that 75 percent of Tatars live outside of Tatarstan, moreover mainly in their historic homeland, that is on the territory of the former Kazan', Astrakhan', Kasimov and Siberian khanates. In that way, a significant part of Russia · appears as much Tatar as Russian." Again, in contrast to Bairamova and the militants of the Ittifak movement, Khakimov insists that his "republic is not interested in secession," but in remaining part of the "Russian space" (*v rossiiskom prostranstve*).[80]

In addition, Chechnya and Tatarstan offer marked contrasts in the nature of major socioeconomic indicators. As table 5-1 illustrates,

Map 5-1. *The Middle Volga Region*

Tatarstan at the end of the Soviet era was far more urbanized and "modern" than Chechnya, with little disparity between Tatars and Russians in the main socioeconomic indicators, such as education and income. The homogeneity in the Chechen community is illustrated by language use, with virtually all Chechens indicating Chechen as their native language, whereas over 14 percent of Tatars chose Russian. Nearly 40 percent of Tatars spoke Russian at home, compared with a quarter of Chechens.

The superficial structural features of Tatarstan—oil, Islam, crime, its autonomous status within the USSR—would appear to make it resemble Chechnya in its potential for violent secessionism. Yet, as Derluguian points out, a more meaningful set of socioeconomic factors makes that resemblance less tenable. Even so, one could imagine that without the stabilizing, if not particularly democratic, leadership of Shaimiev, Tatarstan's relations with Moscow could have been far more violent. By the same token, a more sensible Boris Yeltsin and a less erratic Dzhokhar Dudaev

Table 5-1. *Socioeconomic Indicators in the Late Soviet Period, Chechnya and Tatarstan*

Indicator	Chechnya	Tatarstan
Population (millions)	1.3	3.6
Major ethnic groups (percent)	Chechens, 59 Russians, 23 (mainly in Grozny) Ingush, 13	Tatars, 48.6 Russians, 43
Share of rural population (percent)	58	26
Discrepancies in levels of socioeconomic indicators among ethnic groups	Significant: Russians are more urban and "modern," Chechens more "traditional"	None since the early 1970s
Children per family	Chechens, 3.8 Russians, 1.6	Both groups, 1.47
Adult literacy (percent)	Less than 70	99
Native language of members of titular nationality, 1989 (percent)	Chechen, 98.9 Russian, 1.1	Tatar, 85.6 Russian, 14.2
Language spoken at home by members of titular nationality, 1994 (percent)	Chechen, 73.4 Russian, 25.2	Tatar, 60.8 Russian, 38.8
GNP per capita (index, Russian average = 100)	65.9 (largely due to oil production)	95.1
Investment assets (index, Russian average = 100)	78.1 (mainly in Grozny)	114.6
Unemployment (percent)	40	In 1990 full employment required importing workers
Rank by combined indicator of socioeconomic development of former Soviet territories (out of 49)	46 (just ahead of Tajikistan)	13 (close to Lithuania)

Source: Adapted from Georgi M. Derluguian, "Ethnofederalism and Ethnonationalism in the Separatist Politics of Chechnya and Tatarstan: Sources or Resources?" *International Journal of Public Administration,* vol. 22, nos. 9 and 10 (1999), pp. 1402–04. Language information from *Chto nuzhno znat' o narodakh Rossii: Spravochnik dli gosudarstvennykh sluzhashchikh* (Moscow: Skriptorii, Russkii mir, 1999), pp. 561–62.

might have gone far toward avoiding the conflagration that engulfed Chechnya. Personalities as well as structural factors influenced the course of events in both republics, including the success of the nationalist independence movement.

As political scientist Mary McAuley has argued, "unless the existing political elite splits, fragments, with a section identifying with the reform-minded nationalists, it is going to be extremely difficult for a popular movement to mount a serious challenge to its power." Instead, "the existing elite, while still in control of the offices of state, and acquiring control of the economic resources, can claim a new legitimacy based on its role as national leader."[81] This generalization seems to account well for the divergent cases of Chechnya and Tatarstan. It also fits the case of Bashkortostan.

Bashkortostan

Like its neighbor Tatarstan, Bashkortostan is rich in natural resources, relatively well developed in industry (including military production), and noted for being one of the few "donor" regions whose tax revenues are redistributed to the poorer areas of the federation. But the republic's physical proximity to Tatarstan and their shared history have made some observers worry that Bashkortostan and Tatarstan might join together to form the nucleus of an "Udel'-Ural Republic," as first proposed in 1917, and thereby assert their independence from Russia. Such an entity would be a military-industrial powerhouse and could pose a real threat to the survival of the Russian Federation.[82]

A Tatar-Bashkir union would face serious obstacles, however, as a basic demographic overview indicates. Out of a total of 4.1 million, Bashkortostan's population includes about 900,000 ethnic Bashkirs, 1.2 million Tatars, and 2 million Russians. Bashkirs are already a minority in their "own" republic. If they joined with Tatarstan, the addition of Tatarstan's 19,000 Bashkirs would still leave them far outnumbered. Given the high level of intermarriage between the two groups,[83] this might not be such a grave issue, but nor would union of the two republics provide any obvious benefit. Meanwhile efforts of the government of Bashkortostan to assert cultural rights of ethnic Bashkirs have come under criticism from Tatarstan. In particular, efforts to make Bashkir and Russian the republic's official languages are perceived by Tatar residents as discriminatory—not unreasonably, given that they represent a larger population than the Bashkirs themselves. Particularly worrisome was the provision that a candidate for the presidency of Bashkortostan must speak Bashkir, a restriction that would limit the field of contenders drastically. It is not surprising that the leaders of neighboring Tatarstan should express concern about the issue, as they did directly to the Bashkortostan parliament. Nor is it surprising that the parliament in turn criticized the Tatarstan officials for unwarranted interference in their republic's internal affairs.[84] In any case, these are the sorts of conflicts that make an easy union of the two Volga-Urals republics an unlikely prospect.

A second factor leading some observers to include Bashkortostan in the category of "regions at risk" is the presence of Islam. But as in Tatarstan, the level of religious practice in Bashkortostan has not historically been high and the population is even more diverse than in Tatarstan, with many non-Muslim peoples and many nonbelievers. Out of a population of nearly 4 million, 22 percent are ethnic Bashkirs, 28 percent are Tatars, and 39 percent are Russians.[85] Among the Bashkirs, 44 percent identify themselves as atheists or agnostics, 31 percent believe in but do not practice Islam, and 25 percent are practicing Muslims.[86]

Perhaps to avoid the use of Islam as a mobilizing factor in a nationalist movement, the government of Bashkortostan sought to co-opt it. Moreover, it made a point of supporting Russian Orthodox institutions as well as Muslim ones. President Murtaza Rakhimov, for example, signed two decrees providing state funding for restoration of both a major cathedral and a mosque. Some observers, nevertheless, raised objections to such a seemingly evenhanded approach. First, it neglects, and perhaps deliberately discriminates against, less well represented religions in Russia, such as Protestantism, Judaism, Buddhism, and Roman Catholicism, as well as various "New Age" spiritual movements. Second, it represents a diversion of scarce funds at a time of "acute social crisis, characterized by delays in wage, pension, and social-benefit payments and an absence of funds for health care and education, and a halt in construction of public housing."[87] Since these are the conditions that often give rise to fundamentalist movements—even in the presence of well-endowed state-sponsored religions—this is a criticism probably worth heeding.

The third main concern about Bashkortostan's separatist potential is the position its government took toward the Federative Treaty. Bashkortostan's leaders negotiated a supplementary bilateral agreement with Moscow, appended it to the Federative Treaty, and only then signed the treaty, as did Boris Yeltsin on behalf of the Russian Federation.[88] Bashkortostan's action was followed by Tatarstan's outright refusal to sign the treaty and by its proposal of a bilateral treaty as an alternative. When the treaty between Moscow and Kazan' was signed on February 15, 1994, it set off what one critic called a "chain reaction," as other ethnic republics, and even Russian-majority provinces, sought to negotiate bilateral arrangements.[89] Bashkortostan itself concluded a treaty with the Russian Federation on August 3, 1994.

The text of Bashkortostan's supplement to the Federative Treaty and the bilateral treaty with Moscow reveal that the main issue for the republic is not secession or any deliberate undermining of the Russian Federation. Instead, Bashkortostan's leaders seek to raise the status of the republic's residents and, especially, to secure control of the territory's resources and economic activity. Thus the supplementary agreement to the Federative Treaty begins with some symbolic, and seemingly contradictory, language to the effect that Bashkortostan is an "independent subject of a renewed Russian Federation." It then gets to the heart of the matter: the republic's claim on its land and natural resources as the "property of its multinational people." Again there is no suggestion that Bashkir people should be favored over Russians, Tatars, or other nationalities, but just that the wealth of the republic should be under local control.[90]

Since the value of Bashkortostan's resources depends on the ability to export them abroad, there is further provision that the republic be "an independent participant in international and foreign economic relations, except those voluntarily transferred by agreement to the Russian Federation." The same provisions applied to the systems of criminal justice, law, and taxation, with all rights reserved to the republic unless formally granted to the relevant organs of the federal center.[91] Additional legislation, differing from the federal laws, is intended to encourage foreign investment.[92]

Critics have suggested that the Bashkortostan government's insistence on control over the republic's resources is less a function of a nationalist striving for autonomy than the result of the individual greed of its president, Murtaza Rakhimov. In September 1998, for example, Rakhimov consolidated control over five major energy firms in the republic to form the Bashkir Fuel Company, even though the government held a controlling stake in only two of the five firms. One might argue that Rakhimov's intent "to gain control over the main revenue producers in the republic" was driven primarily by the need to bolster the economy in the wake of the drastic decline in the value of the ruble and the central government's default on its debts the previous month.[93] Most observers have not been so generous.

Bashkortostan, like its neighbor Tatarstan, is a prime example of what one observer has called the "regionalization of autocracy" in Russia.[94] As such, it should be of concern to democratically minded citizens and leaders in Moscow as well as the regions themselves. Yet concerns about auto-

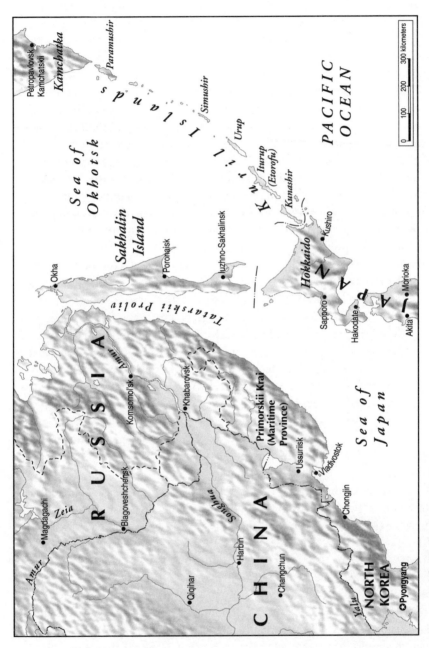

Map 5-2. The Russian Far East

cratic rule are a different matter entirely from the risks of separatism and the breakup of the Russian Federation—risks that Bashkortostan did not pose. Thus one can doubt the wisdom of Russian leaders who pursued a war in Chechnya ostensibly to eliminate such nonexistent risks.

The Far East: Primor'e and Sakhalin

Concerns about separatist tendencies in the Russian Federation have not been limited to the Islamic republics. The regions of the Russian Far East have also asserted their autonomy, even though they lack the formal status of the republics, by thwarting the policies of the federal government on a range of economic and political issues. Consider this somewhat sensationalist vignette: "A power-hungry governor in the Russian Far East demands control of the Kuril Islands, upsetting delicate negotiations and the establishment of closer relations between Moscow and Tokyo. The same local autocrat denounces Moscow's agreements on border demarcation and strategic partnership with Beijing and instructs local militia to intimidate Chinese traders." The implication is that Moscow has lost control of distant regions, with serious implications for its foreign policy, if not for the federation's very survival.[95]

The "local autocrat" in question was Evgenii Nazdratenko, then governor of Primorskii krai, the "Maritime Territory." Primor'e, as it is known, is located at the distant eastern reaches of the Russian Federation, bordering the Pacific Ocean and China, in close proximity to Japan and the Korean peninsula. Its capital, Vladivostok, is as far from Moscow as Moscow is from New York. The only Russian territory further east is the island of Sakhalin, known to European Russians for generations as the "end of the world."[96]

Examining the Russian Far East—Primor'e and Sakhalin *oblast'*—offers an opportunity to "control" for the effect of Islam and non-Russian ethnic identities on the prospects for separatism. Sakhalin, with a population estimated at 631,000 in 1996, is predominantly Russian, but it has plausible reasons to assert its autonomy from Moscow.[97] Its natural trade partners are in the Far East, and the exploitation of its resources (gas, oil, fish) was hindered for years by bureaucratic and political intransigence in Moscow. Moreover, the government of Sakhalin resents the federal government's efforts to negotiate the status of the Southern Kuril Islands with Japan, without taking Sakhalin's interests into account.[98] If material incentives play an important role in separatist movements, they should be evident in Sakhalin. If, on the other hand, there exist countervailing factors that contribute to the preservation of the Russian Federation despite strong fissi-parous tendencies, the Sakhalin case should reveal them.

Primor'e, with a population of about 2.2 million, makes an even more compelling case of a potentially separatist region. It enjoys a "usable history" of independent political status, however brief, and a distinctive regional identity.[99] Its now former governor Nazdratenko had portrayed himself as a defender of regional interests against Moscow's incompetent interference, had pursued economic sovereignty, and had threatened to hold a referendum to decide the territory's relationship to the Russian Federation. When the Kremlin finally managed to oust Nazdratenko in 2001—by offering him a lucrative job running Russia's fishing industry from Moscow—it was unable to keep him from getting his chosen successor, Sergei Darkin, elected against the favored candidate of President Putin.[100] Thus Primor'e remained a potential problem for Moscow even after Nazdratenko.

Primorskii krai

The prima facie case for taking seriously the separatist tendencies of Primor'e is nicely laid out by political scientists Mikhail Alexseev and Tamara Troyakova. Physical distance from Moscow—the administrative center of the Soviet Union and post-Soviet Russia—posed many practical problems for Primor'e's economy. Prices for everything were higher than in European Russia because transportation costs were calculated with the assumption that Moscow should be the natural hub. As then Governor Nazdratenko once suggested, "Why don't we start counting distances in Russia not from Moscow (the political center), but from Vladivostok (where the sun rises first)? Then our [transportation] tariffs would be zero and we'd be prospering!" Instead, Primor'e's vast wealth of natural resources was also channeled through Moscow rather than traded with local partners in China, Japan, or even the United States.

Economic sense would seem to dictate a new orientation for Primor'e, once the hypercentralized Soviet system was abandoned. Similar arguments were made by the separatist movements in Estonia, Latvia, and Lithuania in the years of perestroika. As Alexseev and Troyakova pose the question, "If proximity to European economies was a powerful motivation behind the Baltic secession, why shouldn't proximity to Pacific Rim economies . . . engender political separatism in the Russian Far East?" The leaders of Primor'e "had a clear incentive to do the same thing as Estonia did in 1988: declare economic sovereignty and attract hard currency and superior industrial equipment from abroad."[101]

In addition to economic considerations, the Russian Far East enjoyed a distinctive regional identity—*oblastnichestvo*, in Russian—upon which its leaders could have drawn to bolster a case for sovereignty. Aside from practical consequences, such as higher prices, the sheer physical distance implied a certain psychological difference: "Breakfast in Moscow is dinner in Vladivostok." In Siberia and the Far East people tended to favor individual initiative and self-help, whereas the psychology of the European heartland emphasized collective values and communal decisionmaking. Moreover, the historical experiences of the Russians of the East distinguish them from their European compatriots: "The collective memory in the Far East is shaped by stories of frontier settlement and resistance against external threats that echoed only distantly in Moscow." Finally, history records several efforts to establish a distinct political entity, separate from Russia. In 1865, just a few years after the tsarist empire had finally defeated Imam Shamil' and crushed the resistance of the mountain peoples of Dagestan and Chechnya, a new specter of separatism appeared in the East. The police imprisoned two advocates of Far Eastern regionalism "for an alleged conspiracy to detach Siberia from Russia and set up an American-style republic." In the early years of the twentieth century, the United States again appeared as a model when proposals for a new tariff on Far Eastern ports threatened a revolt of the sort mounted by the thirteen colonies against England.[102]

The most usable historical precedent for Primor'e's separatists was the Far Eastern Republic, a quasi state that emerged in the wake of the Russian Revolution and was later suppressed by the Bolsheviks in the 1920s. Interest in the republic surfaced in the early *perestroika* years, when regional activists launched a newspaper called the *Far Eastern Republic* and published the political writings of Aleksandr Krasnoshchekov, the president of the republic who had been shot during Stalin's Great Purge in 1937.[103]

Yet despite clear economic motives, geographic isolation from the center, and a well-defined sense of regional identity, political separatism in Primor'e was never a serious prospect. There was no effort by regional leaders to establish distinctive political institutions to govern the territory independently of Moscow. Instead, Governor Nazdratenko used the threat of separatism opportunistically to defeat his political rivals and to negotiate with Moscow.

Nazdratenko's background resembles somewhat that of Boris Yeltsin. Trained as an electrician in the construction industry, he worked his way up to foreman, brigade chief, and then director of the Vostok mining enterprise. As an elected people's deputy to the Russian parliament, his political constituencies were the industrial managers and Communist Party *apparatchiki* who became regional administrators after the demise of the USSR, whereas Yeltsin for a time became the darling of the democrats. While working in Moscow, Nazdratenko developed ties to Yeltsin's aide Viktor Iliushin and presidential bodyguard Aleksandr Korzhakov. On their recommendation, and with support of the local Primorskii industrialists and officials, Yelstin appointed Nazdratenko chief of administration of Primor'e in May 1993, before the position of governor was created.[104] Nazdratenko's main rival was Vladimir Kuznetsov, whose "policy called for an incremental transition to self-government in Primor'e through integration with the Pacific Rim economies and concomitant development of free market institutions in the region." According to Alexseev and Troyakova, Nazdratenko played the separatist card and "presented himself as a stronger supporter of regional independence than his political rivals." He advocated "upgrading" Primor'e from a territory (*krai*) to a republic, in order to claim the prerogatives that Tatarstan and Bashkortostan, for example, enjoyed.[105] At the same time, Nazdratenko's supporters convinced the Russian president that their candidate would back Yeltsin against his opponents in the Supreme Soviet (even though Nazdratenko's initial sympathies were with vice president Aleksandr Rutskoi and the opposition).[106] Thus Yeltsin evidently ignored the separatist rhetoric in favor of the guarantee of support from Nazdratenko's backers.

In any event, Nazdratenko's vows to create a maritime republic were sheer opportunism. "While arguing for economic sovereignty, Nazdratenko refused to back any measures on free economic zones that had not received his political approval and that did not directly enhance his political standing in the region." His main concern as chief executive of Primor'e was to defeat his political rivals in the regional legislature. Boris Yeltsin had a similar problem with the Supreme Soviet in Moscow, and he resolved it by ordering army tanks and helicopter gunships to fire on the parliament's headquarters in October 1993. "Nazdratenko replicated Yeltsin's strategy—albeit without tanks and helicopters—and dissolved the region's assembly." With it dissolved Nazdratenko's interest in a maritime republic. Once he had achieved political supremacy for the executive branch, and himself personally, he canceled the referendum on upgrading the status of Primor'e.[107]

Nazdratenko's subsequent interest in regionalism was driven by his own political goals. His conflict with Moscow over demarcation of the border with China and his intimidation of Chinese traders, cited at the beginning of this section as evidence for purported separatist tendencies, are more plausibly explained by local political exigencies. As political scientist Michael McFaul put it, "Nazdratenko has capitalized on ethnic tensions between Russians and Chinese to legitimate his regime's gross violation of individual human rights," and has used the border dispute as "a convenient 'nationalist' issue to rally local support behind his authoritarian regime."[108] Primor'e is thus another shining example of the regionalization of autocracy.

Critics in Moscow, such as former deputy prime minister Egor' Gaidar, described Nazdratenko's as "the most criminalized regime in Russia"—an epithet normally reserved for Chechnya.[109] But as Galina Kovalskaia reported from talking to people in the region, in the late 1990s Nazdratenko's regionalist, anti-Moscow antics seemed to yield some benefits:

> The population is rather calm with respect to Nazdratenko. He is not liked, but "Moscow" is hated to such an extent that they will support Nazdratenko if only to spite the devil-reformers. He is also ranked among the mafia, but at the same time "he is not the main mafioso; those are in Moscow." Almost everybody you ask says that if the governor is dismissed, things will get even worse.[110]

As in many cases of center-regional relations in Russia, local autonomy seemed to come at the expense of democracy.[111]

In 1994, in the other example raised at the start of this section, Nazdratenko argued that the Kuril Islands should be transferred from the jurisdiction of Sakhalin *oblast'* to Primor'e. The southern Kurils had long been a matter of dispute between Tokyo and Moscow since Japan was obliged to cede them to Soviet control at the end of World War II.[112] From time to time, Moscow had attempted to resolve the issue by compromise of some sort. The most promising moment came with the advent of *perestroika* and the official repudiation of much of the legacy of Soviet foreign policy, but Mikhail Gorbachev never managed to fulfill the promise. Nor did his successor, even though Yeltsin seemed in a stronger position to make concessions, at least initially.

In any case, Nazdratenko's intervention complicated Russian diplomacy, but he appears to have had more parochial motives. Gaining administrative control over the fishing and shipping resources of the southern Kurils would have allowed Nazdratenko to reward his political supporters in those industries. The more important point, however, is that Nazdratenko's ploy undermined his position as a promoter of economic autonomy, free trade, and foreign investment for Primor'e. "A separatist strategist in Nazdratenko's place would be more likely to support the return of the islands to Japan, thus scoring political points with Tokyo and securing major Japanese investment in Primor'e."[113] Thus Nazdratenko's separatism was illusory and no danger to the territorial integrity of the Russian Federation. Since his departure—and despite replacement by his chosen successor—the situation is even less threatening, as Kremlin-linked financial interests increase their political control over the region.[114]

Sakhalin oblast'

In Sakhalin *oblast'*, as in Primor'e, one might expect local leaders to have favored a rapprochement with Japan for economic reasons. Yet they did not. In fact, the issue of secession came up precisely when the Yeltsin regime seemed on the verge of finding a territorial compromise with Japan. In 1992 Valentin Fedorov, then governor of Sakhalin, threatened that his region would have to consider seceding from the Russian Federation if Yeltsin returned the southern Kuril Islands to Japan.[115] Since then something of a nationalist backlash throughout the country has hindered efforts to resolve the dispute, with a vigilant mainstream press alerting the public to the slightest signs of Russian flexibility.[116] One popular magazine article in May 2001 took the occasion of some remarks by a former Japanese prime minister about his hopeful meeting with President Putin two months earlier to trot out all of the arguments against ceding any of the disputed territory to Japan. Particular emphasis was put on the economic resources that Russia would have to forgo and the dangerous military implications for Russia's Pacific Fleet if it had to give up its bases on the islands in the face of a continuing U.S. military presence in Japan. The article concluded by repeating a crude ditty that had appeared on a recent television broadcast: "On the Kurils it's hardly a paradise, but at least there aren't any Samurais!"[117]

In fact, popular attitudes in Sakhalin *oblast'* toward the Japanese have been far more sympathetic than the media discussions would suggest. One poll in 1998 indicated that only 7.7 percent of the respondents disliked Japan, 66.7 percent liked it, and 77.7 percent wanted to visit.[118] Igor' Farkhutdinov, Fedorov's successor as governor, was no more enthusiastic about territorial compromises. As political scientist Steven Solnick points out, "The Sakhalin governor has used his opposition to territorial concessions as a tactic for extracting greater economic resources or privileges from the federal government."[119] In early 1999 Farkhutdinov responded cautiously to Moscow's proposal to create a special economic zone in the southern Kurils to encourage Japanese involvement in joint ventures there. Perhaps fearing that a special status for the islands was merely a prelude to partitioning the *oblast'* and giving back some of it to Japan, he suggested instead that the whole of Sakhalin be granted the benefits of a free economic zone.[120]

Like Primor'e, Sakhalin would appear to have solid economic incentives for seeking autonomy from Russia. Rich in natural resources—with offshore energy reserves that could rival those of the North Sea—Sakhalin has nevertheless had trouble convincing foreign investors that the region is a reliable partner. Moscow seems to be a big part of the problem. Throughout the 1990s the Russian parliament, dominated by opposition communist deputies, was extremely sluggish in approving the legislation necessary to secure investment by foreign energy companies. They were wary that "the law gave foreign investors an unfair advantage over domestic producers."[121] "They're against it because Yelstin wants it," complained the manager of Mobil Sakhalin Ventures.[122] Because of such political and bureaucratic barriers, and despite the enormous potential wealth, Sakhalin ranked seventy-sixth among Russia's eighty-nine regions in investment climate, according to one major bank survey.[123]

Under the circumstances, one might expect the Sakhalin authorities to take matters into their own hands, as in Tatarstan or Bashkortostan, and cut the foreign deals themselves, without Moscow. Sakhalin's residents suffered particularly badly from the August 1998 economic crisis, much of which could be attributed to mistakes and crimes committed in Moscow.[124] Yet in an interview just months later, its representative to the federal government was unwilling even to consider acting on foreign involvement without Moscow's permission. He insisted that investments in Sakhalin's main oil projects had not declined, despite the crisis. He was particularly keen to have Rosneft', a Moscow-based oil company, participate in the so-called Sakhalin-1 project. That way, skeptical Duma members would be less justified in criticizing the project as one benefiting only foreigners.[125]

Ordinary residents, who saw little benefit from the oil investments, took a different tack in their approach to Moscow. On Shikotan, one of the disputed Kuril Islands, 3,800 residents sent a petition to President Yeltsin suggesting that if Moscow did not address their economic crisis, they would lease the island to Japan for ninety-nine years in return for aid. The petitioners cited provisions of a 1992 presidential decree allowing ninety-nine-year leases as a way to attract foreign investment.[126] The move was evidently a bluff to get the attention of the authorities, as there does not seem to be much desire by residents to become Japanese subjects.

Not all of the barriers to foreign investment, particularly in the energy sector, are Moscow's fault. Environmental destruction from oil production is likely to be substantial—there have already been significant spills. Activists have expressed concern about the impact on the fishing industry as well. Finally, many residents do not expect to benefit from foreign investment in the energy sector and are therefore indifferent about creating conditions to favor it. In autumn 1999 Mikhail Alexseev reported from his conversations with ordinary Russians in Sakhalin—"hotel employees, taxi drivers, salespeople, phone operators"—that all of them dismissed his "suggestions that some day the energy wealth would trickle all the way down to them."[127]

If Sakhalin were an autonomous republic, with a titular nationality, rather than a mainly Russian *oblast*, one might expect some effort to assert economic sovereignty in the interest of local control of natural resources, the basic model of Tatarstan and Bashkortostan. In fact, Sakhalin Island is the homeland of several indigenous peoples, among which the Nivkhi, in particular, have been studied extensively since the tsarist era.[128] Nivkhi were designated as one of the (numerically) "small peoples"—or "Children of the North" (as a Sakhalin government program that supports their cultural activities is rather patronizingly named). Toward the end of the second millennium there were somewhere between 2,400 and 3,200 Nivkhi on Sakhalin.[129]

Even if the Nivkhi were numerous enough to stake a claim on Sakhalin's oil resources, as the Chechens have done in their republic, for example, they would probably not do so. The Nivkhi still regard the discovery of oil in their homeland as "the great misfortune" because of the damage the oil industry has caused to their native habitat and because of the flood of outsiders it brought.[130] Although not seeking a share in the oil wealth per se, some Nivkhi activists have demanded that Russia and Japan apologize and pay reparations for the land they stole from the indigenous peoples as they colonized the territory over the past two centuries. Vladimir Sangi, a novelist and Nivkh leader, has suggested figures of $80 million for Russia and $30 million for Japan. Furthermore, countries whose oil companies "broke Nivkhi laws and came to our territory without permission" should chip in an additional $5 million each as compensation.[131] Although these amounts represent a small fraction of the billions of dollars of anticipated revenue from oil production, no one is lining up to pay. Nevertheless, indigenous protests are unlikely to have much impact on relations between the center and Sakhalin.

Both Primor'e and Sakhalin would appear to share some of the basic elements of potentially successful separatist movements: regional identity, economic incentives, and a plausible historical model to emulate (at least in the case of Primor'e, with the Far Eastern Republic). But these factors must be understood in their political context. In particular, they are subject to manipulation by regional leaders to serve their own political agendas: "economic incentives and regional political identity matter in the emergence of regional separatist strategies, but only in as much as they are perceived by subnational elites as something that would advance their political objectives."[132] Only in the case of Chechnya did such objectives include outright secession—and even there, as the previous chapters have suggested, there was room for compromise.

The End of the "Parade of Sovereignties"

In the wake of the August 1998 financial crisis, fissiparous tendencies in the Russian Federation showed a marked decline. As Vladimir Shapoval, Sakhalin's representative to Moscow, put it to me in November of that year, "The crisis showed that not one of us, even the richest, is yet ready to survive independently in today's world." He believed that "the period of the 'parade of sovereignties' is over." The government has "a real chance to create a normal structure of a federal state, in which each unit will know the rights it has and the responsibilities it bears." Shapoval criticized "the rosy democratic slogan our President [Yeltsin] put forward: 'Take just as much sovereignty as you can handle.' I consider that this was simply a populist slogan and it hasn't the remotest relationship to real life."[133]

Tatarstan's experience confirms Shapoval's judgment that even the richest regions suffered from the August meltdown.[134] Mikhail Stoliarov, first deputy plenipotentiary of Tatarstan to the Russian Federation, expressed similar views. As for the August crisis, "we really suffered from it, and we do suffer from it now. We are not separate; we cannot close the border and seclude ourselves from the economy of the Russian Federation." The crisis confirmed that "we are part of Russia, and we are Russian, and therefore all the problems that have been faced by the Russian Federation, they are also the problems of Tatarstan." Moreover, "being in the center of the Russian Federation, we cannot separate." Stoliarov expressed confidence that Tatarstan would be able to work out its differences with Moscow, including reconciling divergent constitutions and laws.[135]

The leadership in Bashkortostan also took a fairly conciliatory line in the wake of the August crisis. It was particularly anxious to defend against charges that the republic had secured unwarranted privileges through its negotiated agreements with the center, in the realm of taxes, for example. Irek Ablaev, Bashkortostan's representative to Mosocow, explained that the republic's decisions to withhold certain tax payments to the center were usually intended to offset subsidies that Moscow was no longer providing. For instance, a major industrial complex in Blagoveshchensk that produced important polyether compounds for the construction industry and for the military had not received the necessary funds to modernize its facilities or even to cover basic social services for the employees. Whatever funds the republic provided to make up for what Moscow failed to send would then be withheld from its tax obligation.[136] The situation with Blagoveshchensk resembles on a smaller scale what Tatarstan faced in its efforts to maintain the enormous Kamskii automobile works (KamAZ) in Naberezhnye Chelny. Without support from the federal center to maintain production, unemployment could threaten the livelihoods of thousands of people, about 100,000 in the case of KamAZ, including workers and their families.[137] Dependence on the federal government in these cases tends to mute any calls for secession.

Despite their insistence on their republic's "sovereignty," Bashkortostan's officials, like those of Tatarstan, acknowledged how completely the region was integrated into the Russian system. As Irek Ablaev pointed out to me, out of a population of 4.1 million, nearly 1 million of Bashkortostan's citizens are pensioners. They spent their lives working throughout the Soviet Union and then returned home to retire. Who should be responsible for paying their pensions, the republic or the center? On these sorts of matters, Bashkortostan is happy to maintain its links with Moscow. Even in areas where the republic does enjoy advantages, such as in its level of industrial development and endowment of natural resources, its officials are willing to admit that "we perfectly well understand that these are not the achievements of our republic alone. They were created in the course of seventy years by the entire Soviet people." Ablaev particularly drew attention to the scores of factories that were moved into Bashkortostan during World War II to escape destruction by the German armies and the vast investments in oil processing that were "created by the efforts of the entire Soviet Union." Ablaev was sensitive to the charge that Bashkortostan's wealth accords it a certain privileged position in its relations with Moscow. But he also stressed the negative side of his republic's Soviet-era economic development. Industrial pollution poisons the land, water, and air. According to Ablaev, every second child in Bashkortostan is born unhealthy, the victim of an environmental disaster that the central government in Moscow ignores. "And they speak of 'privileges,'" he complained. "If we had healthy children, that would be a privilege."[138]

It is evident that there was no great rush on the part of the regions actually to secede from the Russian Federation—not in the early years of the Yeltsin regime and certainly not at the dawn of the Putin era. The Chechen example was one that no other region sought to emulate. Moreover, the overall level of integration and mutual dependence between the center and the regions was recognized by the leadership of even the most privileged republics. They sought to use whatever leverage they had to improve their status, but they had no intention of abandoning the federation. The concerns that both Yeltsin and Putin raised to justify going to war against Chechnya—the imminent disintegration of the Russian Federation—appear unfounded. Moreover, as chapter 6 suggests, the reforms that Putin has instituted to reestablish central control—or the "vertical of power," as he calls it—could do more harm than good.

6

Dictatorship of Law

The first effect of centralization . . . is to make any kind of indigenous character in the diverse regions of the country disappear . . . all of the provincial and municipal freedoms are confiscated to benefit the supreme power that is the government.
—Pierre-Joseph Proudhon, 1862

The central authorities are not letting us hold these elections in peace. We want to live together with Russia, but we want to choose our president ourselves, while the Kremlin is literally imposing its candidate.
—Madina Merzhoeva, a teacher from Ingushetiia, 2002

The state lies, it is unable to offer any cogent policies or enforce its decisions. But citizens still believe in the state.
—Representative of a nongovernmental organization in Pskov, 1999

In August 1990 Boris Yeltsin traveled to Kazan', the capital of Tatarstan, to urge the local authorities to "take as much autonomy as you can swallow."[1] Ten years later, newly elected president Vladimir Putin visited the same city during a festival and dunked his head into a bucket of fermented mare's milk as part of a local folk ritual. But he was not swallowing any of his predecessor's pro-autonomy rhetoric. Propelled into office by popular support for revival of war against the separatist republic of Chechnya, Putin pledged from the start to bring the rest of the regions into line as well. Although a noticeable departure from Yeltsin's laissez-faire approach, Putin's intention to strengthen the center at the expense of the regions was hardly unprecedented. His stated views were consistent with those of most of the prime ministers who served under Yeltsin, as well as of national political leaders across the spectrum.

Russian leaders' preoccupation with the weakness of the center in relation to the regions is part of the explanation for two brutal wars in Chechnya. Yeltsin evidently believed that he had gone too far in his rhetorical
embrace of regional autonomy. He tried to draw the line at Chechnya. For
Putin, who insisted on the need to rebuild a strong state, regaining Russian
control over Chechnya was the sina qua non of statehood, defined in
Weberian terms as the monopoly of force over a given territory.

Putin's attempt to recentralize Russia and do away with Yeltsin's legacy
of "asymmetric federalism" could prove counterproductive, reintroducing
authoritarian methods, but without producing improvements in people's
quality of life. An alternative to Putin's approach would require the recognition that ruling the world's largest country from a single capital city is
unrealistic. Some form of genuine federalism—perhaps still a negotiated,
asymmetric federalism—is Russia's best hope.

This chapter begins with a review of Russian approaches to federalism
since the demise of the Soviet Union, both Yeltsin's policies and Putin's
reforms. It highlights concerns that Putin's system of regional super-
regions—headed mainly by former KGB, police, and military officials—
puts individual rights and regional autonomy at risk without providing
compensating improvements in the overall quality of life. In combination
with increasing government control over the media—especially the formerly independent television networks that had played such a key role in
criticizing the first Chechen war—Putin's "reforms" threaten to bring back
some of the authoritarian nature of the Soviet Union.

Yeltsin's Legacy

In 1990 Yeltsin was president of a Russian republic still formally part of the
Soviet Union. He seemed so intent on rattling his rival, Soviet president
Mikhail Gorbachev, that he was willing to fan the flames of separatist sentiment in order to do so. Once he had contributed to the destruction of the
Soviet Union and emerged as leader of an independent Russia, Yeltsin still
faced serious political opposition—this time from the Russian parliament.
In October 1993 he disbanded the parliament by military force and then
sought to remove regional leaders who had supported the opposition. But
overall his message to the regions, especially those that had remained loyal,
only served to encourage their aspirations for further autonomy: "The
regions have to deal with their own problems on their own, by, among
other things, raising their own status." He acknowledged that "the government has no coherent regional policy."[2] Yeltsin's approach led to a situa-

tion of "asymmetrical federalism," with regions seeking to establish special privileges in relation to the central government, particularly in the realm of tax collection and the control and sale of natural resources.

Yeltsin's indulgence of the regions, especially the national republics (with the glaring exception of Chechnya) owed less to ideological conviction than to political and economic expediency. He turned a blind eye to regional leaders who engaged in fraud and other undemocratic means to maintain their power (such as Magomedali Magomedov of Dagestan), as long as those leaders supported Yeltsin's own political aspirations, particularly his reelection campaign in 1996. Under Yeltsin the federal government signed "treaties" with many of the twenty-one ethnically defined and self-styled sovereign republics to govern matters such as taxation and trade that normally would have fallen under the purview of routine domestic legislation. Moscow's concessions to rich industrial powerhouses such as Tatarstan and Bashkortostan seemed driven by weakness. Better to give them some benefits than to risk provoking further separatist tendencies. Better to allow the relatively wealthy "donor" regions to keep a substantial portion of their tax revenues than to risk receiving none to redistribute among the vast majority of poorer regions, particularly if the central government lacked the means for efficient taxation anyhow.

Political and economic incentives motivated the regional leaders as well in their contribution to the evolution of asymmetric federalism. Figures such as Tatarstan's president Mintimer Shaimiev used the threat of radical separatism to extract more resources from the center and used those resources to buy off the separatist opposition. The ambiguous status of Tatarstan bolstered his own personal political position. In the wake of the August 1998 financial crisis, Tatarstan sought an improvement in relations with the center; its representatives in Moscow seemed committed to working with the government, for example, to reconcile important discrepancies between the constitutions of the Russian Federation and the Tatar Republic.[3] At the same time, Shaimiev began to exhibit ambitions for a national political role, as a leader of the All Russia-Fatherland bloc.

Even nominally independent Chechnya had reason to take a conciliatory approach to Moscow after the first war. The August 1998 financial crisis only compounded the economic and social problems the republic was already suffering. In the autumn of that year, the Chechen "embassy" in Moscow was run by Vakha Khasanov, a former factory manager from the Nadterechnyi district, an area that, as he put it, tried to maintain "neutrality" during the war. In an interview, Khasanov explained to me that he was not trained to be either a diplomat or a politician. His outspoken views suggested as much. He readily criticized the late Chechen leader Dzhokhar Dudaev, whose eccentric behavior and megalomania contributed much to the outbreak of the war. He was forthright in admitting that the crime rate in the republic was so high as to discourage any foreign investment. Indeed, he had recently told a commercial delegation from Malaysia that they would need a small army of security guards even to consider a potential site visit to the republic. The prerequisite for solving Chechnya's problems, in Khasanov's view, lay in improving relations with Russia, and he seemed willing to try, on behalf of the Maskhadov government.[4]

Whatever conciliatory effect the August 1998 crisis had on formerly recalcitrant regions, it was not enough to satisfy central government officials. In September, in his inaugural speech to the Duma, newly appointed prime minister Evgenii Primakov insisted that his "government must first and foremost pay special attention to preserving Russia as a single state. . . . We are facing a serious threat of disintegration of our country."[5] In January 1999, anticipating the language that Putin would use just months later, Primakov called for the "restoration of the vertical state power structure, where all matters would be solved jointly by the center and local authorities" and insisted that separatist trends "must be quelled, liquidated, and uprooted."[6] Primakov did not remain in office long enough to carry out that agenda. It was left to his successor, Vladimir Putin, to relaunch a brutal war against Chechnya in August 1999, and once elected president in March 2000, to begin an ambitious reform of center-regional relations.

Putin's Project

Putin enunciated several goals for regional reform: to bring regional laws into compliance with federal legislation and the Russian Constitution; to provide for impeachment of regional leaders who abused their power; to effect a redistribution of tax revenues to favor poorer regions, by revoking the special tax status of many of the republics; to limit the regions' ability to conduct foreign trade independently of Moscow and to solicit foreign credits; and to reform the Federation Council, the upper chamber of the parliament, where most of the regional leaders sit, along with representatives from regional legislatures. Putin wanted especially to remove governors and republic presidents from the Federation Council, not least so that their parliamentary immunity would not protect them from the law.

The initiative that created the biggest impression was Putin's presidential decree of May 2000. It established seven federal districts among which all of the eighty-nine subjects of the Russian Federation would be divided.

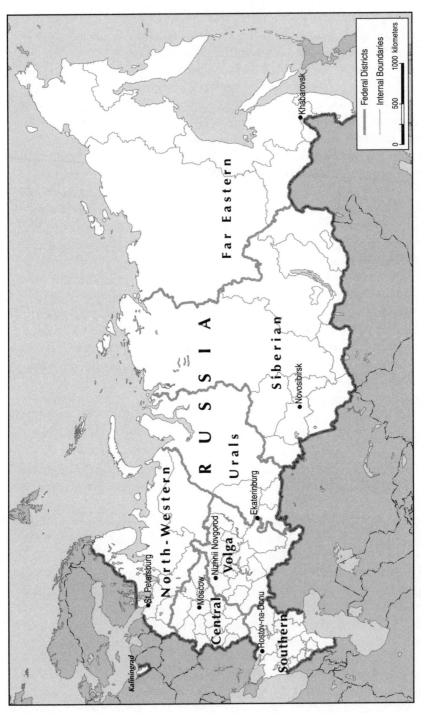

Map 6-1. *Russia's Federal Districts*

The seven districts have designated capital cities that serve as the bases for the president's "plenipotentiary representatives" and their staffs. The districts (with their capitals) are Central (Moscow), Northwest (St. Petersburg), South (Rostov-na-Donu), Volga (Nizhnii Novgorod), Ural (Ekaterinburg), Siberia (Novosibirsk), and Far East (Khabarovsk). The new districts corresponded fairly closely to the economic regions known as "associations of economic cooperation," but even more closely to the country's military districts, with only a couple of capital cities differing.[7]

Proposals for replacing the system of ethnic-territorial divisions that characterized both the old Soviet Union and the present Russian Federation have been around for some time. Perhaps the best-known one came nearly a decade earlier from the fascist politician Vladimir Zhirinovskii, who suggested a return to the tsarist system of *gubernii*. Democratic political figures, such as the late Galina Starovoitova, were also sympathetic to proposals to reorganize Russian political divisions to deemphasize the ethnic factor, although she had come to believe that such a reform would be impossible to implement.[8]

Zhirinovskii claimed that Putin's decree coincided exactly with what he had proposed, but in fact the president's plan differed in a key respect: the new federal districts did not replace the existing eighty-nine subjects of the federation, but rather imposed an additional layer of administration between them and the central government in Moscow. As one observer from Bashkortostan noted, "The decree just creates one more bureaucracy with thousands more employees."[9]

Reactions from the Regions

Regional leaders responded to Putin's initiatives in various ways, depending apparently on the same sorts of economic and political considerations that had influenced their behavior during the Yelstin years. Many were understandably unnerved by the prospect of losing parliamentary immunity, as anticipated in Putin's proposal for reform of the Federation Council. Concern for maintaining their own personal political status seemed to loom large in their calculations—as Putin evidently recognized.

Many governors claimed to favor giving the central government the power to appoint regional leaders, presumably hoping that their support for such an initiative would secure their own reappointment. But Putin rejected this option. As he put it, "I have thought and still think that the heads of the constituent members of the federation must be elected by popular vote. This practice is already in place. It has become a part of our democratic state system."[10]

Even if he chose not to give himself the power to appoint regional leaders, Putin found other ways to reward his favorites. On April 26, 2000, a month after his election victory, Putin presented awards to twelve regional leaders. Why were these particular leaders chosen? The official justification referred to their "significant contribution to the social and economic development" of their regions. Observers immediately noted, however, that "all of the regions have at least one thing in common": Putin received more than 51 percent of the vote in each in the presidential election (the only exception was one region where Putin drew 49.5 percent).[11]

Because Putin's specific proposals were not always announced in advance, some regional leaders found it difficult to calculate their best course of action. President Shaimiev of Tatarstan, for example, initially welcomed the plan for seven federal districts because he reportedly expected to be named head of the Volga district, in return for not running for a third presidential term (and risking a violation of the Russian Constitution). He resisted the reform of the Federation Council until it became clear that the regional governors and presidents expelled from that body would find a new home in the State Council (and presumably keep their Moscow apartments and chauffeurs). Putin invited all eighty-nine regional leaders to join the new body, making some observers wonder if he were not just re-creating the Federation Council. But Putin made clear that the State Council would have only consultative status and would meet only four times a year. Shaimiev, while claiming to support the creation of the new body, vowed to push for constitutional amendments to grant the State Council "real powers."[12]

Regional leaders such as Shaimiev were reassured when it became clear that the State Council would have a small presidium consisting of representatives of the seven federal districts, and that the presidium would meet every month. Putin cleverly chose some of the most skeptical and potentially oppositional regional leaders to serve on the first presidium: Moscow mayor Iurii Luzhkov, St. Petersburg governor Vladimir Iakovlev, Dagestan's Magomedali Magomedov, and Shaimiev himself. Their status secured, the regional leaders emerged from the first session of the State Council with words of praise. The new organization would be "much more efficient" than the Federation Council, according to Luzhkov. Shaimiev predicted that it would be a "very serious, influential organ."[13]

As mentioned in chapter 5, one result of asymmetric federalism was that leaders of the ethnic republics enjoyed considerable freedom from Moscow's political scrutiny as they secured their hold on power. That hold was reinforced by whatever economic benefits they could negotiate, particularly in the realm of tax policy, control over natural resources, and foreign trade. Tatarstan and neighboring Bashkortostan are among the richest regions in the Russian Federation, thanks to substantial oil and natural gas deposits and high-technology industries inherited from the Soviet military-industrial sector. They were particularly successful in extracting concessions from Moscow that would allow them to retain much of their wealth. Putin's new regional policies threaten to undermine their achievements.

The potential for conflict over the economic implications of Putin's reforms came in September 2000 when the president revealed his budget and tax proposals. Some sixteen of the poorest regions—the recipients of federal subsidies—expressed support for Putin's budget because it appeared to entail a redistribution of funds in their favor. On the other hand, leaders of economically successful regions, such as Novgorod's governor Mikhail Prusak, were incensed that the government sought to revise the provision of the tax code that allowed for a 50/50 split in the distribution of tax revenue. Bashkortostan's leaders were even more upset. They were obliged to void previous agreements with Moscow, and, for the first time in years, turn over tax revenues to the central government; previously they had retained those funds in lieu of various payments and subsidies from Moscow (such as support for the Blagoveshchensk polyether complex in Bashkortostan, mentioned in chapter 5).

As opposition mounted from the wealthier "donor" regions, Putin's finance ministry evidently began cutting side deals, making promises, to St. Petersburg and Tiumen, for example, to provide additional subsidies to make up for the decline in receipt of tax revenues. Smoothing over such potential conflicts through bilateral negotiations was a hallmark of Yeltsin's regional policy, but too many exceptions of this sort could undermine the coherence of Putin's reforms.

Freedom versus Order?

Putin's intention to rationalize the governing institutions of the Russian Federation and to bring regional laws into compliance with the constitution would seem to command widespread support. His initial appointments to the new positions of plenipotentiary representatives have caused some observers to wonder, however, whether Putin's imposition of order comes at the expense of individual freedom and democracy. Five out of seven of the presidential representatives he appointed were former military, police, or security service officials, including KGB and Interior Ministry officers and two generals who had commanded forces in Chechnya. One of the two exceptions (the other is a former diplomat) was Sergei

Kirienko, who served as acting prime minister under Yeltsin in 1998, and before that in Nizhnii Novgorod, now the center of the new Volga federal district. But even Kirienko put former KGB officials on his staff, including most notably Major General Marsel Gafurovich Galimardanov, who was appointed federal inspector in Tatarstan.

Many observers have speculated that the backgrounds of the people Putin appointed (and his own experience as a KGB officer), in combination with his own inclinations, make it likely that the president's regional reforms will favor imposition of order rather than the strengthening of democracy. For some of his supporters, this aspect of Putin's regional policy is the most attractive. In a radio interview, Valerii Velichko, the head of an association of former KGB officials, maintained that officers of the Federal Security Service are best suited for imposing top-down authority on the regions. They are the best hope for helping Putin establish an "enlightened autocracy" in Russia. Such a political system would be "neither the coarse militarized communism of Pol Pot, nor the fascist or half-fascist regime of Pinochet" (although some of what transpired in the course of Putin's war in Chechnya would be familiar to the victims of those regimes).[14]

In February 2000 then acting president Putin told Justice Ministry officials that "the only sort of dictatorship to which we must be subject is the dictatorship of law." He complained that "the system of state authority is neglected, slack and ill-disciplined," and he stressed the need to relieve popular anxiety and insecurity. "There is only one way to achieve this—by turning Russia into a strong state." Putin's commitment to a strong state has enjoyed support among most Russians, but his reference to dictatorship, even a dictatorship of law (whatever that could mean) left others uneasy. They seemed to be in the minority, however. According to public opinion polls, Russians have given clear precedence to order over freedom. At the end of May 2000, just as Putin was launching his campaign for regional reform, the All-Russia Public Opinion Center (VTsIOM) asked respondents whether it would be "to the benefit or to the detriment of Russia" if "the President gets full control of the parliament and governors and concentrates in his hands virtually unlimited power." More than half considered such a course beneficial. In April 2000, 81 percent of those polled told VTsIOM that "it is more important for Russia today to bring law and order, even if it will be necessary for this purpose to encroach on some democratic principles and limit citizens' personal freedoms."[15]

Many observers gave Putin's neo-tsarist/military/KGB plan for regional reform the benefit of the doubt. They hoped it would help build a strong law-governed state to protect the freedom and economic well-being of Russia's citizens. But an "enlightened autocracy," even one that avoids the extremes of Pol Pot and Pinochet, would be another matter. Russians could end up with the worst of both worlds: an authoritarian regime that fails to bring order and peace to the fractured Russian Federation.

Making Matters Worse

When Galina Starovoitova was alive, she devoted much of her work in the Russian parliament to monitoring antidemocratic tendencies in the regions. Many regional governors have, for example, manipulated electoral laws to eliminate any challenges to their rule. At the most basic level, they violate the Russian Constitution or their own regional constitutions by seeking third terms and wielding power in such a way as to render challenges unrealistic. Putin has seized on this issue to impose Moscow's control over regional electoral processes. Unlike Starovoitova, however, he seems less driven by principle than by the desire to put his own people in power.

In November 1998 Starovoitova told me of a particularly blatant, but not unusual, technique employed by one regional leader, Vladislav Zotin, when he was president of the small ethnic republic of Marii El. He sponsored a law requiring that any candidates for the presidency of the republic be fluent in Russian as well as two dialects of the Marii language. With ethnic Marii people a minority in the republic (43 percent of the population), the law would eliminate candidates from other groups—such as Russians, who made up 48 percent—as well as the many Marii who had lost their native language. Starovoitova had made her political reputation in the late 1980s by supporting the cause of autonomy for the Armenian enclave of Nagorno-Karabagh in Azerbaijan. But she was not one to offer blind support for ethnic chauvinism at the expense of democratic principles. In one of her last achievements in the service of democracy before her murder, she challenged the Marii El electoral law as unconstitutional, and the Russian Constitutional Court ruled in her favor.[16]

Concerns about the "regionalization of autocracy" discussed in chapter 5 would constitute a plausible counterargument to those worried about Putin's attempted recentralization of the Russian Federation.[17] Unfortunately, under both Yeltsin and Putin, manipulations of local elections and other antidemocratic practices have received only selective attention and condemnation. They have often gone unremarked by the Moscow authorities, especially if the regional leaders have supported the president's electoral efforts in the past.[18] Moreover, unlike Starovoitova, who relied on strictly legal means to challenge regional illegality, Putin, the former KGB agent, employs a wider range of techniques. Moreover, his objectives favor central control rather than the local democracy that Starovoitova promoted.

Ingushetiia: Putin's Regional Policy in Practice

The case of Ingushetiia illustrates Putin's methods for reimposing central control in the regions—and suggests the counterproductive results they might yield. The republic borders Chechnya, and, as noted in chapter 2, was until 1991 part of the same Soviet institutional entity, the Checheno-Ingush Autonomous Soviet Socialist Republic. Like the Chechens, the Ingush were deported en masse by Stalin during World War II. During the post-Soviet era, Ingushetiia suffered a great deal from Moscow's wars against Chechnya, particularly the second one, when it became home to some 150,000 desperate refugees. Ingushetiia might well have been considered a prime candidate for a "region at risk" for secession.

Yet the Ingush republic managed to maintain stability as it balanced itself between the radical extremism of Chechnya and the crude militarism of Moscow. Much of the credit for keeping Ingushetiia from going the way of Chechnya or even Dagestan belongs to Ruslan Aushev, the former Afghan war general and its president during the decade following the collapse of the Soviet Union. According to Georgi Derluguian, Aushev recognized early the threat of militant Islam. After the onset of the first Chechen War in late 1994, Aushev watched as "volunteers from Arab states, including veterans of the Afghan war, arrived in the Caucasus with money, the ideology of jihad and terrorist tactics." Aushev recognized that the al-Qaida militants posed a danger not only to the Russian authorities but also to the nationalist regime in Chechnya. He "saw the promise of cooperation between Russia and secular separatists against the common threat of foreign-inspired terrorist militancy."[19] Yet Aushev remained a consistent critic of Moscow's heedless use of force in Chechnya and the Russian authorities never forgave him for that.

Aushev pursued policies intended to undermine militant Islamic movements in his own country. In particular, he sought to keep young Ingush men out of trouble—not easy in a place where unemployment reached 90 percent—and to undermine the influence of the foreign mercenaries and ideologists. With the consent of village elders, he closed mosques that had been funded by external Arab money. As Derluguian describes, Aushev "used his charismatic authority to plead with families of the born-again

Islamic puritans to take good care of their sons, to keep them busy, to get them married. He implored their communities to help them build houses, to purchase farmland, livestock, taxicabs and trucks." In violation of Russian law, Aushev legalized the Islamic custom of polygamy and the Ingush tradition of clan vendetta. Russia's Constitutional Court threatened to remove him from office, but Aushev's moves proved popular at home and he held onto power.[20] Although hardly a textbook democracy, Aushev's Ingushetiia managed to maintain stability while enjoying greater freedom of the press than most of Russia's regions.[21]

In Vladimir Putin, however, Aushev finally met his match.[22] Putin seemed determined to oust Aushev from office. In late 2001 Aushev was faced with a government-inspired court challenge to the length of his term as president and steady pressure from Viktor Kazantsev, the presidential representative to the Southern Federal District. In addition to doing Putin's bidding, Kazantsev had his own reasons to want to be rid of Aushev. Kazantsev had served as a leading commander in Moscow's war in Chechnya, whereas Aushev remained one of the war's severest critics. At the end of December 2001 Aushev finally resigned. He accepted, as a sort of consolation prize, a position on the Federation Council, expecting, evidently, that his chosen candidate would be elected to succeed him. This was the pattern by which the Putin regime had sought to ease out other entrenched regional leaders.

In the case of Ingushetiia, however, Putin had more ambitious plans. Moscow refused to let Aushev's candidate win. Initially Aushev supported Ingush minister of the interior Khamzat Gutseriev, a representative of one of the most powerful clans in Ingushetiia, whose brother Mikhail ran the state-owned Slavneft' oil company. He was heavily favored to win. The Kremlin intervened, however, in several ways. Moscow objected that Gutseriev was not allowed to run for president while remaining interior minister. On April 3, 2002, armed men from Kazantsev's staff forced their way into the Ingush Supreme Court while it was considering Gutseriev's case. They argued that the Russian Supreme Court should decide the case and demanded that all the relevant materials be handed over to it. On April 5 the Russian cabinet sacked Mikhail Gutseriev, accusing him of financing his brother's campaign with Slavneft' funds. That same day, the Russian Supreme Court disqualified Khamzat Gutseriev from the election, just two days before the first round of voting.

The Kremlin's favored candidate was Murat Ziazikov, a general in the Federal Security Service (successor to the KGB) and deputy to Kazanstev. Moscow's machinations were insufficient to get him elected in the first round, however. In fact, Ziazikov polled only 19 percent of the vote, compared with 32 percent for Alikhan Amirkhanov, a State Duma member and Aushev ally. With Amirkhanov poised to win in the runoff, Moscow reverted to its usual repertoire of tactics to defeat him. Armed security forces raided Amirkhanov's offices following the vote, seeking evidence that he had engaged in bribery and otherwise violated electoral laws. This time, however, the Supreme Court rejected the charges. The final vote produced a predictable "surprise" outcome: The Kremlin's candidate Ziazikov won with 53 percent of the vote to Amirkhanov's 43 percent. Amirkhanov's supporters charged fraud, and several national newspapers provided corroborating evidence. The headline in the daily *Izvestiia* said it all: "Ingushetiia's President Elected by Russia's President."[23]

Even before the outcome was known, Aushev himself had provided an explanation for what would happen, citing the Kremlin's use of "new technologies involving judicial, law-enforcement and government bodies to eliminate candidates that are unsuitable" to Putin's administration.[24] Four days before the runoff election, Aushev resigned his seat on the Federation Council, describing it as "a chamber that decides nothing." He also complained of the Putin administration's unwillingness to deal with Ingush concerns over the Prigorodnyi district and accused Moscow of "accepting atrocities" committed by federal troops in Chechnya.[25]

Putin's methods for removing a popular and successful regional leader would be cause for concern in any case. But some observers have suggested that the removal of Aushev served only as a means to an end and that the end is of even greater concern. An obvious goal was the restoration of central authority. As Ziazikov indicated after his victory, his priority was to create a "vertical of power" in Ingushetiia. "The federal center is the federal center," explained the general, "and there can be no questions of contradictions or misunderstandings here." He also expressed his intention to deal with the crisis of Chechen refugees, but gave no hint of how he would cope with such a seemingly intractable problem. Some observers worried that he would use methods suitable for a former KGB officer to compel the refugees to return home: "The authorities apparently plan simply to cut off their food supplies or possibly even deport them," suggested one report.[26]

Most observers believe that the Kremlin's heavy-handed intervention in the Ingush presidential elections was linked in some way to the Chechen situation. Putting an intelligence officer in charge of the republic would make it easier to control and expel journalists who might provide critical reports on the nearby war, a process already under way before the elections.[27] Aushev expressed a further concern that under Ziazikov,

Ingushetiia would become a base for Moscow's military operations in Chechnya—that all of his efforts to avoid "another Chechnya" would be undermined by Putin's insistence on imposing Moscow's control. Russian journalist Anna Politkovskaia suggested a more extreme variant: that the Kremlin would eliminate Chechnya as an administrative unit and fuse it with Ingushetiia, essentially re-creating the Soviet-era Checheno-Ingush republic. According to Politkovskaia, Moscow authorities came up with the idea at the start of the second Chechen War and offered Aushev the job of president of the new "Vainakh Republic," to be named after the ethnolinguistic group to which both Chechens and Ingush belong.[28] Aushev rejected the proposal, but his successor, handpicked by the Kremlin, indicated from the outset his intention to do Putin's bidding, whatever that may entail.

Unfortunately, Ingushetiia is not the only example of how Putin's drive to bring the regions to heel could have counterproductive effects on Russia's stability. Dagestan, whose unusual system of ethnic representation is arguably an important reason for its avoidance of wide-scale conflict, has been under increasing pressure from the Putin administration to bring its constitution into line with the federal one, regardless of the consequences: "genuine federal principles are being replaced by centralized, sometimes authoritarian, means of control" that threaten "to eliminate features of a political system that has successfully provided for representation and proportionality." In particular, Moscow's policies favor an increasingly narrow elite in a republic where the gap between rich and poor is already a major source of potential conflict. According to some observers, "Moscow might be better advised to renew its efforts to eliminate corruption at the top of Dagestan's political structure, while ignoring the successful ethnic electoral system at the bottom, at least for another decade or two."[29] This would be good advice for many of Russia's regions—that Moscow fight corruption while tolerating local peculiarities that lead to stability—but Putin seems unlikely to heed it.

The system of asymmetric federalism that Boris Yeltsin fostered was hardly the most elegant or efficient way of organizing a multiethnic state of Russia's size and complexity. On the other hand, the Russian Federation did not enjoy the luxury of being able to start from scratch. It inherited its basic federative structure from the Soviet Union. The "asymmetric" aspect of Yeltsin's policy represented an attempt to conciliate restive populations and opportunistic leaders who promoted greater autonomy with threats to secede. Under the circumstances, Yeltsin could have done worse. Indeed,

he did do worse in Chechnya—suggesting what might have happened elsewhere if Moscow had not shown some flexibility in dealing with the
regions.

Vladimir Putin inherited Yeltsin's system of regional deals but was not
happy about it. Within two months of his election, he instituted a system
of seven federal districts and appointed mainly police and military officials
to head them. He threatened regional governments to bring their laws and
constitutions into conformity with federal law. He engineered the removal
of several powerful republican leaders, including one—Ruslan Aushev—
who had served as a bulwark of stability in the volatile North Caucasus.
There are many valid reasons for seeking to rationalize the system of center-regional relations in Russia, but also good reasons to wonder about
Putin's intentions. His emphasis on discipline and dictatorship (even "of
law") and the undemocratic means he has employed to impose Moscow's
control give serious cause for concern. Perhaps Putin's project to
strengthen the state and impose order would have raised fewer worries if it
had not coincided with the renewal of the Chechen War. The lawlessness,
disorder, and wanton violence of Russia's second military campaign in
Chechnya—the subject of chapter 7—could prove a more enduring symbol of Putin's legacy than his half-baked regional reforms.

7

War Crimes and Russia's International Standing

The fact that national propaganda everywhere so eagerly cloaks itself in ideologies of a professedly international character proves the existence of an international stock of common ideas, however limited and however weakly held, to which appeal can be made, and of a belief that these common ideas stand somehow in the scale of values above national interests. This stock of common ideas is what we mean by international morality.

—E. H. Carr, 1946

It is forbidden to use the army against civilians. It is forbidden to shoot against the people.

—Major General Ivan Babichev, 1994

Despite the claims of Russia's leaders, the wars in Chechnya are hard to justify as necessary to preserve the Russian Federation from going the way of the Soviet Union. Whatever metaphor one prefers, Chechnya never did start a brushfire of secessions or knock down a row of dominoes. Russia has suffered a great deal from Chechen separatism, but much of the damage was self-inflicted, the consequence of overreliance on military force and inadequate attention to political and economic means to resolve the conflict. The wars in Chechnya, and what they reveal about the weakness and venality of Russia's rulers, explain a lot about the sorry state of the Russian Federation more than a decade after the collapse of the Soviet Union.

What about the international implications of the Chechen Wars? In the late 1990s Serbia's war against Muslim separatists in Kosovo—including deliberate use of force against civilians and a policy of mass expulsions—provoked international outrage and led to military intervention by the North Atlantic Treaty Organization (NATO). That intervention, particularly the U.S.-led bombing campaign, in turn came under scrutiny for its effect on innocent civilians and the role it played in exacerbating a serious refugee crisis. A couple of years later, revelations by a retired general about France's policy of torture and extrajudicial killings of Algerian separatists in the mid-1950s led to considerable embarrassment in Paris and implausible expressions of shock at what was in fact well known at the time.[1] In the spring of 2002 the world's attention was drawn to the situation in the Middle East, where Israeli reprisals against Palestinians suspected of engaging in terrorism entailed widespread destruction of homes and high civilian casualties. Given the apparent sensitivity of international opinion to the impact of modern warfare on innocent civilians, one might have expected that Russia's wars against Chechnya would have brought widespread condemnation and damage to the country's international standing.

In his classic definition of the state, Max Weber associated its rise with the emergence of a monopoly on the legitimate use of force over a given territory. Especially for a leader such as Vladimir Putin, whose rhetorical commitment to rebuilding the Russian state was the main—perhaps only—discernible goal of his political project, the reassertion of central control over the rebellious territory of Chechnya must rank above any considerations of international prestige.[2] Nevertheless, the way the Russian army has waged war against Chechnya could undermine the goals of state-building and internal cohesion, especially if Russian actions led to a decline in the country's international standing.

In fact, despite incontrovertible evidence that the Russian armed forces have committed systematic atrocities and war crimes in the course of both Chechen Wars, Russia's international prestige has apparently not suffered much. This chapter seeks to explain the relative lack of international condemnation by focusing on the way Western journalists and experts have interpreted Russian behavior for policymakers and the broader public. I argue that many Western commentators—with the notable exception of human-rights activists—have misunderstood the laws of war and Russia's legal obligations. They have been inclined to give Moscow the benefit of the doubt, a stance that accords with the Realpolitik interests of many of the major powers as well.[3]

Before developing this argument, I review the body of international law relevant to such conflicts as the wars in Chechnya. The laws of war are not without some ambiguity, but given the degree to which they have been misunderstood in the popular media, it is worth reviewing them. I then summarize official Western reactions to evidence of war crimes committed during both wars in Chechnya; the response from the Russian government, including its campaign against domestic journalists and activists who have criticized Moscow's policy; and the responsibility of the Chechen side for provoking atrocities by deliberately deploying fighters in the midst of the civilian populations. Then I return to a discussion of how Western misunderstandings of Russia's war crimes have benefited the Russian government, at the expense of Chechen and Russian civilian victims of the wars. Even before the events of September 11, 2001, rendered Vladimir Putin's "antiterrorist operation" somewhat more palatable to the major Western powers, the wars in Chechnya had done little damage to Russia's international prestige. The ongoing war is likely, nevertheless, to have a long-lasting corrosive influence on Russian society and domestic political institutions, even if it poses no significant threat of the country's further disintegration.

Laws of War

That Russia is legally bound to observe the laws of war, even in an internal conflict, is not in doubt. According to the Russian Constitution, "The commonly recognized principles and norms of international law and the international treaties of the Russian Federation shall be a component part of its legal system. If an international treaty of the Russian Federation abides by rules other than those stipulated by the law, the rules of the international treaty shall apply."[4] As Captain Vladimir Galitskii, professor of law at the Russian Academy of Military Sciences, has pointed out, "Our state, acknowledging the priority of international over national law (articles 15 and 17 of the Russian Constitution of 1993) ratified all of the currently active international conventions on the laws and customs of war, defense of victims of war (May 10, 1954, and September 29, 1989) and took upon itself the obligation strictly to observe them." Thus "the military command is directly obliged to apply and carry out the demands of the laws of war. Unfortunately, many in Russian state, political, and military circles do not always correctly understand the essence of the laws of armed conflict."[5]

The main bodies of international law relevant to the war in Chechnya are common Article 3 of the 1949 Geneva Conventions, relating to cases of "armed conflict not of an international character occurring in the territory" of one of the parties to the conventions, and the two Geneva Protocols, added in 1977.[6] That the conflict in Chechnya is not an international one is suggested by the fact that virtually no countries have recognized

Chechnya's independence.[7] Galitskii agrees that "the events in Chechnya in 1994–1996 and 1999–2000 should be classified as an internal armed conflict, in the course of which it is obligatory to adopt article 3, common to all four Geneva Conventions from 12 August 1949 and Protocol II from 8 June 1977 in its entirety."[8] The Russian government, however, has sought to underplay the relevance of Article 3 by referring to the war in Chechnya as an "antiterrorist operation" or the suppression of a rebellion, rather than an armed conflict.

Even if one accepts the dubious claim that the Geneva Conventions are not applicable to the Chechen conflict, there are other international laws and conventions that apply. In December 1994, just days before the attack on Chechnya, Russian representatives signed the "Code of Conduct on Politico-Military Aspects of Security," sponsored by the Organization for Security and Cooperation in Europe. The OSCE code of conduct, which is binding upon its signatories, came into effect on January 1, 1995. Thus, states one analyst, Russia violated the code's "most fundamental principles within days of having signed it."[9] In addition, the Council of Europe found Russia in violation of the European Convention on Human Rights and the European Convention for the Prevention of Torture and Inhuman or Degrading Treatment or Punishment.[10] A plausible case can be made that Russia has also violated the Genocide Convention for "acts committed with intent to destroy, in whole or in part, a national, ethnic, racial, or religious group." Its jurisdiction covers internal as well as international armed conflicts, and, indeed, cases where there is no armed conflict at all.[11]

Background to the Geneva Protocols

The 1977 Geneva Protocols resulted from a perceived need to reaffirm and develop rules applicable to armed conflicts that were not obviously international in character. Of particular concern were so-called wars of national liberation, waged against occupying colonial powers in the period following World War II. National liberation movements had staged major uprisings and fought guerrilla wars. Colonial powers such as Britain, France, and the Netherlands, along with the United States, had engaged such movements militarily, often without much apparent respect for the laws of war. In 1974, when the Swiss government convened the diplomatic conference that led to the adoption of the Geneva Protocols, it invited participation from national liberation movements, although only representatives of states were allowed to vote.[12]

One consequence of the involvement of nonstate actors in these deliberations was a concern that national liberation movements and the like would be accorded the protections of the Geneva Conventions. Thus Article 96, paragraph 3 of the first protocol stipulates that parties to a conflict with a state army can unilaterally declare that they want the 1949 Geneva Conventions and 1977 protocols to apply. This offers greater protections than if the conflict were considered internal, or "noninternational." Parties eligible to make such a unilateral declaration are ones involved in "armed conflicts in which people are fighting against colonial domination and alien occupation and against racist regimes in the exercise of their right of self-determination."[13]

Chechen representatives have sought to portray their opposition to Russian control as an anticolonial struggle. This view was expressed by Akhmad Kadyrov, the chief mufti of Chechnya who supported Dudaev and Maskhadov in the first war. Even after switching sides to work with Moscow in the second war, Kadyrov stressed the colonial aspect of Chechnya's relationship with Russia. In February 2000 he told an interviewer, "As far as I know, there isn't a single document to prove that Chechnya voluntarily became part of Russia." To decide the question of Chechnya's relationship to the Russian Federation, he maintained that "the Chechen people must be taken into consideration" and, a year or two after the war ends, "a referendum should be held" to determine the republic's status.[14]

Even if Russia and the international community do not recognize the Chechen conflict as a war of national liberation or an anticolonial war, Chechen fighters and civilians are still covered by international law. The minimal protections afforded by Article 3 of the original Geneva Conventions of 1949, for example, include prohibitions on inhumane treatment of noncombatants, including members of the armed forces who have laid down their arms. Specifically forbidden are "murder of all kinds, mutilation, cruel treatment and torture; taking of hostages; outrages upon personal dignity, in particular, humiliating and degrading treatment;" and extrajudicial executions. Finally, provision must be made for collecting and caring for the sick and wounded.[15]

Even within this narrow scope of international law—the protections provided by Article 3—Russian human-rights activists have documented an overwhelming pattern of abuses and crimes committed by the Russian armed forces.[16] International nongovernmental organizations, such as Human Rights Watch, have also prepared several reports, some of which have received broad media attention. Finally, according to Article 1(2) of the first Geneva Protocol, even in cases not covered by the agreement, "civilians and combatants remain under the protection and authority of the principles of international law derived from established custom, from the principles of humanity and from the dictates of public conscience."[17] Fortunately, many of the most active journalists and human-rights activists who have uncovered Russian atrocities appear to be motivated by conscience, aside from considerations of international law.

International Responses to the Wars in Chechnya

In the first war, international criticism of Russia's attack on Chechnya was quick in coming. Yeltsin's staff took note of the various responses and documented them. On December 27, 1994, for example, a group of Finnish parliamentarians expressed their concern to governments and presidents of Russia and the United States, to the United Nations, and to the OSCE.[18] The next day, an assistant to President Yeltsin met with officials from the International Committee of the Red Cross who conveyed their view to the Russian president that the situation in Chechnya now attained "the legal status of an armed conflict of non-international character." That status, according to the Red Cross, "above all signifies that the government authorities involved in the conflict must adhere to specific humanitarian obligations."[19] From this point, as Yeltsin's advisers have documented, Russia's president was made aware of his international legal obligations with language taken directly from the 1977 protocols to the Geneva Conventions. Expressions of international concern intensified in the next few days, as German foreign minister Klaus Kinkel made an "emotional call" to his Russian counterpart Andrei Kozyrev on behalf of Prime Minister Helmut Kohl and the European Union.[20]

Reports from nongovernmental organizations, such as Helsinki Watch, as well as intergovernmental bodies, such as the Council of Europe, provided great detail on the damage to civilians inflicted by Russian attacks. OSCE representatives who conducted a fact-finding mission to Chechnya "were appalled by the magnitude of destruction and compared the condition of Grozny with that of Stalingrad during World War II."[21] Others saw similarities with the situation in Bosnia when its capital city was under siege by Serbian militia forces and the Serbian army, actions that eventually provoked NATO intervention. In the winter of 1995, "at the height of the shelling of Sarajevo there were thirty-five hundred detonations a day, while in Grozny the winter bombing reached a rate of four thousand detonations an hour."[22]

In contrast to the Germans, the Finns, and the various international organizations, the U.S. government responded quite late to the Russian invasion. President Bill Clinton did not contact Yeltsin to discuss the situation until February 13, two months into the conflict. His remarks, according to the summary by his press secretary, were not particularly hard-hitting: "President Clinton reiterated the importance of an end to the bloodshed and the start of a process leading to a peaceful settlement of the dispute." Making even that statement more palatable, "he stated once again that Chechnya is part of Russia, but noted the legitimate international concern over the humanitarian toll the fighting has taken."[23]

The U.S. response to the first war in Chechnya rested by and large on the assumption that everything must be done to support President Yeltsin as the only hope for Russian democracy. Electoral gains by communists and supporters of the fascist politician Vladimir Zhirinovskii were particularly worrying to U.S. officials who sought to avoid weakening Yeltsin any further with their criticism. U.S. policymakers, from President Clinton on down, referred to the war in Chechnya as an "internal matter" and compared it to the U.S. Civil War, implying that all-out war, with massive civilian casualties, was fully justified to preserve the country. Warren Christopher, the U.S. secretary of state, explained that Yeltsin was in full control of his military forces, that "Russia is operating in a democratic context," and therefore the United States should "not rush to judgment."[24]

Contrast the position of American officials with the views of Russian opponents of the war. In March 1995 a group of mathematicians and physicists distributed by electronic mail an open letter to colleagues in the West expressing their concern. It represents views widely held in Russia at the time. The letter begins, "We are compelled to write to you from the feeling that the terrible crimes committed by Russian authorities and armed forces in Chechnya are not accidental and that we are all responsible for them." Already less than three months into the first war, "journalists, defenders of human rights and mothers of the soldiers fighting there" were reporting not only indiscriminate bombing of towns and villages, "but also the capturing of hostages, robberies, organization of filtration camps where people, incarcerated on the basis of their race, are cruelly beaten, tortured, maimed and murdered." The authors of the letter characterized these actions as genocide and crimes against humanity and insisted, therefore, that they not "be considered merely as an internal affair of Russia." They criticized the dominant view of Western governments that "Russia is moving towards democracy and reforms and unless Yeltsin is supported fascists of the Zhirinovskii type will take over."[25]

Such expressions of concern became even more urgent in the wake of the Samashki massacre of April 1995, when Russian troops assaulted a village in western Chechnya and carried out widespread atrocities.[26] Russian officers apparently believed the village, whose population was estimated at about 7,000, was sheltering guerrilla fighters. The Russians ordered the village to surrender, to hand over the fighters, and to turn in their weapons. Village elders met with the Russian authorities and explained that the fighters had left the previous month and that the village did not have the hundreds of weapons or the armored personnel carrier that the Russians were demanding. The Russians then issued an ultimatum to turn over the weapons, and when the elders were unable to do so, Russian forces pounded the village with artillery and mortar fire for three days. In the meantime hundreds of villagers tried to escape. When the Russian forces began attacking some members, the village's small self-defense force returned fire. The Russian troops reacted in keeping with the vow of their minister of defense Pavel Grachev: "We shall respond to every Chechen shot with thousands of our own."[27] This vow, consistent with Russian practice throughout both wars, offers clear intention to violate the principle of proportionality that undergirds the laws of war.

Disproportionate use of force, however, was the least of the crimes committed against Samashki. When the Russian troops entered the village, they met little resistance from the forty-strong self-defense force. Nevertheless, the Russians proceeded to carry out a *zachistka*, or "mopping-up" operation, randomly killing civilians, including elderly Chechen veterans of World War II, women, children, and three middle-aged ethnic Russians who were machine-gunned in a bedroom of their house. Soldiers hurled grenades into basements and houses without warning and burned down nearly 200 homes. The overall death toll from the Samashki massacres was estimated by some sources at more than 200. The Russian authorities insisted that all were rebel fighters, yet most witnesses maintain that no more than two or three of the victims were armed and most were killed in their homes or shot point blank after being rounded up.[28]

The U.S. response even to such massacres was weak. The Clinton administration did acknowledge that Russia had "not fulfilled all of its commitments under the OSCE and the Helsinki Final Act," but it made no mention of war crimes.[29] The timing of the Samashki massacre was especially inconvenient for Western leaders. Boris Yeltsin had invited them to Moscow to celebrate the fiftieth anniversary of the defeat of Nazi Germany on May 9, 1995. It would have been difficult to decline the invitation to honor the millions of Russians killed in the fight against fascism without creating a serious rift in relations with Moscow and risking a popular anti-Western backlash. Paradoxically, the approach of the anniversary might itself have contributed to the Russian decision to terrorize Samashki in order to speed the end of the war before the Western visitors arrived.[30] In the event, Western leaders attended the victory celebration, including a major parade of military equipment and soldiers on Red Square, as the war continued to rage in Chechnya. President Clinton made some mildly critical remarks about the Russian conduct of the war, but they had no effect.

With the war still raging a year and a half later, Sergei Kovalev, one of the most outspoken critics of Russian policy, denounced the "senseless diplomatic steps in the Western tradition counting on cultivated partners. We are not cultivated partners," he insisted. "We are not! When you criticize us politely, we perceive it as a compliment."[31] It did not help that Western actions spoke louder than the restrained words of criticism.

The actions that seemed most meaningful to Moscow were the U.S. administration's commitment of money ostensibly to aid Russian economic reform. The Clinton administration was unwilling to link economic aid to Russian compliance with its international treaty obligations and observance of humanitarian law in Chechnya. On the contrary, it supported continued assistance from international financial institutions. Six months into the war, for example, Moscow received a $6.8 billion loan from the International Monetary Fund. As Rachel Denber, the Moscow representative of Helsinki Watch, pointed out, "Despite the Chechen conflict, 1995 must be considered a jackpot year for the Russians as far as funds from the international community are concerned." The 1995 loan was followed by a further $10.2 billion from the IMF in early 1996. The two loans combined exceed most estimates of the total cost of the first war, leading some observers to argue that the West actually "paid for the Russian invasion."[32]

Private corporations were also in a position to help Russia pay for the war, especially those in the oil industry—the crucial source of Russian foreign currency. Their actions, as much as those of governments, can convey whether in the face of accusations of war crimes it is acceptable to continue literally to conduct "business as usual" with Russia. Journalist Seymour Hersh, in his investigation of the practices of Western oil companies in the former Soviet Union, turned up an illuminating example. Hersh claims that in January 1995 Lucio Noto, the chief executive officer of Mobil Oil Corporation met with Viktor Chernomyrdin, Russia's prime minister. As Hersh interprets the meeting, "Russia was then in the midst of a currency crisis and the war in Chechnya, and Noto offered to help by lending the government a billion dollars. In return, he asked for a five-year

supply of crude oil on preferential terms."[33] Although Noto's alleged proposal fell through, it would have been an indication to the Russian government that not only was a U.S. corporation willing to look the other way as
Russia prosecuted its brutal war in Chechnya, but Mobil was actually offering to relieve the financial pressure that many observers argue constituted
the main constraint on Moscow's continuation of the war.

External financial aid was not as crucial to Moscow's prosecution of the
second war in Chechnya because a rise in oil prices provided adequate
funds. In any case, the international financial institutions, dominated by
the United States, expressed little interest in trying to influence Russian
policy in Chechnya. In late January 2000 the Parliamentary Assembly of
the Council of Europe (PACE) overwhelmingly adopted a resolution calling on Moscow immediately to halt military operations in Chechnya and
to open a political dialogue with the Chechens. Two days later Stanley Fischer of the International Monetary Fund indicated that his organization
would not get involved in the issue and would not seek to penalize
Moscow for its brutal war in Chechnya. "If Russia meets the [economic]
conditions, it gets the money," Fischer said.[34]

Russian critics of the wars in Chechnya tend to argue that a more forthright Western position could have influenced Russian policy. Egor' Gaidar,
who served as acting prime minister under the early Yeltsin administration, has made such an argument for the first Chechen War. He claimed
that a strong Western response could have made a difference in the key
period between the introduction of Russian troops in November and the
storming of Grozny at the end of December 1994: "I am convinced that in
December, right up to 31 December, the beginning of the assault on
Grozny, everything hung in the balance. It was possible, by coordinated
force of pressure, to change the course of events to one of negotiations on
the basis of a demonstrated threat. It was the moment when we had to,
and we could have used all channels and levers of influence to convince
Yeltsin that he had made a mistake—as they say, it was worse than a crime,
it was a mistake. And at that moment the West was silent."[35]

In summing up the Western countries' response to the first Chechen
War, a group of Yeltsin's liberal advisers wrote that it seemed to follow a
formula: "You there, straighten things out quickly please, while we close
our eyes a little."[36] Their perception of Western responses to the second
war, starting in September 1999, was that it was, at least at first, "uniformly
negative."

In fact, official Western responses to the second war were rather cautious. The motive to support Yeltsin at any cost no longer applied, given

that his regime was not threatened with possible electoral victory by communists or fascists as in the mid-1990s. Moreover, the defensive orientation of the initial Russian military campaign was evident. Concern only came as the Russian government used the incursion into Dagestan as a pretext to mount an all-out invasion. On October 28, 1999, as Russian air strikes against Chechnya reached 150 per day, President Clinton expressed his hope that "we will see a minimumization [*sic*] of the casualties" in Chechnya and ultimately a "negotiated solution." On November 2 he warned that "Russia's international reputation could suffer."[37]

In January 2000, as Vladimir Putin took over the Russian presidency from the retired Yeltsin, he issued an ultimatum to the Chechen side. If the rebels in Grozny did not surrender, "all will be killed." That threat seemed to attract the international community's attention. According to one Russian journalist, "The ultimatum was angrily condemned internationally. U.S. President Bill Clinton and European Union leaders announced that the policy—killing everyone in a city where thousands of helpless civilians were holed up in basements—was totally unacceptable." Yet when no surrender was forthcoming, the Russian side carried out its threat, reportedly using fuel-air explosives that can clear out buildings and basements with high temperatures and shock waves more commonly associated with nuclear weapons.[38] Unlike nuclear weapons, however, fuel-air explosives have no stigma attached to them. The United States had used them extensively in the 1991 Persian Gulf War, for example, so its response to Russia's second massive destruction of Grozny was rather muted.[39]

Other segments of the international community expressed greater concern. In April 2000 the Parliamentary Assembly of the Council of Europe again criticized Russia's conduct of the war. This time it suspended the voting rights of the Russian delegation and called on members to exclude the country from PACE if it did not meet certain conditions. These included a commitment to "initiate political dialogue without preconditions or prior restrictions with a cross section of the Chechen people, including the elected Chechen authorities, seek an immediate cease-fire, allow independent enquiries into allegations of human rights violations, ensure access by all detainees in the region to independent legal assistance."[40] The Committee of Ministers, responsible for taking such action, declined to do so. The PACE leadership sent delegations to Russia to consult with officials there, to inspect refugee camps in Ingushetiia and detention centers in Chechnya, and to establish a joint commission with members of the Russian Duma. It also regularly denounced acts of terrorism from the Chechen side and urged a peaceful resolution of the conflict.

Although useful in providing information on the ongoing crisis in Chechnya, the PACE reports did not have a noticeable effect on Russian policy. Indeed, by the end of January 2001 the Russian delegation had its PACE membership restored, even though the atrocities continued apace.

Russian Government Response to War Crimes

The impact of international opinion on Russia's conduct of the war in Chechnya can be gauged in part by the reaction of Russian political and military leaders. Some theorists of international relations, especially from the Realist school of thought, do not expect public opinion to have any impact. A more nuanced analysis, however, was provided many decades ago by E. H. Carr, often considered the founder of modern political realism. Carr argued that "every state concludes treaties in the expectation that they will be observed; and states which violate treaties either deny that they have done so, or else defend the violation by argument designed to show that it was legally or morally justified." For Carr, "violation of treaties, even when frequently practised, is felt to be something exceptional requiring special justification. The general sense of obligation remains."[41]

Even within a general sense of obligation, however, we should distinguish between the dishonest denial of violations of international law, the attempt to excuse the violation, and the recognition of violation and promise to remedy it. An example of the first behavior—outright mendacious denial—came at the very outset of Moscow's first war against Chechnya, when military authorities denied the bombing of Grozny. In fact, they went a step further and tried to pin the blame on the Chechens themselves. Report 27, issued at 12:30 P.M. on Friday, December 22, 1994, claimed:

> The city of Grozny was not bombarded. However, the [Chechen] militants imitated the bombing of residential areas. About 1 A.M., an administrative building and an apartment house were blown up. People living in it, Chechens and Russians, were not warned. The imitation of a bomb was done to prove the notion of the "war against the Chechen nation being waged by the Russian leadership."[42]

Many accusations of war crimes initially met with such denials and fabrications of alternative accounts by the Russian authorities; some were followed eventually by reluctant acknowledgment, usually accompanied by attempts to excuse Russian behavior.

For the most part, Moscow's excuses framed the Chechen conflict as a war against terrorism. This characterization was not merely a response to the events of September 11, 2001, for it was prominent in the first war as well. Indeed, Western governments have evinced greatest sympathy for the Russian side when it alluded to the war in this fashion. A January 1996 raid into Dagestan illustrates the point. A group of Chechen guerrillas, led by Salman Raduev, after failing in their assault on a Russian helicopter base at Kizliar, rounded up hundreds of hostages and threatened to kill them if they were not allowed safe passage back to Chechnya. William Perry, then U.S. secretary of defense, expressed support for Russia's response—without, of course, knowing in advance what it would entail. "We reject the right of any group to take hostages as a means of implementing their policies," he said. "So therefore we believe the Russian Government is entirely correct in resisting this hostage-taking effort and resisting it very strongly."[43]

The Russian response in this case was certainly strong, if not wise or honorable. Seeking to negotiate their way home, the Chechen fighters had escaped with their hostages, including many kidnapped from a hospital, into the village of Pervomaiskoe. The Russians seemed more interested in revenge than saving the civilians' lives. At one point, Aleksandr Mikhailov, speaking for the Federal Security Service, claimed that the Chechens had executed all of the hostages. "We believe the hostages are dead," he said. "And now we will destroy the bandits." As the village came under withering attack from Russian Grad missiles, Mikhailov bragged that the Russians were counting Chechen casualties not by the number of corpses "but by the number of arms and legs."[44] In fact, the Chechens had not killed their hostages—although at least twenty-eight of them died in the Russian assault—and Mikhailov later acknowledged that he had deliberately lied to justify the attack.[45]

At the highest level, official Russian responses to charges of war crimes included both denial and putting the blame on the other side. Even after his retirement from office, Boris Yeltsin continued to maintain that "we have never committed mass executions of unarmed people in Chechnya. There have been no ethnic cleansings or concentration camps. The main reason for the missile strikes and bombs that have brought pain and grief to ordinary citizens is the war unleashed by the terrorists against the Russian people."[46]

During the course of the second Chechen War, the Russian government put increasing emphasis on the theme of terrorism. In August 2001, appearing before a panel considering Russia's possible membership in the

European Union, one Russian official described Chechnya as an "aggressive center of international terrorism and political extremism." General Vladimir Potapov, deputy secretary of the Russian Security Council, had served as chief of staff of the North Caucasus military district, with first-hand involvement in the wars in Chechnya. As the Viennese newspaper *Die Presse* reported, Potapov's "interpretation of the bloody events in the northern Caucasus was not contradicted by the panel," suggesting an acceptance of the Russian framing of the war by officials of the European Union, an important representative of the international community.[47]

Nevertheless, a number of international organizations, particularly nongovernmental human-rights groups, continued to criticize Russian conduct of the war. Moscow could have gone a long way toward relieving the pressure of international public opinion if it had taken responsibility when its forces committed war crimes by prosecuting the guilty parties. This has been a rare occurrence indeed.

A year and a half into the second war, Colonel Iurii Budanov was the only Russian military official put on trial for war crimes. He was accused of raping and strangling to death an eighteen-year-old Chechen woman, Elza Kungaieva, after kidnapping her from her home in the middle of the night. The incident began on March 26, 2000, when Budanov and his troops went on a drinking binge in double celebration of Vladimir Putin's electoral victory and the birthday of Budanov's daughter. At one point Budanov's drunken assistant ordered Lieutenant Roman Bagreev to fire an artillery barrage at a neighboring village, ostensibly to test the military preparedness of his soldiers. When the lieutenant refused, he was beaten up and thrown into a pit for the rest of the night. He became the main witness against Budanov.[48]

Although the colonel was arrested, the reaction from Russian leaders and the general public did not augur well for further prosecution of war crimes. Defense Minister Sergei Ivanov "voiced his support and sympathy" for Budanov when he was put on trial, calling him "a victim of circumstances."[49] Ivanov, a fellow Petersburg resident and former KGB agent, has been called Putin's "eye and arm," and his views are probably not far from the president's on this matter.[50] Indeed, a sizable proportion of Russian public opinion sympathized with Budanov. Forty-two percent of those questioned about the colonel's murder of the young Chechen woman— the earlier rape charge was dropped—claimed that he "was justified in doing so and should not be punished. Thirty-two percent said the trial was arranged to smear the military, with only 11 percent saying that they believe the colonel is guilty and should be punished."[51]

Vladimir Kalamanov, Russian human-rights ombudsman for Chechnya, indicated in April 2001 that the Budanov case was far from unique. He "called for a careful investigation of mass graves found in Chechnya and for the punishment of all found responsible for such atrocities."[52] Three months later Russian troops engaging in *zachistki* arrested and "disappeared" so many people in Chechnya that the popular outcry was finally heard in Moscow. As correspondent Maura Reynolds, in a thorough examination of the issue in the *Los Angeles Times*, wrote:

> Even Russian President Vladimir V. Putin's personal human rights representative, Vladimir A. Kalamanov, who tends to emphasize abuses attributed to Chechen rebels, acknowledges the "disappearance" problem. His office is trying to track down hundreds of missing people and has forced authorities to open investigations into at least 110 such cases. But according to Human Rights Watch, 79 of those cases have been suspended because investigators say they "cannot identify a suspect." [53]

In January 2001 Putin had transferred operational control of the Chechen campaign from the armed forces to the Federal Security Service, or FSB, the main successor agency to the KGB. The FSB was supposed to ensure that *zachistki* were conducted legally, for example, by seeing that a representative of the prosecutor's office was present during sweep operations. But, according to Reynolds's sources, the situation only deteriorated under FSB control, with prosecutors rarely available and, at all events, unable to influence the military's behavior. In a number of cases, "civilian administrators were reportedly locked in their offices to prevent them from keeping an eye on the soldiers."[54] When Chechen civilians did file complaints with the local prosecutors, the army often responded with intimidation. "Federal forces with guns and dogs visited the houses where people made statements," one young man reported to a journalist from the BBC. "They asked: 'Are you sure you don't want to withdraw your complaint?'"[55]

The events of July 2001 prompted a rare exception to the official Russian practice of denying war crimes.[56] Lieutenant General Vladimir Moltenskoi, acting commander of Russian forces in the North Caucasus, assembled his subordinate officers and members of the Russian press at the main Russian military base in Khankala, near Grozny, to acknowledge that Russian forces had engaged in "widespread crimes" against Chechen civilians in the course of *zachistki* in the villages of Assinovskaia and Sernovodsk. After some Russian soldiers were killed by remote-controlled

mines in the vicinity, a column of more than a hundred armored personnel carriers, with their identifying numbers covered over, arrived and set
up mass "filtration" centers in open fields and pits. Troops arrested some
1,500 villagers, mainly men and boys between the ages of fifteen and fifty-
five, beat them, tortured them with electric shocks, and left them in the
blazing sun all day. While ostensibly searching for those who had placed
the mines, soldiers looted homes, a school, and a hospital; stole cars and
trucks; blew open safes to steal money; and raided drug cabinets. General
Moltenskoi claimed that "those who conducted the searches did so in a
lawless fashion, committing numerous outrages and then pretending that
they knew nothing about them."

In fact, according to witnesses, Moltenskoi's original response was similar to that of his subordinates. Local Chechen officials who met with him
to complain about the assaults reported that Moltenskoi sat silently and
"admitted nothing." In the meantime, villagers filed hundreds of complaints with local prosecutors. Evidently they reached the attention of
authorities in Moscow, who ordered a change in approach. In addition to
Moltenskoi, a number of other officials spoke out. Sergei Iastrzhembskii,
an aide to President Putin, even suggested on Russian television that "the
very practice of mopping-up operations should be changed, and perhaps it
should become a feature of the past"—although nothing came of that suggestion. Moreover, there were countervailing voices seeking to play down
the gravity of the crimes. The newspaper *Izvestiia,* for example, quoted
Anatolii Shkirko, a former Interior Ministry commander, suggesting that
the outcry over military abuses was "inspired by the guerrillas, directly or
indirectly."

Not surprisingly, even Chechen officials working with the Russian government remained skeptical of Moscow's change of heart. Akhmad Kadyrov, the Moscow-appointed head of the Chechen government, warned that
"if we don't punish the culprits I will not be able to face my people." Aslan-
bek Aslakhanov, who served as Chechen deputy to the Russian Duma, told
a Russian television audience that "I am not sure that those who are guilty
will be punished." He cited examples of numerous previous mopping-up
operations "accompanied by mass pillaging" and "violations of human
rights" and complained that "nobody has reacted to these." Aslakhanov
called for negotiations with Aslan Maskhadov, the elected president of
Chechnya—something other pro-Moscow Chechens had been unwilling
to do.

By August 2001, Vladimir Kalamanov, President Putin's commissioner
for human rights in Chechnya, reported that eighty-two criminal cases

had been opened against members of the armed forces for crimes committed against civilians. Of those, only twenty-five had come to court, and in only eleven cases had the perpetrators been sentenced. It is not surprising that Kalamanov was not taken seriously by most Chechens, who considered him a "Kremlin stooge."[57]

Thus fully two years into the second war, only eleven Russian soldiers had been convicted of crimes against Chechen civilians, while more than a thousand complaints had been registered with the authorities.[58] In September 2001 presidential aide Iastrzhembskii sent a list of the eleven soldiers to officials of the Council of Europe for use during a meeting of its Parliamentary Assembly. The government blamed many of the crimes on soldiers' drunkenness, denying that their activities received any official authorization.

At about the same time, various government officials issued conflicting reports about the extent to which other cases of war crimes were being prosecuted. Iastrzhembskii's office, for example, reported a figure of 82 criminal cases under investigation since October 1999, among them 30 murders. Twenty cases were handed over to military courts and 60 more were still under investigation. Lieutenant General Iurii Iakovlev, first deputy prosecutor for the Ministry of Defense, claimed in October 2001 that his office had reviewed 1,700 criminal cases since the start of the second Chechen War. Of those, 345 were dismissed for various reasons, including amnesty for the suspects, and 360 cases were passed on to the courts.[59] In the meantime, Russian troops continued to commit atrocities, and Chechen civilians continued to complain. In November 2001, for example, 1,500 residents of the Chechen town of Argun protested a raid by FSB forces during which 6 civilians were killed, 21 were wounded, and 40 houses were destroyed. The authorities promised to investigate.[60]

By any measure, the Russian government has fallen far short of its international obligation to pursue war criminals. The Geneva Conventions require its signatories to "provide effective penal sanctions for persons committing, or ordering to be committed, any of the grave breaches" listed in the Conventions and Protocol I, and "to search for persons alleged to have committed, or to have ordered to be committed, such grave breaches, and shall bring such persons, regardless of their nationality, before [their] own courts."[61] But as Human Rights Watch points out, Russia "has refused to establish a national commission to investigate charges of serious abuses by Russian troops against Chechen civilians" and "has directly flouted the resolutions of the United Nations Commission on Human Rights, including by refusing to allow U.N. monitors access to Chechnya."[62] In the spring of 2002, concerned that Moscow would never adequately prosecute those guilty of war crimes, officials of the Council of Europe and Carla del Ponte, chief prosecutor of the war crimes tribunal for former Yugoslavia, suggested that some kind of international role might be required.[63]

The vast discrepancy between the large number of complaints and eyewitness accounts of war atrocities and the minuscule number of prosecutions and convictions has led Russian observers to doubt Vladimir Putin's much-vaunted commitment to law and order. As journalist Evgeniia Albats wrote,

> Early in his presidency, Putin became dubiously associated with the phrase "dictatorship of law." Back then, I raised the question of whether that meant law and order or just order without law. Recently, the Duma passed the long-awaited judicial reform, which, although limited, was a Kremlin initiative. However, several days later, federal troops killed, tortured and robbed dozens of innocent civilians in Chechnya, clearly demonstrating the concept of order without law even to the extreme extent of inflicting the death penalty without due process. Putin has not said a word about these incidents, just as he has said virtually nothing about any other atrocities committed in Chechnya over the last two years.[64]

Few Western governments have been so forthright in their criticisms of Putin for Russia's conduct in Chechnya. Nor have they considered, as Albats did, the implications for internal Russian politics. International and transnational nongovernmental organizations have been much more critical of Russian policy, but their impact has been limited.

The Russian Armed Forces and the Laws of War

In early December 1995 Russian military leaders were reminded of international concern about the invasion of Chechnya when they received a "curious communication from Stockholm":

> Charges of crimes against humanity will be brought against Boris Yeltsin, president of the Russian Federation, Minister of Defense Pavel Grachev, former minister of the interior Viktor Erin, secretary of the Security Council Oleg Lobov, former minister of nationality affairs Nikolai Egorov. It is not excluded that charges will be brought against Andrei Kozyrev [Russian foreign minister] and Dzhokhar Dudaev, the president of Chechnya. International public hearings of

the general tribunal will take place 15–16 December 1995 in Stockholm with support from the Olof Palme International Center.

Colonel Viktor Baranets, who read the document at the General Staff headquarters, suggested that for such a tribunal to charge "many representatives of Russia's top leadership, starting with Yeltsin, was bad news for the Kremlin."[65] But he did not believe that General Grachev worried much about it. "More frightening for him were the curses of the many thousands of mothers of those soldiers who are looking at us today from their gravestones in Russian cemeteries."[66]

Nor did Russian officials need any international condemnation to become aware of the abuses carried out under their authority. The Interior Ministry, for example, knew of war crimes committed by its troops within weeks of the initial Russian invasion. A document distributed to its forces in February 1995 referred to cases of "looting, extortion, and atrocities committed by servicemen with relation to the civilian population."[67]

To what extent are high Russian military officials sensitive to the impact of such charges of war crimes on Russian international prestige? What do they even understand about international humanitarian law governing warfare?

In July 1995 the Constitutional Court of the Russian Federation heard a case brought against Boris Yeltsin by members of the Russian Duma for illegal use of armed force in launching the war against Chechnya in November 1994. Although Yeltsin was ultimately exonerated, the court posed many questions about the conduct of the war to the witnesses who appeared before it. Some of the answers provide insight into Russian military thinking about morality and law in warfare. Particularly revealing were the remarks of Marshal Viktor Kulikov. For twenty years Kulikov had served as deputy minister of defense in the Soviet armed forces, as chief of the General Staff, and as commander in chief of the combined armies of the Warsaw Pact. His understanding of the morality and legality of the Chechen conflict should reflect that of the top ranks of Russian military command.

Kulikov began by posing the basic problem associated with the conduct of a guerrilla war: "It is very, very difficult to make sharp distinctions between bandit formations, militia forces, and the regular army"—not to mention civilians. Thus soldiers and officers face a tough situation. "This morning they receive an order to shoot, and the next day they're told, you shot at peaceful inhabitants."[68] A sympathetic questioner asked Kulikov whether the army was prepared to deal with cases where the Chechens used human shields to defend themselves. The marshal acknowledged that such situations put a "particular psychological burden on servicemen," but he did not indicate how they were expected to act in such circumstances. Nor did he acknowledge instances in which Russian troops themselves used Chechen civilians as shields.[69] There is some indication that the Chechen fighters abandoned the deliberate use of civilian shields because "it was simply useless—Russian attacks took place notwithstanding civilian casualties."[70]

Another questioner asked Kulikov what kind of training the armed forces received for dealing with civilian populations during military operations. "Which methods can be used and which not?" Is it allowed, for example, "to drop bombs on a city, or mount a massive fire attack on villages? Is it regulated in any way, at least at the level of training, or of some kind of theory, or at the level of some kind of norms?" Kulikov responded that the commander in charge of the operation must take everything into account when making such decisions, but that there were no particular guidelines provided. "In our regulations, in our instructions, there's no such conception." Then, demonstrating what he had learned well from the Soviet system, he deflected the question into a criticism of the United States. "This conception" of norms governing attacks on populated areas "isn't in the regulations of foreign states" either, he argued. "An example of this is the complete destruction of Dresden" and other cities "by American forces, when the population was completely destroyed, with no conceivable military objective."[71]

Kulikov would address the notion of inadvertent civilian casualties only in the context of a situation where Russian troops were being attacked. He had discussed this matter with many commanders, he said, and they described the decisions they faced. The commander "identifies a target from which powerful artillery and machine-gun fire is being carried out. But there's no data on whether civilians are there or not. A decision has to be made to carry out the strike or not. The strike is carried out, and then it turns out that there were civilians. It's a nonstandard [*nestandartnaia*] situation, but he fulfilled the task in principle correctly because he had suffered losses."[72] In fact, if this scenario poses the question of war crimes at all, they are not the sort that attracted most international attention: the high-altitude indiscriminate bombing of population centers, on the one hand, and face-to-face massacres and maltreatment of civilians, on the other.

Boris Yeltsin used a similar rhetorical technique when he dismissed accusations of Russian war crimes. In one volume of his memoirs he acknowledged: "There are reams of evidence proving that civilians have suffered in what is called the second Chechen War. People have lost their homes and their property. Many civilians have lost their lives or their health. But should the Russian army bear responsibility for these woes? Could anyone have imagined a situation in which Russian soldiers would hide in the homes of civilians and shoot at an armed enemy, putting women and old people in the line of fire? I think no one could."[73]

The more problematic questions of massive bombing of cities such as Grozny, Kulikov only addresses by saying in effect that other countries have done it, so Russia is no worse than them. Indeed, because the United States relies so heavily on aerial bombing, even for putatively humanitarian initiatives, such as the Kosovo intervention, it has been difficult for critics of Russia's bombing practices to make much headway. Nevertheless, numerous more clear-cut cases of illegal acts that transpired within the course of bombing campaigns have become the focus of international attention. In a number of instances, Russian aircraft have deliberately bombed columns of refugees fleeing Grozny and other towns, sometimes after Russian authorities have announced the opening of a corridor and urged civilians to leave. There are documented cases of Russians firing upon cars flying white flags and killing unarmed civilians—including elderly people and children—and then broadcasting on television that the victims were in fact guerrilla fighters.[74]

These cases constitute clear examples of possible war crimes that should require, at a minimum, thorough investigations. Russian authorities undermine international perceptions of their credibility and integrity when they either ignore the cases or report deliberate falsehoods about them. Yet such behavior pales before that of Russian officials who forthrightly justify or advocate war crimes. Some of them have played prominent roles in the Chechen Wars and have made their views very public.

One such individual is General Gennadii Troshev, who commanded Russian forces in Chechnya for the first twenty months of the second war, before taking over as head of the North Caucasus military district. In June 2001 Troshev gave the newspaper *Izvestiia* his solution for how to deal with continuing attacks by Chechen rebels. "Here's what I would do," he said, "collect them all on the square, string the bandits up and let them hang, and let everyone see them. The word bandit's too good for them. They're scum."[75] A policy of summary executions would violate the most minimal protections of the laws of war, as Russian military jurists themselves have acknowledged.

Among the most explicit advocates of deliberate killing of civilians is Lieutenant General Vladimir Shamanov, whom Boris Yeltsin awarded the

"Hero of Russia" medal for commanding the Western group during the second Chechen War. Shamanov later took charge of the 58th Army, stationed in Vladikavkaz, the capital of North Ossetiia. At forty-three, he was Russia's youngest general when Anna Politkovskaia, a reporter for the popular *Novaia gazeta* newspaper, interviewed him in June 2000. She began her interview by asking him how he felt about the way the whole country now referred to him as "cruel Shamanov" whereas the other leading general in the Chechen War was known as "kind Troshev" (as incredible as that seems). "For me it's praise," responded Shamanov.

The journalist went on to pose direct questions about his views on a series of reported atrocities, which Shamanov dismissed as "much exaggerated by the media." She pressed him on the particular case of Alkhan-Iurt, where Russian bombs had killed many civilians as well as guerrilla fighters. Shamanov replied that the case had been investigated, graves were opened, and "only 20 bodies were found. Of those, 12 were bandits." "Six weeks later," he said, "the prosecutor's office issued a finding about the remaining eight bodies: they were people connected in one way or another with the bandits." Politkovskaia questioned that formulation—"connected with"—and persisted: "In your view, who is the wife of a Chechen fighter?" "A female bandit," he responded. "If she's not a female bandit then she should leave him." "Is the child of a bandit also a bandit?" she asked. "Certainly," he answered. Then he posed his own rhetorical question. "Tell me something: how can you tell someone's wife from a woman sniper?" Politkovskaia suggested that "ordinary soldiers don't reason that way and don't even share your point of view. That's why, later on, they commit suicide." Shamanov denied knowing any such soldiers.[76]

Chechen Strategy: Inviting War Crimes?

Chechen leaders apparently believe that the Russian army is so afraid of taking casualties that the Chechens put their own civilians at risk in order to deter Russian attacks. This practice, intended to protect civilians, actually risks inviting further Russian war crimes. Aslan Maskhadov, the besieged president of Chechnya, explained his thinking to journalist Anne Nivat in September 2000. The Russian soldiers "avoid all contact with the enemy, with us." Instead, "they take out all their aggression on innocent civilians." According to Maskhadov, whenever the Russian military leaders learn that Chechen fighters, the so-called *boeviki*, "are in a certain area, they cease firing" for fear of being attacked themselves. This observation led Maskhadov to give counterintuitive instructions to his village chiefs. "Whatever you do, don't admit that you're not harboring rebel fighters.

They'll bombard you. Tell them instead that you're hiding at least two hundred rebels. That way they'll leave you alone." Maskhadov even went to the point of reversing an earlier order forbidding Chechen troops to open fire from village centers. "Better that we ourselves should open fire than that we should stand by silently while the Russians rob and pillage and commit acts of barbarism."[77]

Maskhadov's policy, even if it saved lives by deterring Russian attacks, could help the Russian government avoid some charges of war crimes. Whereas it is against international law to attack an undefended population center, it is acceptable to attack a defended one in the interest of defeating the military forces based there. Moreover, Maskhadov, by ordering his troops to fire from civilian population centers, is himself guilty of a war crime. The Geneva Conventions bar use of "civilian shields." Does it matter that Maskhadov's claimed intention was to use the fighters to shield (defend) the villagers, rather than vice versa? Or that even if he did intend to use the civilians as shields, the tactic had not worked? The Russian forces had long since demonstrated themselves willing to destroy any number of Chechen civilians.

Indeed, Maskhadov's boasts about his side's military strength and deployment serve to justify the apparent Russian belief that every village is a legitimate target and every Chechen male a presumptive combatant: "We have exactly 420 villages in Chechnya. In each one of them we have at least 50 combatants and 30 or so reservists. That's around 33,000 persons I can count on, in addition to my commanders and their staffs."[78] Such calculations, even if exaggerated, might deter Russian forces from attacking Chechen population centers. Or they might serve as further stimulus to the brutal *zachistki*, where every male Chechen from the age of fifteen to fifty-five is treated as a presumed guerrilla fighter.

Government Response to Domestic Critics

Some of the sharpest criticism of Russian conduct of the wars in Chechnya has come from domestic sources—especially from journalists such as Politkovskaia and from human-rights activists such as Kovalev. Supporters of the war in Chechnya within the Russian government in turn have sought to stifle any media criticism of Russian policy—often resorting to violence to do so. Scores of journalists were killed under mysterious circumstances or "disappeared" during the first war.[79] Perhaps as a result, the second war saw fewer journalists taking risks to report on activities that cast Russian policy in a negative light, and those who did often suffered the consequences.[80]

Andrei Babitskii, a reporter for Radio Liberty, was one of the very few Russian journalists to report on the impact of the second Chechen War on the civilian population. For his trouble, he was arrested by Russian security forces in January 2000 and "disappeared" for a month. In order to demonstrate that he was a traitor, the Russian authorities set up a fraudulent exchange of Babitskii to a bogus group of Chechen "rebels" in return for supposed Russian prisoners of war.[81] Vladimir Putin made clear his government's position on journalists who criticize official policy on the war when he was asked about Babitskii by Russian journalists. Putin claimed that Babitskii "was working directly for the enemy. He was not a neutral source of information. He was working for the bandits." When the journalists suggested that Babitskii was only trying to report the truth of the war, Putin declared that "what Babitskii did is much more dangerous than firing a machine gun." He insisted, "He's not a Russian journalist."[82]

Another journalist who suffered for her courageous reporting from Chechnya was Anna Politkovskaia. In February 2001 she traveled to Chechnya to investigate stories of mass detentions in underground pits, torture, and summary executions. Not only did she verify the stories, but she herself was arrested by the FSB and threatened with rape and "execution." Unbowed, she continued to issue critical reports about the behavior of Russian forces in Chechnya.

In October 2001 Politkovskaia had to flee the country after receiving threats on her life. She had published more controversial articles on the Chechen War, including the interview with Shamanov.[83] In September she wrote about alleged summary executions and torture committed by a unit of Interior Ministry troops from Khanty-Mansiisk, serving in Grozny in January 2001. The report contained detailed accusations of torture by Sergei Lapin; an officer who allegedly shaved his nickname "Kadet" on the back of the head of Zelimkhan Mourdalov, a twenty-six-year-old Chechen man in his custody, before breaking his arm and thorax and cutting off his right ear. Supposedly transferred to the hospital, Mourdalov was never seen again. When officials from the Grozny prosecutor's office came to question Lapin, his police colleagues refused to turn him over. Later he was sent back home to Nizhenevartovsk, where the local authorities continued to protect him from Grozny's prosecutors. Subsequently, the editors of *Novaia gazeta* received anonymous information that a police official, trained as a sniper and going by the code name "Kadet," had been sent to Moscow, where Politkovskaia worked. Another anonymous call demanded that the newspaper print a retraction of Politkovskaia's article. Instead the editors sent the reporter abroad for her safety.[84]

Politkovskaia had managed to anger other top officials with another report from September 2001, entitled "Grozny under Blockade." She suggested that a helicopter carrying a visiting delegation of ten General Staff officers was deliberately shot down by local officials who were afraid of what the generals would report back to Putin. From her own observations, the main square of Minutka was completely sealed off when the attack occurred, rendering implausible the official explanation that a lone Chechen fighter had downed the helicopter with "an antiaircraft gun of foreign manufacture." Politikovskaia wondered, "Who could have carried an anti-aircraft gun into a space where no one was being allowed to go?"[85] The reaction to her public speculation presumably contributed to her decision to flee abroad.

Other journalists have criticized Moscow's conduct of the wars in Chechnya and have explicitly accused Russian officials of war crimes. Pavel Fel'gengauer, a specialist on military policy, attributed Russian behavior in part to poor training:

> The Russian armed forces have lots of guns, bombs and ballistic missiles, but they do not have the well-trained infantry to match the rebels. Because of this weakness and because of pressure to capture Grozny and declare "victory" at any cost, Russian generals are virtually forced to resort to illegal means, to commit war crimes and to substitute for well trained and motivated infantry with increasingly more powerful bombs.[86]

In Fel'gengauer's view, the indiscriminate bombing of Grozny, in particular, violated the second protocol of the Geneva Conventions, which protects civilians caught in internal armed conflict. Thus, he argued, the Russian military command is implicated in war crimes, "and Putin—who has publicly said he was personally involved in planning Russian tactics in Chechnya—most likely is a war criminal too." Fel'gengauer was disappointed in the Western response. "The international community is all but silent," he complained. He found it particularly galling that Clinton's secretary of state Madeleine Albright had referred to Putin as "one of the leading reformers," echoing the rhetoric that the administration had substituted for criticism of Boris Yeltsin during the first war.[87]

Media criticism of the conduct of the second Russian war in Chechnya has been more the exception than the rule. One Russian journalist pointed out that the Russian media and government officials have even apparently coordinated their efforts to underplay the significance of the war crimes:

"Some central newspapers have published material, distributed also by official information sources, justifying practically any actions of the federal forces."[88] Given the dangers that critical journalists such as Politkovskaia and Babitskii have faced, it is not surprising that most journalists prefer to cooperate with the government. Many were accustomed to doing so during the Soviet era, when the consequences of criticizing the official line rarely included the risk of physical extermination, at least after Stalin's death.

The corrupting influence of the Chechen Wars extends beyond relations between the government and the media. Russian officials evidently have come to consider not only journalists as potential enemies, but also foreign humanitarian workers. In February 2001, Petra Prohazkova, a Czech citizen married to a Russian, was expelled from the country and denied a visa to return. When members of the Russian parliament intervened on her behalf, they were told that Prohazkova was banned under a law that permitted such actions "when necessary for the purposes of maintaining state security." What had Prohazkova done to pose such a threat to the Russian state? From 1992 to 2000 she worked as a journalist and reported, often critically, on the war in Chechnya.[89] From the summer of 2000, however, she gave up journalism to run an orphanage in Grozny. Which activity Russian officials perceived as more threatening is unclear. The government also banned the head of a Japanese Buddhist society who had been running soup kitchens in Chechnya and Ingushetiia since 1995 and a British humanitarian worker whose Center for Peacemaking and Community Development ran schools for refugee children, provided psychological counseling, and repaired schools in Chechnya itself.[90]

War Crimes and the International Community

Human-rights activists and critical Russian journalists, such as Fel'gengauer and Politkovskaia, have expressed dismay over the inadequate response from the international community to the extensive evidence of war crimes in the Chechen Wars. I have already mentioned the Realpolitik motives that influenced the Clinton administration during the first war as it sought to bolster a political regime that it considered friendly to U.S. interests. What accounts for the international community's relatively mild reaction to the second war, particularly in comparison with its response to the situation in Kosovo just months earlier? How has Russia managed to avoid the status of international pariah that Slobodan Milošević earned for Serbia by his prosecution of wars in the former Yugoslavia? Has Russia in fact survived the Chechen Wars without damage to its international prestige?[91]

Before that question can be answered, one needs to define the "international community." Some observers use the term as a synonym for "the West"—the United States and its allies—but the practical definition is even more narrowly limited to the governments of those countries. Others have in mind the United Nations, as the representative of all countries. Still others think of a "global civil society"—the nongovernmental groups and social movements that seek to influence the behavior of states.

Whatever the sources of international opinion—governments, corporations, or activist groups—it tends to be expressed through the news media. Typically, judgments of Russia's behavior are conveyed by journalists, retired diplomats, and academic specialists who seek to share their expertise with a broader popular audience. Human-rights activists try to disseminate their views through press releases and press conferences, but many of their detailed reports never receive much media coverage.

Standards and Double Standards

The standards by which such observers judge Russia are not always apparent. One could imagine two main types. First, Russian behavior could be evaluated on the basis of international law governing situations such as the wars in Chechnya. This is the approach human-rights organizations tend to take. Second, Russia's responses could be judged in the light of how other major powers have dealt with similar situations, one example being the bombing of Dresden cited earlier. The problem is that representatives of other countries that have violated international laws of war cannot ask Russia to adhere to those laws without being accused of using a "double standard." Human-rights groups or journalists who do not represent governments when they criticize Russia for violations of international law are less susceptible to that charge.

One barrier to clear perceptions of the extent of Russian war crimes in Chechnya is Western observers' poor understanding in general of international law. Many who supply information on and analysis of the country are journalists and experts on Russia, including scholars and former government officials, with little knowledge of the laws of war.

Just War: Do the Ends Justify the Means?

Much of international humanitarian law, or the laws of war, derives from Just War Theory as developed by Catholic theologians, beginning with St. Augustine. Its key distinction between just ends (*jus ad bellum*) and just means (*jus in bello*) provides a useful framework for examining international reactions to the Chechen situation.[92] Just War Theory's language of ends, means, and justice appears throughout discussions of the Chechen Wars. For example, many observers who were unwilling to condemn Russia's conduct of the war believed the campaign to bring Chechnya under control was justified, as reflected in the comparisons some American officials have made between Boris Yeltsin and Abraham Lincoln. That sentiment was even stronger in the second war, which began in response to an attack against Russian territory from Chechnya. It also coincided with a series of terrorist bombings of apartment buildings in Russian cities, widely attributed to Chechens. Furthermore, the situation in Chechnya after the withdrawal of Russian troops in 1996 had deteriorated to such an extent—particularly with the epidemic of kidnappings of Russians, Chechens, and foreigners—that it seemed irresponsible not to try to restore order there.[93] Nevertheless, although Russia is not the only country to have experienced a kidnapping epidemic, few others have responded with all-out war.[94]

Not every observer distinguishes between just ends and just means as intended by Just War Theory and international humanitarian law. Yet doing so enables one to make independent judgments about the morality or legality of each aspect considered separately. A war can be fought for a just cause but with unjust means. By the same token, objectives can be unjust but the means of fighting for them just. A key feature of Just War Theory is that it deliberately undermines arguments of the ends-justify-the-means sort often found in commentaries on the wars in Chechnya. This is the case made by Robert Bruce Ware, a U.S. specialist on Dagestan, in evaluating the second Chechen War:

> It is particularly difficult to accept Moscow's objectives when its methods are brutal, and admittedly, at times, unconscionable. But if we accept the objectives then it appears that we must tolerate some of the methods, for it is unlikely that the objectives could be achieved with methods that were substantially different. It would be difficult for Moscow to dispense with indiscriminate bombing and shelling since 1) Chechen militants purposefully take refuge among, and are often indistinguishable from, civilians, 2) Russia lacks the capability for remote precision attacks, and 3) it would be difficult or impossible for Russia to achieve its objectives by fighting largely in close quarters.[95]

Ware was never insensitive to the crimes and abuses committed by the Russian armed forces in seeking to subdue Chechnya. But he was particularly concerned that observers not paint a picture in black and white, but instead recognize the threat posed by rampant kidnapping, the slave trade, and cross-border incursions by armed gangs. Two years into the war, if Ware (as many others) still acknowledged the just ends of Russia's military campaign, he expressed considerably more skepticism about the means. He compared the U.S. war against al-Qaida and its Taliban supporters in Afghanistan to the Russian war in Chechnya and found much to emulate in the U.S. example: the attempt to win over the population and convince it to abandon its militant leaders, the concern to avoid civilian casualties, and the provision of food aid. "Moscow did none of this," and thereby missed an opportunity to combine just means with just ends.

> Many Chechens suffered from the chaos in their country, and were fed up with the warlords and extremists who ran it. Especially in the early stages of the war, Russia had the support of some of these people, and it might have had the support of more had it made an effort to assure their protection. Instead Russian attacks have been characteristically brutal and indiscriminate. Efforts to identify militants in "pacified" areas of Chechnya have resulted in the regular abuse of civilians. These tactics have inspired Chechen resistance and undermined any popular support that Moscow might otherwise have cultivated. So long as these tactics continue there can be no hope for peace in Chechnya.[96]

Ware's observations highlight an important relationship between ends and means. From a pragmatic perspective, the injustice of Russia's means can undermine achievement of its more easily justifiable ends.

Are Some War Crimes Less Criminal than Others?

Some observers argue that the morality and legality of Russia's wars in Chechnya depend in part on the types of war crimes involved. For them, killing of civilians by aerial bombardment is not as serious a violation as direct killing of civilians on the ground, especially if it includes a system of camps where people are rounded up and tortured before being killed. Furthermore, killing of civilians in order to protect one's own troops seems hardly a crime at all, in the view of some analysts, and is sometimes described even as a duty.

The Russian government has reinforced the tendency to forgive the killing of innocents by following the U.S. lead in emphasizing, at least at the rhetorical level, the protection of its troops. This move was intended to prevent a resurgence of the popular opposition to the first Chechen War, when the army seemed to lack any regard for the lives of its soldiers.[97] The Chechen side has taken advantage of this heightened Russian sensitivity to casualties. As the Chechen guerrilla leader Shamil' Basaev told the French journalist Anne Nivat, the Russians "can't bear heavy troop losses. They know that, if this happens, the Russian people will eventually rise up against this war."[98]

One of the most prolific proponents of the distinction between aerial bombing and face-to-face killing of civilians is Anatol Lieven. The author of a detailed account of the Russian war against Chechnya in 1994–96, in which he rather romanticized the Chechen resistance, Lieven expressed very different views about the second war. Lieven has also written extensively on U.S. military strategy, and his views about what is required and acceptable for "the West" to do seem to have influenced his arguments about Chechnya.

First, Lieven argues, much Western criticism of Russia's conduct of the war in Chechnya is self-serving, constitutes a double standard, and reflects an ingrained "Russophobia."[99] Lieven recommends that Western observers play down Russia's indiscriminate aerial bombardment of urban areas on the grounds that "several Western states, the United States included, have engaged in it at certain times and may have to do it again." Lieven put these words into a report of the Carnegie Endowment for International Peace, but few other nongovernmental organizations interested in peace and human rights would endorse them.[100] Most human-rights organizations do not believe that in the twenty-first century Russia's international reputation should be determined on such a least-common-denominator basis, by putting the country up against the (possibly rather low) standards set by other world powers and deciding that it does not look so bad in comparison.

The ready acceptance among some Western observers of Russia's indiscriminate bombing is a bit surprising. In an article written just before the 1994 Russian invasion, and published as the bombs were destroying Grozny, a leading scholar of military affairs had predicted a very different future for warfare: "It is highly unlikely that advanced powers will again resort to the wholesale devastation of cities and towns, whether to shatter enemy morale or as a by-product of efforts to hit other target systems, such as railroad yards or factories."[101] If this expectation were widely held, one might have anticipated greater public shock at the Russian bombing, and a reluctance to accept it as business-as-usual.

Lieven is not insensitive to the desirability of avoiding civilian casualties, but his reasons are entirely political and pragmatic, with little moral or legal substance. He is critical of the U.S. tendency to protect its own troops ("force protection") by using excessive military force ("firepower"), especially from high-altitude bombing. Lieven argues that these "linked obsessions with firepower and force protection are likely to lead to a politically disastrous level of civilian casualties." American military practice posed a particular problem for what Lieven considers "the most dangerous battlefield of the future"—"the sprawling modern city, with its endless possibilities of ambush and car bombs, and its unlimited capacity to produce large-scale and deeply embarrassing civilian casualties."[102]

In the wake of the September 2001 attacks against the World Trade Towers in New York and the Pentagon in Washington, Lieven turned his attention to Afghanistan, where the United States led a war against the Taliban regime that protected members of the al-Qaida network believed responsible for the attacks. His firsthand knowledge of the Soviet Union's war in Afghanistan added weight to his point about the politically embarrassing effects of indiscriminate urban bombing, and he drew a parallel to the Russian assault on Chechnya from 1994 to 1996. "When I visited Herat on the government side in June 1989," he wrote, "I looked out from the government machine gun nests in the ancient fortress over an immense field of ruins—from which the Mujahedin went on sniping. We had better hope that such horribly destructive urban battles do not develop, because as in the case of Grozny, scenes like this would not have a good effect on important sections of international public opinion."[103]

Priority Protection of Soldiers: A Law of War?

In recent years people in the West, particularly the United States, have appeared to believe that the lives of innocent civilians in enemy countries—or even countries that are the target of "humanitarian" intervention—are worth less than the lives of their own country's soldiers. Evidence suggests that Russian leaders have sought to promote this belief in their prosecution of the war in Chechnya. Even though the war is supposed to ensure that Chechens remain Russian citizens, it has been fought as if the lives of Chechen civilians (and Russian civilians caught in Chechnya) are expendable compared with those of Russian soldiers (whose lives are also considered quite cheap, judging by the way Russian political and military leaders waste them).[104] A number of influential Western observers of the situation in Chechnya have come to accept the argument that a country is allowed, or even obliged, to protect its soldiers first, even at the expense of killing innocent civilians.

U.S. military and political leaders—in their policy toward recent wars and in their reminiscences about past ones—have increasingly emphasized that protecting soldiers should be given top priority. This belief lay at the core of U.S. and NATO policy during the intervention in Kosovo in 1999. General Wesley Clark, the Supreme Allied Commander, Europe, during the Kosovo war, "issued a secret order that NATO's first requirement was to avoid the loss of any aircraft." As the *New York Times* reported, Clark's "preoccupation with avoiding NATO military casualties limited the effectiveness of the air campaign and increased the prospect of civilian casualties, because allied warplanes bombed from high altitudes." Nevertheless, "General Clark defended the order in an interview as necessary to maintain public support for the war."[105] Similarly, another officer involved in the Kosovo campaign—General Klaus Naumann of Germany, who was chair of the NATO Military Committee at the beginning of the war—defined NATO's "three guiding principles" as follows: "we had first of all to avoid if possible any of our own casualties and fatalities; secondly we were told to avoid collateral damage to the extent possible; and thirdly bring it to a quick end."[106]

The fact that such prominent military leaders should openly give first priority to avoiding casualties among soldiers and lower priority to avoiding deaths of innocent civilians suggests unfamiliarity with the basics of Just War Theory and international law. A similar ignorance of the laws of war probably explains the public reaction to revelations that former U.S. Senator Bob Kerrey participated in the killing of more than a dozen women, children, and elderly people when he led a commando team in Vietnam in 1969. Kerrey's unit was on a mission to assassinate Vietcong leaders supposedly living in a hamlet among the civilian population. When he and his soldiers were discovered en route to the hamlet, they murdered the people who had seen them—an elderly couple and their three grandchildren—so as not to compromise the mission and put their own lives at risk. "Standard operating procedure was to dispose of the people we made contact with," Kerrey explained. "Kill the people we made contact with, or we have to abort the mission." There is some dispute among the soldiers in Kerrey's unit as to whether they killed a subsequent group of civilians in a firefight or rounded them up and executed them. The first incident is already adequate, however, to support a charge of war crimes against Kerrey and his soldiers. And if it is true, as Kerrey claimed, that it was "standard operating procedure" to "dispose of" civilian noncombatants, then his political and military superiors could be guilty as well.[107]

When Kerrey's actions were exposed, he pondered whether "what I did was militarily allowable or morally ethical or inside the rules of war" and decided, "I can make a case that it was." In fact, as the reporter who broke the story explained, "the [U.S.] Army's Field Manual is explicit" in describing the legal obligations of a commander in Kerrey's situation:

> A commander may not put his prisoners to death because their presence retards his movements or diminishes his power of resistance by necessitating a large guard, or by reason of their consuming supplies, or because it appears certain that they will regain their liberty through the impending success of their forces. It is likewise unlawful for a commander to kill his prisoners on grounds of self-preservation, even in the case of airborne or commando operations, although the circumstances of the operation may make necessary rigorous supervision of and restraint upon the movement of the prisoners of war.[108]

Note that these rules apply to enemy soldiers taken as prisoners of war. The protections accorded to civilian noncombatants should be even greater. As political theorist Michael Walzer describes, "The war convention requires soldiers to accept personal risk rather than kill innocent people." Moreover, "self-preservation in the face of the enemy is not an excuse for violations of the rules of war. . . . The crucial point is that soldiers cannot enhance their own security at the expense of innocent men and women."[109] Thus Kerrey's assertion finds no basis in the laws of war.

Kerrey is not the only Vietnam War veteran who believes that killing Vietnamese civilians was justified to protect American soldiers, independently of whether any specific military objectives were involved. Consider this excerpt from a memoir of one soldier's Vietnam experience:

> I recall a phrase we used in the field, MAM, for military-age male. If a helo [helicopter] spotted a peasant in black pajamas who looked remotely suspicious, a possible MAM, the pilot would circle and fire in front of him. If he moved, his movement was judged evidence of hostile intent, and the next burst was not in front, but at him. Brutal? Maybe so. But an able battalion commander with whom I had served at Gelnhausen, Lieutenant Colonel Walter Pritchard, was killed by enemy sniper fire while observing MAMs from a helicopter. And Pritchard was only one of many. The kill-or-be-killed nature of combat tends to dull fine perceptions of right and wrong.[110]

This soldier's perceptions of right and wrong were certainly dulled if he can justify the routine killing of "remotely suspicious" peasants as a preventive measure to decrease the risk of occasional sniper attack. As Walzer explains, "The dangers of enemy fire are simply the risks of the activity in which [soldiers] are engaged, and they have no right to reduce those risks at the expense of other people who are not engaged."[111] Yet Colin Powell, the soldier in question, went on to become chairman of the Joint Chiefs of Staff and U.S. secretary of state. It is not surprising that his views on legal and moral matters related to war should be widely held among U.S. journalists and the public, even if they are erroneous.

International humanitarian law prohibits methods of warfare that cannot discriminate between civilians and combatants, but also accepts that civilian casualties incidental to a proportionate pursuit of a legitimate military objective are acceptable. Within limits, a country can, in the process of attacking legitimate military targets, choose to protect its forces through military tactics that harm civilians. States are not required to fight wars using the means least likely to injure innocents. The question is whether the target is legitimate and whether the unintentional damage to civilians is proportionate to the benefits of destroying the military target. As with much in the laws of war, this formulation leaves a large gray area. The case of the U.S. air campaign in Kosovo, for example, is hardly clear-cut.[112]

Interpreting Russia for the West

The four points discussed in this section—double standards, ends justifying means, the relative status of indiscriminate bombing as a war crime, and the priority of protecting soldiers—help explain why some Western journalists and Russia experts have sought to rationalize Russia's wars in Chechnya. Among this group are Anatol Lieven and Jack Matlock.

Lieven strongly criticizes Western human-rights activists, journalists, and politicians for condemning the Russian destruction of Grozny, but several of his arguments reflect some confusion about the laws of war. Lieven compares the situation of Russian soldiers in Chechnya to that of U.S. soldiers in Somalia in October 1993. Dropped into an urban market in Mogadishu to capture clan leader Mohamed Farrah Aidid, the U.S. troops encountered unexpectedly stiff resistance. To save themselves, the soldiers indiscriminately killed many civilians. In one instance, as author Mark Bowden depicts it,

> Private David Floyd was shooting at everything that moved. At first he had hesitated firing into crowds when they massed downhill to the south, but he had seen the Delta guy, Fillmore, get hit, and Lieu-

tenant Lechner, and about three or four of his other buddies, and now he was just shooting at everybody. The world was erupting around him and shooting back seemed the only sensible response.[113]

In this case, one might be justified in resisting moral condemnation of the U.S. soldiers, because many of the "civilians" at whom they were indiscriminately firing were themselves armed, albeit with primitive weapons, and were seeking to do harm. Moreover, the politicians and military leaders who gave the soldiers such an ambitious mission for which they were ill-prepared deserve considerable blame.

Lieven evinces sympathy for the U.S. soldiers in Somalia, but goes well beyond that. He seems to suggest that the behavior of the soldiers who killed Somali civilians was morally superior to that of people who have criticized the Russian bombing of Grozny: "The United States tactics used in Mogadishu and elsewhere do not reflect any discredit on the American commanders and troops concerned," writes Lieven, because their "overriding duty was to the lives of their own comrades. The discredit attaches only to those Western commentators and politicians who, willfully ignorant of their own military history, have portrayed the Russian bombardment of Grozny as an act of brutality, a war crime, or both."[114]

Here Lieven conflates the laws of war with the issue of double standards. In fact it is illegal under international laws of war for soldiers to protect their comrades if it means disproportionate killing of innocent civilians in relation to the likely achievement of the intended military goal. Likewise, indiscriminate bombing of cities and villages leading to the loss of civilian life disproportionate to the military objectives achieved (a fair description of the Russian bombardment of Grozny and other Chechen population centers) is illegal, whether carried out by Russia or by Western powers. Contra Lieven, the Russian destruction of Grozny was arguably both an act of brutality and a war crime, regardless of whether it was Human Rights Watch or Colin Powell making the charge. The military value of bombing Grozny to rubble was minimal in relation to the civilian casualties involved. As everyone predicted, the Chechen rebels simply retreated to the mountains to continue fighting from there.

A number of Russian journalists and human-rights activists have suggested that the atrocities committed by Russian forces in Chechnya would justify putting top officials, including President Vladimir Putin, on trial for war crimes. Few Western journalists or specialists on Russia would go so far. Part of the explanation may be their limited understanding of command responsibility in war, as is evident in the writings of Jack F. Matlock

Jr., a former career State Department official and ambassador to Moscow and Prague, who comments frequently on Russian affairs. In a review of a book by Christopher Hitchens outlining the case against Henry Kissinger for commission of war crimes in Vietnam and elsewhere, Matlock revealed a limited grasp of the principle of command responsibility. He also seemed unwilling to acknowledge that what Hitchens described—such as the knowing destruction of unarmed civilians—were genuine crimes. Note his quotation marks: "To the degree that American armed forces or clandestine operatives were involved in these 'crimes,' it was under the authority of the president, not that of his assistant for national security or secretary of state [Kissinger]."[115]

Hitchens's book makes clear that Kissinger was involved directly in planning military operations that resulted in well-foreseen disproportionate civilian deaths. This behavior is well within the realm of command responsibility. In a historical review of that topic, a professor of law at the U.S. Naval War College summarized the consensus on this issue:

> There seems to be little doubt that modern international law embodies the principle that, in addition to the individual responsibility of those who may actually perpetrate such crimes, criminal liability will also accrue to any political or military superior who orders, colludes in, condones, or fails to take steps to prevent their commission or repress and punish the actual offenders.[116]

The excuse that they were just following orders or the policy of their superiors did not work for perpetrators of war crimes during World War II (at least those on the losing side), and it did not save those tried for committing such crimes in places such as Rwanda, Bosnia, or Kosovo.[117] When the question of command responsibility for war crimes in Chechnya comes up, one would hope that Ambassador Matlock would have a better understanding of this basic component of the laws of war.[118]

Matlock, like Ware and Lieven, also overlooks the basic distinction between just ends and just means: "Normally, those who start a war are held responsible for the violence, not those who resist the invaders and terrorists. Whatever criticism may be properly directed at the way the United States fought the war in Vietnam, it is a travesty to characterize the attempts to resist communist aggression as criminal acts."[119] The point here is not Matlock's highly partisan characterization of the Vietnam War—depicting the United States as the defender against Vietnamese terrorist-aggressors. Rather, it is his claim that whoever started the war (*jus ad bellum*) is morally and legally responsible for subsequent actions of both sides (*jus in bello*). Matlock ignores the fundamental point that the legality of both ends and means of war must be judged independently. Only by conflating the two can he argue that "the way the United States fought the war" could be subject only to "criticism" but certainly not to accusation of criminal responsibility.

The deference to government officials revealed in his discussion of the Hitchens book seems to have influenced Matlock's policy advice regarding Russia's wars in Chechnya.[120] In testimony before the U.S. Congress in March 1996, Matlock expressed the uncontroversial belief that "the Russian Government has a right to suppress armed rebellion within its borders." He acknowledged, however, that "the methods used have violated solemn commitments undertaken by the Russian Government, in the Helsinki Final Act, in particular." But he stressed that the Helsinki accords "are political commitments which do not have the force of law or treaties," thereby ignoring the extent to which Russia's methods had also violated international treaties, including the Geneva Conventions. As already mentioned, other Clinton administration officials, including the president himself, also tended to cite the Helsinki agreements rather than the Geneva Conventions in their rather mild criticisms of Russia.

As for policy prescriptions, Matlock explained, "some Americans argue that the U.S. Government should do more overtly to put Russia under pressure to end the war in Chechnya, by such steps as curtailing economic and political cooperation with Russia as long as the war persists." This approach, he suggested, "would not be wise." He favored quiet diplomacy and "private dialog [*sic*]" between U.S. and Russian officials because "private pressure can often be more important than public pressure." Matlock averred that "unofficial non-governmental human rights organizations have a very important role to play" and "should bring to light atrocities when they occur." But he insisted that "they should be evenhanded about it. It is just as much an atrocity to kill and kidnap innocent civilians by acts of terrorism as it is to bombard defenseless cities, though more people may die from the latter."[121] Here again a distinction between ends and means could be helpful. Russian leaders justified the bombing as a means of achieving a certain end—the eradication of terror and kidnapping in Chechnya. But if the means—bombardment of defenseless cities—not only fails to achieve the declared end, but meanwhile destroys thousands of innocent lives, should not that fact figure somehow into the moral and legal calculus? Even a simplistic ends-justifies-the-means argument would expect the means to contribute to achieving the ends.

The Ends of the Chechen Wars

The international community, as represented by the major Western powers, has done little to question Russia's international standing despite continuing reports of war crimes. As the *Washington Post* put it in a hard-hitting editorial on the eve of a July 2001 summit meeting, "The politically savvy Mr. Putin is obviously concerned about his image in the West, yet he clearly felt no pressure to temper his Chechnya campaign or even his description of it just days before a summit meeting with the presidents and prime ministers of the United States, Britain, Germany, France, Italy, Japan and Canada. You can hardly blame him: After all, none of these governments has had anything significant to say as reports about the bloody cleansing operations have poured in." The *Post* criticized President George W. Bush for his "extraordinary—we would say shocking—public endorsement of Mr. Putin." Bush told reporters that he sympathized with the Russian president's deep "concern about extremism and what extremism can mean to Russia." As the *Post* editorial noted,

> Those words were delivered on July 6 [2001]—the day after the pro-Moscow [Chechen] mayors of Sernovodsk and Assinovskaia resigned in protest over an operation that even Russia's commander in Chechnya acknowledged was "lawless." Mr. Bush's public support has had the effect of virtually silencing almost all other criticism of Chechnya by Western governments, and it has emboldened Mr. Putin to deliver ever-more-inflated falsehoods about the situation there. At his press conference Wednesday he said that Russian cleansing operations "boil down to passport checks and measures to identify people who are on the federal wanted list"; in fact, what happens is that hundreds or thousands of boys and men are rounded up in fields or placed in pits, where many are tortured and some are summarily executed.

The editorial concluded by pointing out that the Bush administration's commitment to build a system of national missile defense could help explain its unwillingness to criticize Putin. "In a great hurry to win Moscow's acquiescence to a modification or abrogation of the Anti-Ballistic Missile Treaty," the *Post* argued, "Mr. Bush has abdicated U.S. authority to speak out about human rights in Russia and given Mr. Putin a free pass to pursue the most bloody and criminal campaign of military repression now in the world."[122]

When Russian defense minister Sergei Ivanov was asked in June 2001 how long the second war in Chechnya would last, he replied with a question of his own: "How long did it take to eliminate the Lithuanian partisans after World War II?"[123] The answer was revealing in more ways than one. The anticommunist fighters resisted Soviet rule in Lithuania well into the 1950s. Their resistance was eventually overcome by a combination of military and police measures, including deportations to Siberian prison camps. But more significantly, Lithuania ultimately broke free of Soviet control as the USSR disintegrated, and the partisans are now considered national heroes. If Ivanov really believes in the analogy implied by his question, the Chechen War—seen as a war of national liberation by Chechens—should drag on for years and ultimately result in Chechnya's independence from Russia.

When then U.S. president Bill Clinton visited Moscow in June 2000, he posed the question "whether any war can be won that requires large numbers of civilian casualties and has no political component bringing about a solution."[124] The question goes to the heart of the issue that troubles many Western analysts who believe that Russia's cause is just: how to fight against rebels who hide in populated areas and are protected by civilians.

Michael Walzer pondered precisely this question in his classic study of Just War Theory: "What if the guerrillas cannot be isolated from the people?" His answer was that "the anti-guerrilla war can then no longer be fought—and not just because, from a strategic point of view, it can no longer be won. It cannot be fought because it is no longer an anti-guerrilla war but an anti-social war, a war against an entire people, in which no distinctions would be possible in the actual fighting."[125] Here considerations of just ends and just means come together. If the Russian government cannot conduct its "anti-terrorist operation" without turning it into a genocidal campaign against all Chechens—including many who are residents of Moscow and other places far from the battlefields—then it must seek an alternative means to resolve the problem.

8

Russia and the West
after September 11

How did the Russians become the No. 1 good guys so soon after they
were the No. 1 bad guys? It's easy, because Bush can get Vladimir Putin
on the phone anytime he wants to—but Osama bin Laden never returns
his calls.
                                          —Art Buchwald, February 2002

What is wanted here is law, good faith, order, security. Any one can
declaim about these things, but I pin my faith to material interests. Only
let the material interests once get a firm footing, and they are bound to
impose the conditions on which alone they can continue to exist. That's
how your money-making is justified here in the face of lawlessness and
disorder. It is justified because the security which it demands must be
shared with an oppressed people. A better justice will come afterwards.
                                                      —Joseph Conrad

I n the wake of the attacks of September 11, 2001, the
first foreign leader to telephone President Bush and
express his condolences was Vladimir Putin, the president
of Russia. It seemed both a touching personal gesture and
a symbol of potential importance for the future of Russia's
relations with the West. Despite the end of the cold war
and the demise of the Soviet Union, Russia never managed
to become integrated into Western institutions and
accepted as a "normal" member of the international community, at least not to the extent that the reformers of the
perestroika era had hoped. Would the common interest—
newly rediscovered after September 11—in defending
against international terrorism lead to a greater acceptance of Russia by the West and a more profound integration? Or would Moscow's war in Chechnya, prosecuted

amid widespread charges of war crimes and atrocities against civilians, serve as an example—especially for democracies—of how not to fight terrorism?

What about the perspective from Moscow? Had Putin, as many observers suggested, definitively thrown his lot in with the West, abandoning once and for all the Soviet legacy of support for groups and states that sought to challenge U.S. hegemony? One Russian journalist suggested that Putin's "crucial and prompt decision to join the American-led anti-terrorist coalition after September 11" was intended specifically "to speed up integration with the West."[1] In the case of Osama bin Laden and his al-Qaida network, the Soviet legacy hardly posed a constraint to cooperation with the West: bin Laden's forces, supported in those days by the United States, helped contribute to the defeat of the Soviet army in Afghanistan and remained enemies of post-Soviet Russia. Moscow was already backing the Northern Alliance as it sought to overthrow the Taliban regime that sheltered bin Laden; the Russians had long tried to make common cause with the United States against al-Qaida.[2] But how far would such cooperation have gone before September 11? Could one even imagine Russia welcoming U.S. military bases along its periphery of former Soviet republics that Moscow still considers within its sphere of influence? How much further could such cooperation go?[3]

Chechnya and September 11

Before September 11 the differences in perspective between Russia and the West on the Chechen War were fairly clear. The dominant European perspective viewed Russia's war in Chechnya as, at best, a human-rights disaster, or worse, a deliberate policy of war crimes and atrocities. For its part, Moscow justified the war by appeal to the vital national interest of territorial integrity, which no Western power disputed, and further sought to characterize the conflict as an "antiterrorist operation."

European institutions called on Moscow to pursue negotiations in good faith to end the war, to protect the peaceful population, and to bring to account the perpetrators of crimes against innocent civilians. They sometimes reinforced their demands with stronger, albeit largely symbolic, measures. The European Union, for example, delayed implementation of the 1994 Partnership and Co-operation Agreement, the formal basis for EU-Russian relations, until December 1997, owing to the ongoing war in Chechnya.[4] As noted in chapter 7, in April 2000, in the midst of the "second" Chechen War, the Parliamentary Assembly of the Council of Europe suspended the Russian delegation's voting rights for a time and threatened to expel Russia from the body.

Not surprisingly, in the wake of September 11 the Russian government has given higher prominence to the terrorism "frame" in its interpretation of the Chechen War.[5] Moscow has sought to persuade the West that the conflict in Chechnya is an acceptable and necessary part of a global war against terror. The Russian government seeks, at a minimum, noninterference from the West as it pursues its war. Beyond that, it would apparently welcome cooperation and an explicit endorsement of its fight against what it considers internationally sponsored terrorists.[6]

Within days of the al-Qaida attack against the United States, Russia's effort to portray itself as a victim of terrorism rather than a perpetrator of war crimes seemed to pay off. On a visit to Germany on September 26, 2001, President Putin was pleased to hear Chancellor Gerhard Schröder appear to endorse Moscow's line: "Regarding Chechnya," claimed Schröder, "there will be and must be a more differentiated evaluation in world opinion."[7] In diplomat-speak, Schröder was promising to tone down the criticism of Russia's military occupation of Chechnya, much of which had come from Europe. Schröder's démarche elicited criticism from some human-rights organizations, but it seemed to accord with the wishes of the U.S. government.[8] Had Putin successfully reframed the debate to persuade the West to adopt his view of the Chechen conflict?

Reframing and Reevaluating the Chechen Conflict

September 11 offered Putin the opportunity to cast the war in Chechnya in a new light, as part of a common struggle against international terrorism. As he told Barbara Walters, "In 1999, we were the victims of a terrorist attack. And I'm not just referring to Chechnya and the Caucasus. I'm referring to the explosion of residential buildings in Moscow and other cities as a result of which hundreds of innocent people died."[9] Putin's government highlighted the connections between Osama bin Laden and the Chechen fighters, some of whom were trained in al-Qaida camps in Afghanistan. What Putin's account fails to reveal is that these explosions, which solidified public opinion behind Moscow's war effort, have never been conclusively linked to Chechen, let alone al-Qaida, terrorists. In fact, as pointed out in chapter 4, there is considerable suspicion, and some evidence, to link them to the Russian secret services. Nevertheless, Western leaders, led by the German chancellor, seemed sympathetic to Putin's interpretation.

Chancellor Schröder's remarks about reevaluating the Chechen War suggested to many observers that this was a clear example of Realpolitik in action. The "German chancellor paid a political price for Putin's willingness to participate in the international coalition against terrorism," wrote one journalist, summarizing the views of various political analysts. "The trade-off appears clear," wrote another: "The West needs Russia's help to launch an effective war on terrorism, and Russia is willing to offer that help if criticism of its actions in Chechnya is hushed."[10] In retrospect, however, the trade does not seem so clear-cut. First of all, in the first months after the September 11 attack, Western institutions did not noticeably diminish their criticisms of Russia's policy in Chechnya. Human-rights organizations and the parliamentarians of the Council of Europe kept up the pressure, and various media outlets continued to report on atrocities and war crimes.[11] In the U.S. State Department's annual review of human rights, the country report on Russia devoted considerable attention to abuses in Chechnya.[12] It represented a victory by those who argued that the common war against terrorism should not excuse Moscow's human-rights violations. Thus the U.S. institution charged with conducting the diplomacy behind the antiterrorist alliance was itself unpersuaded to accept Moscow's line.

Russia's reactions to the continued criticisms of its policy in Chechnya varied from superficially conciliatory to openly hostile. In the first category, the Russian government vowed to bring under control the "sweep" or "mopping-up" operations (*zachistki*) that had led to extrajudicial killings and torture and the terrorizing of many innocent civilians. Moscow even hinted that it would consider opening negotiations with representatives of Chechen president Aslan Maskhadov.[13] But the new regulations on *zachistki* were violated as soon as they were instituted, and the conditions imposed on the negotiations with Maskhadov made it unlikely that he would participate.[14] In the second category, the response of the Russian Foreign Ministry to the U.S. State Department's report was highly inflammatory. It mimicked the style of Soviet-era pronouncements, intended to call attention to U.S. double standards rather than to address the issue at hand. The Foreign Ministry's press office declared that the United States "should better focus on its own domestic problems, primarily on the issue of capital punishment, prior to claiming the role of a judge in the sphere of how other countries should observe human rights."[15] Russia's heated response to U.S. criticism made clear that at least one major Western power had not significantly reevaluated the Chechen situation to Moscow's satisfaction.

The Puzzle of Russia's Potential Leverage

It should be apparent that if Russia were anticipating a Realpolitik deal on Chechnya, it did not get what it expected. More surprisingly, Moscow did not seem interested in exerting the leverage it held regarding the U.S. war in Afghanistan. It could, for example, have threatened to limit U.S. access to air bases in Uzbekistan and Kyrgyzstan, former Soviet republics within Moscow's sphere of influence, and thereby have undermined the war effort if the United States failed to deliver the "more differentiated evaluation" of the Chechen conflict that the German chancellor promised.

How might one explain Russia's apparent willingness to give the green light to an extensive U.S. presence in its "near abroad" without an obvious quid pro quo? It seems likely that the prospect of a U.S.-led war in Afghanistan against international terrorism led to a serious rethinking of Russia's understanding of its own security. In trying to justify the harsh measures that Moscow imposed on Chechnya, President Putin had highlighted the connections between the Chechen rebels and the al-Qaida terrorist network based in Afghanistan (although information available to the U.S. government suggests that those links are not particularly extensive).[16] Though he achieved only limited success in making Europe and the United States complacent about the Russian atrocities in Chechnya, he may well have convinced himself of the need to disrupt the connection between Chechnya and the Afghan terror network—and that the U.S. war represented the best option for doing so. The Chechnya–al-Qaida link was objectively no different before September 11 than after, but Putin's effort to reframe the Chechen War led to a reframing of Afghanistan and the "near abroad" as well.[17] Whereas U.S. bases on Russia's periphery and U.S. military action in a neighboring country would have seemed intolerable in early September, they seemed desirable after September 11. As he explained in his State of the Nation address in April 2002, "For our state, which has long been confronted with terrorism, there was no difficulty in deciding whether to support efforts to destroy its lair or not—especially as these measures did indeed help to strengthen security on the southern borders of our country and, to a considerable extent, helped to improve the situation."[18]

There is presumably a limit to how far such rethinking can take the Russian government, given widespread suspicions in the Russian media about U.S. intentions. The limit appears to have been approached as the United States sent military trainers to Georgia at President Eduard Shevardnadze's request in February 2002. They were intended to prepare

Georgian forces to pursue suspected terrorists hiding in the Pankisi Gorge on the border between Georgia and Chechnya. Some Russian analysts supported the action as consistent with a cooperative effort to destroy the terrorist network, whereas others claimed that the U.S. intervention would be a long-term and self-interested one, oriented toward securing routes for transshipment of Caspian Sea oil.[19] The leader of the communist opposition went so far as to accuse Putin of "giving up the geopolitical space that Russia has been defending for almost 1,000 years."[20]

Russian cooperation in the international campaign against terrorism does not apparently hinge on the West's turning a blind eye to the war in Chechnya. Moreover, a peaceful resolution of the conflict there would do more to hinder the spread of terrorism than giving Putin a free hand to escalate the war. Regardless of the West's attitude toward Chechnya, Moscow has good reason to cooperate to break the al-Qaida network and to undermine extremist versions of Islam. A fifth or more of the population of the Russian Federation consists of people of Muslim heritage and several republics have sizable Islamic constituencies. It is in Moscow's interest to make sure that the country's Muslims are not driven to embrace extremist movements that engage in terrorism.

Shared Values and Norms?

At a meeting of world economic leaders in New York in February 2002, Russian prime minister Mikhail Kasianov echoed Putin's line about Russia's understanding of the U.S. situation and associated it with shared values. "People realize that we have common values, and that there is room for cooperation," said Kasianov. "Russia understands better than any other nation what has happened in America."[21] His focus was not, however, on common values of respect for human rights—a difficult case to make in light of the Chechen situation—but rather common economic interests. Kasianov urged Western investors to take advantage of the improved economic situation in Russia, and he revealed an important Russian concession. Reversing the commitment Russia had made to the Organization of Petroleum Exporting Countries to restrict its sale of oil in order to keep the world price from falling, Kasianov announced that Russia would boost its production. Lower energy prices would benefit the United States and Europe during a difficult time.[22]

In his State of the Nation address in April 2002, Putin provided some insights into his understanding of the shared values and norms that undergird the international community that Russia seeks to join. He began his discussion of foreign policy with the observation that "for a fairly long time many politicians and citizens" of Russia were convinced "that the end of the period of military and political confrontation in the world would almost automatically open up a road to Russia for the world economic system, that it would throw wide open its economic embrace." Instead, despite the fact that Russia seeks "constructive, normal relations" with all countries, "norms in the international community, norms in the modern world, also mean harsh competition—for markets, for investment, for political and economic influence."[23]

In their dealings with President Putin, European leaders have done little to discourage him from thinking that they place a higher value on economic cooperation and competition than human rights. Perhaps the extreme case—as in so many other respects—was Italian premier Silvio Berlusconi. On a visit to Russia in April 2002, Berlusconi gushed that meeting Putin was like meeting an old friend: "Even though we've known each other only a short while, our relations are sincere and intense."[24] Berlusconi told Putin that "among European leaders I am probably the most convinced supporter [of the view] that Europe and the EU should open up to Russia." He told reporters, "I am a convinced propagandist of President Putin's objectives." Putin's economic reforms, argued Berlusconi, provide "enormous potential for growth."[25]

The subject of war crimes and human-rights abuses did come up in the conversations between Berlusconi and Putin. Berlusconi pointed out that "the list of innocent victims is growing." He said, "I persist in reasserting the call to reasonableness and a sense of responsibility, convinced, as I am, that there is no other way than a political solution."[26] As it turns out, however, the topic was not Chechnya—which, judging by news reports, did not come up—but the situation in the Middle East. The destruction wrought by Russian forces in Chechnya is many times what Israel has carried out in the occupied territories (and Chechen fighters have killed far more Russians than Palestinians have killed Israelis), and the tactics are even more indiscriminate in the risk to civilian lives. It is not clear how Berlusconi could consider Putin an international leader capable of bringing "reasonableness and responsibility" to the Middle East when he fails to do so in his own country.

The approach of European leaders to Russia seems driven largely by economic motives and a desire to play a major role on the world stage. European leaders seem to compete for status as privileged interlocutor with Moscow. German chancellor Schröder, for example, evidently enjoyed a special relationship with Vladimir Putin, a fluent speaker of German from his days as a KGB spy stationed in communist East Germany. Russia is an important economic partner for Germany—both for its provision of energy and for the enormous amount of Soviet-era debt it owes. Tony Blair, Britain's prime minister, took pride in being the first to phone to congratulate Putin when he won the presidential election in March 2000, and he hastened to travel to Russia to meet him. As one critic complained, "For Britain to be first into Putin's Moscow is the kind of vacuous coup diplomats dream of. It also plays to the leader's ambition to be out in front."[27]

Berlusconi seemed driven by similar motives. The Italian press played up his apparent success in being the first Western leader invited to visit Putin at his dacha in Sochi, on the Black Sea, "an honor until now denied" even to such prominent figures as Germany's Schröder and France's Lionel Jospin.[28] In his meeting with Putin, Berlusconi expressed the view that the European Union should be enlarged to include "Great Russia." He also voiced support for Russia's entry into the World Trade Organization. This position is consistent with Italy's growing role in the economies of the former Soviet bloc.[29] Overall, EU-based firms represent half of all foreign direct investment in Russia.[30]

Overtures to Russia on the part of Blair, Berlusconi, and other European politicians should not be understood as primarily a reaction to September 11 or as the result of any perceived need to secure Russia's cooperation in the coalition against international terrorism. Long before the campaign against international terrorism became a top priority, European leaders had courted Russia unabashedly. Berlusconi, in particular, had long favored Russia's inclusion in both NATO and the European Union, again presumably for the economic opportunities it would provide for Italy (and perhaps also for him, as Italy's richest entrepreneur).[31]

The priority of economic concerns was reflected even in the negative reactions to Berlusconi's remarks about a quick integration of Russia. Romano Prodi, the head of the European Commission, criticized Berlusconi's proposal to include Russia in the European Union. Did Prodi consider that Russia failed to meet the standards that Europe had set for itself in the realm of individual freedom and human rights? No, his concern was also economic. He argued that Russia's market and territory were too large to incorporate into the European Union at this stage without undermining the very structure of the organization.[32] French president Jacques Chirac and EU trade commissioner Pascal Lamy both expressed serious reservations about Russia's early entrance into the organizatoin, but none had to do with the country's human-rights record or the war in Chechnya.[33]

Russia's integration into NATO also faces barriers unrelated to the Chechen War. At a meeting in Rome in May 2002, Russia's relationship to NATO received an "upgrade," along the lines of what Prime Minister Tony Blair first proposed in November 2001: a new Russia–North Atlantic Council that would meet regularly and serve to coordinate antiterrorism policies and reactions to international crises.[34] This was a far cry from bringing Russia into the alliance as a full member. Present NATO members seemed particularly reluctant to offer Russia a veto over alliance matters, especially concerning the admission of future members. If Russia expected full NATO membership as a quid pro quo for its support of the antiterror coalition, it was certainly disappointed.

Did September 11 Make a Difference After All?

A plausible case can be made that September 11 made little difference in regard to Russia's behavior in Chechnya or the way Western states react to it. Thus Chechnya is not likely to play a role in Western decisions about how far and how fast to integrate Russia into their institutions. As far as Russia is concerned, however, September 11 does seem to have led to meaningful changes in its policy toward the "near abroad." The Russian president, at least, seemed to believe that his country's security was not put at risk by the long-term presence of U.S. military bases along its periphery. On the contrary, to the extent that those bases contribute to the effort to break up an international terrorist network that threatened Russia, they actually served Russian security interests. At some point Putin may come to view the bases, as some Russian commentators already do, as a dangerous opening wedge of U.S. influence in the oil-rich regions of Central Asia and the Caspian Sea. In that case, he will have to balance considerations of the antiterrorism campaign with concerns about economic and strategic interests in the region. So even if the "new thinking" about U.S. bases and intentions is not permanent, it is nevertheless a significant consequence of the events of September 11.

The impact of September 11 on the Chechen situation is far less evident. By the spring of 2002, efforts to call Moscow to account for its abuses in Chechnya had suffered some setbacks, but not much more serious ones than in the period before September 11. On April 10, 2002, for example, the European Parliament debated a resolution to condemn Russian behavior in Chechnya, but barely managed to pass a watered-down version calling on both sides "to negotiate a political solution to the conflict." The report made reference to "some constructive measures" undertaken by

Russian authorities to investigate abuses in Chechnya, a characterization that human-rights groups rejected. As one proponent of the stronger resolution complained, "for the nth time, we 'invite' Russia to behave itself, when we should have demanded that the Council of the European Union exert strong pressure for it to negotiate peace with President Maskhadov," the legally elected leader of Chechnya. Another deputy insisted that "the European Parliament can not be silent as long as there are more deaths in Chechnya than in the Middle East."[35]

A further setback came on April 19, 2002, when the United Nations Commission on Human Rights failed to adopt a resolution on Chechnya. In this case, members of the European Union sponsored the resolution but were unable to pick up sufficient support from other countries to pass it. The vote was 15 to 16, with 22 abstentions.[36] The resolution would have condemned Russia's human-rights abuses, required a national commission to investigate them, and urged Moscow to cooperate with UN rights monitors.

The Parliamentary Assembly of the Council of Europe, for its part, seems to have abandoned efforts at threatening Russia into complying with its human-rights obligations, in favor of a more cooperative approach employing a joint working group including members of the Russian parliament, or Duma. PACE put a positive gloss on the results of such cooperation, but even the tentative nature of its wording rang false: "It is now being recognised that there is no alternative other than a political solution. There begins to be a more general acknowledgment that lasting peace in Chechnya can only be achieved with the support of all significant political forces, including those who sympathise with Mr Maskhadov."[37] The Russian government continued to reject such conclusions, de facto if not de jure, and the Duma participants themselves issued many explicit reservations and disagreements with the supposed consensus.

One could perceive the lackluster effort to hold Russia to account for its human-rights abuses as fulfilling Chancellor Schröder's promise to reevaluate the Chechen situation. In fact, however, the inconsistent nature of Western and international criticism of Moscow's war in Chechnya was nothing new. Since the initial Russian invasion of 1994, the Chechen War has never been at the top of the international agenda. The extent to which it remains in the public eye depends less on the Realpolitik deals that Western leaders seek to cut than on the work of the human-rights activists, parliamentarians, and government officials who feel strongly about the issue and have the wherewithal to call attention to it.

Thus Russia's entry into such international organizations as the European Union, NATO, and the World Trade Organization is unlikely to be hindered much by its conduct of the war in Chechnya. There are already many higher-profile considerations that will make Western leaders limit Russia's engagement, despite the cheerleading of Silvio Berlusconi and various international investors who would like to profit from another speculative bubble of the sort that burst in August 1998.[38] Some of the factors that have made Western firms cautious about direct foreign investment in Russia will also make Western governments cautious about making Russia "an equal partner," as Putin desires.[39]

Putin himself has recognized some of these obstacles, and he discussed them in his State of the Nation address: "We need courts which are respected both inside and outside this country. This is not just a political task, it is very much an economic one . . . an efficient court system is essential so that both Russian and foreign companies can have no doubts about its authority and effectiveness."[40] The emphasis on respect for the rule of law could actually provide an opportunity for opponents of Russian policy in Chechnya to make the link between Moscow's behavior and Russia's suitability for membership in the European Union or NATO. Indeed, one of the key criticisms of Russia's Chechnya policy is that the government is either unwilling or unable to investigate and prosecute well-documented crimes against civilians. Raising questions about the rule of law might be one plausible way for activists strategically to link their concerns about human rights with their national leaders' apparently greater concerns about economics.[41]

The main change in relations between Russia and the West has come not in the West's attitude toward the Chechen war and not in Western countries' willingness to welcome Russia into NATO and the European Union. On Chechnya, the United States and the members of the European Union are not in any case fully capable of delivering the carte blanche that Russia might desire. Much depends on the level of concern of their own citizens and the activity of international human-rights groups. They can continue to criticize and highlight Russia's abuses, despite what their own governments might prefer.

As for Russia's integration into NATO and the European Union, the barriers are already extensive. The conflict in Chechnya will add to those barriers only to the extent that opponents of Russian policy succeed in making the case that lawlessness and violence at home are incompatible with membership in the European and international community.

In recent years European institutions have been particularly sensitive to their member-states' behavior in the realm of immigration and citizenship policy, ostracizing members such as Austria for the xenophobic and racist pronouncements of Jörg Haider, for example, and expressing concern about similar trends in Italy and France.[42] In Russia, the policies of Vladimir Putin and other political leaders have led to a demonization of the Chechens as a nation of terrorists and bandits, an ever-present component of the military campaign. The practice has had inevitable spillover effects. Discrimination is common against anyone "with a Caucasian face"—an expression that, in the Russian context, means a dark-skinned person from the Caucasus region—and there have been many victims of racist violence. Given that member-states of the European Union have been censured for less, Russian policy toward Chechens could certainly present a barrier to further integration into Europe—even without the atrocities associated with the war itself—if other economic and political barriers were not already producing the same effect. The fact that European organizations spend so little time criticizing Russia's policies of discrimination perhaps indicates how far they consider Russia from eligibility for genuine integration into the institutions of Western democracy.

Whether before or after September 11, the United States and the European Union have not made the situation in Chechnya a high-priority item in their dealings with the Russian Federation. Persuading Western states and international organizations to give greater scrutiny to Russia is only part of the matter, however. Whether Russia actually conforms to norms of appropriate behavior in conflict situations depends largely on the domestic political conditions in the country and the material and social leverage that Western states and institutions can bring to bear.[43] I address those issues in chapter 9.

9

Conclusion

In the case of the Soviet Union, federalism failed as the ethnic principle triumphed. In the case of the Russian Federation, federalism faces the opposite danger, that of reflexive centralism, in which even the autonomy of the ethnically Russian regions is at risk if autonomy for the minority regions is not respected. If either extreme prevails, the prospects for democracy in Russia will turn dim indeed.

—Robert V. Daniels, 1997

Russia is an important country. Stretching across eleven time zones from Kaliningrad to Kamchatka, straddling Europe and Asia, it is the world's largest state. Considerably weaker than the Soviet Union, its super-power predecessor, the Russian Federation nevertheless remains the world's second nuclear power and deploys sizable armed forces. The country's economic health and security affect the entire world. Thus it is not surprising that international leaders have attempted to maintain good relations with Russia's presidents, Vladimir Putin, the former KGB agent who was elected in March 2000, and, before him, Boris Yeltsin.

Both Yeltsin and Putin justified pursuit of a military solution to the problem of Chechen separatism by raising concerns about disintegration of the Russian Federation. Western leaders gave those justifications a sympathetic hearing. They endorsed Moscow's ends of maintaining Russian territorial integrity, even if they expressed doubts about the chosen means. I have argued that fears of Russia's going the way of the Soviet Union and breaking up into its constituent parts were largely unfounded. The system of "asymmetric federalism" that Boris Yeltsin improvised as he assumed the task of governing post-Soviet Russia helped maintain the federation rather than threaten to tear it apart. Moreover, the sorts of deals with regional leaders that Moscow used to pacify separatist movements in the other republics should have been pursued in Chechnya as well.

The causes of the Chechen Wars are manifold, encompassing historical, structural, and strategic factors. I have highlighted factors that are often given short shrift in the scholarly study of international relations and political science because they do not lend themselves well to generalization: personal political ambitions and the idiosyncrasies of leaders and their advisers on both sides.

Boris Yeltsin bears the greatest responsibility for his unwillingness to seek a peaceful, negotiated "Tatarstan solution" to the challenge of Chechen separatism after 1991. Dzhokhar Dudaev was hardly the most promising interlocutor on the Chechen side either, but Moscow made a decision early on to support him over his rivals, a mistake that was recognized only after it was too late. Yeltsin also bears responsibility for failing to carry out the peace accords that ended the first Chechen war and to provide adequate funds for reconstruction. Here, however, there is plenty of blame to go around, among Chechens and Russians alike, as the money that was provided disappeared into a black hole of corruption. The breakdown of the Chechen economy and the weakness of the government in Grozny contributed to a climate that fostered kidnapping and organized crime and a desperation among ordinary people that made them susceptible to the ideology of militant Islam, promoted from abroad.

The second war resulted from a failure to learn the lessons of the first war and the interwar period. Inspired by the U.S. bombing campaign in Serbia, Russian military officials became convinced that they could reimpose control over Chechnya by employing overwhelming air power while limiting casualties on the ground. At first the strategy seemed promising and garnered so much popular support in Russia that Vladimir Putin chose to milk it for all it was worth, as he sought election to the Russian presidency. But Putin and his generals overreached. With no viable political strategy to accompany the military one, they refused to negotiate with Aslan Maskhadov, the freely elected leader of Chechnya, and instead sought to impose puppet figures who enjoyed little popular legitimacy. As the war dragged on, and the Chechen fighters increasingly resorted to terror tactics, frustrated Russian soldiers and corrupt officers engaged in numerous atrocities against the civilian population. Yet this tragic situation failed to make Western leaders more critical of Russia and more wary of dealing with the authorities in Moscow.

Indeed, the high level of enthusiasm for the Russian president among European and U.S. leaders is particularly surprising. The need to bring Russia into an antiterrorist coalition constitutes an inadequate explanation, because much of the enthusiasm for Putin predates September 11. Consider the example of U.S. President George W. Bush after his first meeting with Putin at a summit in Slovenia in June 2001. In his opening remarks to reporters, Bush described his Russian counterpart as "an honest, straightforward man who loves his country. He loves his family. We share a lot of values. I view him as a remarkable leader. I believe his leadership will serve Russia well." In an unscripted response to a journalist's question, Bush went further:

> I looked the man in the eye. I found him to be very straightforward and trustworthy. We had a very good dialogue. I was able to get a sense of his soul; a man deeply committed to his country and the best interests of his country. And I appreciated so very much the frank dialogue. There was no kind of diplomatic chit-chat, trying to throw each other off balance. There was a straightforward dialogue. And that's the beginning of a very constructive relationship. I wouldn't have invited him to my ranch if I didn't trust him.[1]

Western leaders seemed to be competing with each other for Putin's favor. They were eager to treat his country as an equal member of the G-7 "club" of advanced industrial democracies, in fact, renaming it G-8 in order to accommodate Russia at its summit meetings. This is a puzzling development, as Sarah Mendelson has pointed out: "Putin enjoyed nights at the opera and pints of beer with Tony Blair, tea with the queen of England, was the toast of the town at the July 2000 G-7 meeting in Okinawa, and was warmly included in the July 2001 meeting in Genoa, although Russia had neither a strong industrialized economy nor a robust democracy."[2]

Meanwhile the toll of victims from Russia's wars in Chechnya continued to mount. Aside from the destruction of Chechnya itself, the Russian bombing provoked a mass exodus of refugees, creating a humanitarian disaster of horrendous proportions. Whereas the first war sent tens of thousands fleeing to Dagestan, most of the refugees from the second war went to Ingushetiia or remained displaced in Chechnya itself. In the spring of 2002, out of an estimated population of 440,000, some 160,000 Chechens were internal refugees with a further 140,000 or 150,000 stranded in Ingushetiia. Tens of thousands were living there in makeshift camps, with up to 20 people to a tent. An estimated 100,000 refugees lodged with Ingush families. Food was scarce and whatever aid was available appeared to come not from the Russian government but from an organization called Islamic Relief. Ingush government officials reported about 500 cases of tuberculosis and local hospitals full of refugees suffering from hepatitis and respiratory illnesses. "The lack of hygiene and bad nourishment have caused an outbreak of intestinal disorders," reported the camp doctor. "We treat approximately 50 people every day suffering mainly from intestinal complaints," a not surprising situation given the provision of only twenty toilets for each 6,000 people, and no shower facilities.[3]

How could the Russian authorities hope to win back the allegiance of people whom they have so abused? In the spring of 2002 Moscow appeared to have given up on trying to help the refugees. With the reimposition of the Kremlin's control over Ingushetiia, the main objective now seemed to be to get the refugees to return home, by whatever means necessary, including cutting off their food supplies.[4]

Back in Chechnya, reports of torture, rape, and murder continued to make the "antiterrorist operation" appear more like an all-out war against the civilian population.[5] The indiscriminate *zachistki*, the kidnappings by Russian soldiers and officers—who demand ransom money even to return the corpses of the victims of their extrajudicial killings—have turned initially sympathetic Chechens against Moscow. One of them recalled "how happy I was when the Russian troops came. I thought they came back to restore law and order for good so that people would have jobs and our children could go to school. But I was wrong. Now I see that they came here not to stop atrocities and destroy the bandits. They came here to destroy all of us, the entire Chechen people." What made her change her mind? Her son was "disappeared" in a *zachistka* and murdered by Russian soldiers. Her attempts to find out what happened or pursue any semblance of justice only met with further abuses.[6]

George W. Bush believes that Vladimir Putin is "deeply committed to his country and the best interests of his country." He views the Russian president as "a remarkable leader" whose "leadership will serve Russia well." Putin's war in Chechnya calls this evaluation into doubt. If Bush and other Western leaders really want to build a "constructive relationship" with Russia, then they had better engage in some "frank dialogue," to use the U.S. president's words, about resolving the Chechen situation peacefully. They must let him know that concentration camps, indiscriminate bombing, torture, and murder are not the way to defeat terrorism—and will certainly not win the hearts and minds of people striving for greater autonomy.

If Western leaders want Russia to play a valuable role in the war against international terrorism, they should encourage Putin to pursue the rule of law at home in his own battle with suspected terrorists. The logic of Realpolitik and the notion that "the enemy of my enemy is my friend" still hold considerable sway in international relations. But they are not enough to sustain the durable relationship between Russia and the West that a protracted campaign against terrorism requires. Citizens of the United States and Europe will find it difficult to support an alliance with a country that engages in the sorts of human-rights abuses and war crimes that Russia has committed in Chechnya. The U.S. government should encourage Moscow to seek a peaceful resolution of the Chechen conflict by engaging in good-faith negotiations with leaders of the separatist movement and broader segments of Chechen society. While the war continues, Moscow must abide by the international laws of war and the Geneva Conventions, as the Russian Constitution itself requires.

Few countries welcome criticism from abroad, and Russia is no exception. Moscow is especially quick to seize on other countries' self-serving motives or double standards as an excuse to ignore their advice. President Bush forestalled such a move on Moscow's part with his decision of February 2002 to apply the protections of the Geneva Conventions to Taliban prisoners held at Guantánamo Bay in Cuba. The previous policy of denying them such protections had inflamed European public opinion. Many Europeans expressed concern that the U.S. not sacrifice its own standards of legality and protection of individual rights to the war against terrorism.[7] Some of the president's advisers recognized that the coalition against terrorism would be difficult to sustain if America's key allies harbored doubts about U.S. commitment to the rule of law—the same argument that I have made in regard to Russia.[8]

By the same token, the Bush administration's decision in May 2002 to "unsign" the treaty establishing an International Criminal Court is likely to undermine any U.S. attempts to criticize Russian war crimes in Chechnya.[9] The court provides a means of bringing war criminals to justice if national courts refuse to do so. By rejecting the court, the Bush administration sent a signal to the Russian government that it could continue to ignore the atrocities committed by its troops in Chechnya without fear of international legal sanction. In order to withdraw from the Rome Statute that established the International Criminal Court, some Bush administration officials thought that the United States was further obliged to "unsign" the Vienna Convention on the Law of Treaties, "a 1969 agreement that requires states to refrain from taking steps to undermine treaties they sign, even if they do not ratify them."[10] By undercutting the basis for international law in such a fashion, the U.S. government made it very difficult for itself to demand that Russia abide by its international treaty commitments—even to such fundamental documents as the Geneva Conventions or the Genocide Treaty. As Senator Russell D. Feingold put it, "Beyond the extremely problematic matter of casting doubt on the U.S. commitment to international justice and accountability, these steps actually call into question our country's credibility in all multilateral endeavors."[11]

Without credible U.S. leadership in fostering respect for international law, it will be left to other countries, in Europe, for example, to put pressure on Russia to cease the war crimes and atrocities in Chechnya. Although inconsistent in their efforts, the European Parliament, the Organization for Security and Cooperation in Europe, and the Council of Europe's Parliamentary Assembly have been most actively involved in seeking a peaceful resolution of the Chechen conflict and holding both sides to account for their crimes.

Ultimately, however, it will be up to the Russians themselves to resolve the situation in Chechnya. The first war ended largely because ordinary Russians judged the cost too great—in lives and money—and they put pressure on the government, particularly vulnerable during the 1996 elections, to make peace. Russian media played a key role during the first war in reporting the hopelessness of the situation on the ground.

The second Chechen War has also proved very costly. The cumulative toll of casualties from both conflicts approach the level of what the Soviet Union sustained in its decade-long war in Afghanistan. Moreover, despite the boon to the war budget provided by relatively high energy prices, one of Russia's leading sources of revenue, the cost of fighting in Chechnya remained substantial: an estimated "$2–3 billion a year—an amount equal to about half of all federal government spending on health and education." Nor should one forget "the evident social costs incurred from large numbers of traumatized former conscripts returning home to Russia's regions without alternative employment and with no programs to assist their reintegration into their communities."[12] Here again the parallel to the Soviet war in Afghanistan is sobering. Much of the violence of the post-Soviet region, from organized crime to civil and ethnic war, has involved the *Afgantsy*, the neglected veterans of the brutal and brutalizing Afghan war. This is one respect in which Russia could well go the way of the Soviet Union, by suffering the enormous long-term social costs of an ill-conceived and futile military adventure.

Could Russia go the way of the Soviet Union in the sense that Yeltsin and Putin had in mind in their fear-mongering about the consequences of Chechen separatism? The evidence presented in this book suggests that the Russian Federation is highly unlikely to break up into its constituent parts, as the USSR did, or even to see any of the other ethnic republics follow the Chechen example. This judgment may not have been obvious at the onset of the first Chechen War, but many sober analysts at the time recognized that Yeltsin and his circle were exaggerating the threat of disintegration and underestimating the risks of attempting a military solution to the Chechen problem. Putin, as Russia's intelligence chief before taking over as prime minister and then president, was certainly in a position to assess the state of the country's center-regional relations. Paradoxically, he drew alarmist conclusions about the federation's fragility but did not seem worried about the impact of a near-genocidal war in Chechnya on the Muslim peoples elsewhere in the Caucasus and throughout Russia.

For the epigraph to my introduction to this book, I used a quote from Robert V. Daniels, one of the deans of Soviet and Russian studies, to the effect that Chechnya—although "an extreme instance in the relations between Moscow and its regions"—nevertheless "serves as a warning that federalism may fail in the Russian republic just as it failed in the Soviet Union as a whole, ground up between the millstones of imperial centralism and ethnic particularism."[13] Was he just another one of many Western and Russian observers predicting the breakup of the Russian Federation? In fact, Daniels's point about the failure of Russian federalism is more subtle, and it is only fitting that I provide the rest of his argument as the epigraph of this concluding chapter. According to Daniels, the danger for Russia at the beginning of the third millennium is not a Soviet-style disintegration, but rather an antidemocratic overreaction to the problems of governing a large and unwieldy federation. This argument accords with my own analysis and with the concerns expressed by many other observers about the threat that Vladimir Putin's government poses to democracy in Russia.[14]

Putin came into office set on "turning Russia into a strong state." Many of his concerns were undoubtedly valid, including the weakness of Russia's institutions, particularly the judiciary; the role of money in politics and the media; the unpredictable and insecure nature of property rights and the problems that posed to foreign investment. At the top of his list was the center's lack of control over the regions and the need to impose a "vertical of power" and a "dictatorship of law." His efforts to reestablish Moscow's influence on the regions have, however, entailed considerable risks to democracy and have threatened a return to some aspects of the centralized authoritarianism of the Soviet era.

Putin's democratic credentials are not solid enough to convince the millions of citizens living in the republics and regions of Russia that his recentralizing efforts will not undermine their democratic freedoms. In many respects, Putin's cure is worse than the disease—and, in the case of Chechnya, it has virtually killed the patient. Putin and his officials underestimated the benefits of the flexible, negotiated federalism that emerged in the wake of Soviet disintegration. Consider the remarks made by Aleksandr Blokhin, Russia's minister of federation affairs, national and migration policies, in Bashkortostan in September 2001. Speaking in the capital city of Ufa, Blokhin denied that Bashkortostan had any right to "sovereignty" because having one sovereign state located within another was "nonsense." Sovereignty resides only in the Russian Federation, he argued, not in any of its constituent parts. As political analyst Paul Goble has pointed out, the experience of the rest of the world's federal states contradicts such an assertion. Moreover, Blokhin can make such an argument only if he believes, as Goble summarized, that "sovereignty is less about popular rule than about the power of the state, an entity which stands above and beyond the society over which it rules."[15]

Indeed, that would seem to be his position, and that of his boss, Vladimir Putin. Such a perspective neglects the positive role that the declarations of republican sovereignty played in the early 1990s in, as Goble put it, "helping to manage the devolution of power from the hypercentralized Soviet state." Not that maintaining the Soviet system was an option. As a Bashkortostan newspaper pointed out in response to Blokhin's remarks, the declarations of sovereignty by that republic and neighboring Tatarstan "helped the republics to affirm popular sovereignty and thus promoted federalism." The alternative to sovereignty and "asymmetric federalism" was not Soviet-style sham federalism and hypercentralization. More likely it would have been a drive toward outright independence, with the prospect of violence and even civil war.[16]

Both Boris Yeltsin and Vladimir Putin waged war against Chechnya for fear of a collapse of the Russian state. Yet the war in Chechnya has not in itself contributed to the strengthening of the state, as wars traditionally are understood to have done. Instead the Chechen conflict shares more in common with a civil war: "while the classic war-between-states tends towards the monopolizing of power, and by every measure strengthens the apparatus of the state, civil war is characterized by the constant threat that discipline will break down and the militias dissipate into armed bands operating on their own account."[17] This description characterizes not only the Chechen side, with its motley mix of warlords and criminal gangs, but also the Russian side, with its undisciplined array of police, army, and interior ministry units, responsible for looting and terrorizing the civilian population.

Here the connection becomes apparent between Putin's antidemocratic policies—carried out in the name of centralized state power—and the intractable nature of the Chechen conflict. The first war came to an end because its brutality and futility were revealed to the Russian public by vigorous print and television media, recently liberated from Soviet censorship by Mikhail Gorbachev's policy of *glasnost'*. Organizations such as the Committee of Soldiers' Mothers mobilized opposition to the war. Under Putin a deliberate policy of restriction and intimidation of journalists seeking to report on Chechnya, and a stifling of independent television, have limited the Russian public's access to information about the war. And the lack of information and accountability creates an atmosphere where war crimes and atrocities proliferate. As Andrei Babitskii, one victim of the government's campaign against journalists, put it, "The main issue is that the Russian military and the Kremlin have banned reports on killings, torture and kidnappings of civilians by the Russian military. The lack of information about Chechnya is one of the most effective ways to create a situation in which killers and kidnappers in epaulets can operate without legal accountability."[18]

In a country where journalists and environmental activists are thrown in jail for blowing the whistle on military polluters, and arms-control researchers with no access to classified information are charged as foreign spies, the prospects for an antiwar movement to bring peace to Chechnya are doubtful. Here international and transnational organizations have a role to play in supporting domestic Russian groups, although their record of success is mixed.[19] And despite the Bush administration's cavalier attitude toward international treaties, the United States and other democracies might influence Russian behavior in providing a kind of role model—by seeking to deal with the threat of violent separatism and terrorism without undermining the fundamental rights and freedoms that their societies value.

There is no easy solution to the Chechen conflict. A history of neglect and abuse by Moscow, including two recent punishing wars, has sharply diminished the prospects for reconciliation and reconstruction. Yet the longer Russia's leaders delay in pursuing a peaceful resolution to the war in Chechnya, the more damage they do to the institutions of their state and to their society.

Notes

Chapter 1

Epigraph is from Robert V. Daniels, "Democracy and Federalism in the Former Soviet Union and the Russian Federation," in Peter J. Stavrakis and others, eds., *Beyond the Monolith: The Emergence of Regionalism in Post-Soviet Russia* (Washington: Woodrow Wilson Center Press, 1997), p. 243.

1. Vladimir Putin, *First Person: An Astonishingly Frank Self-Portrait by Russia's President* (New York: Public Affairs, 2000), pp. 140, 142.

2. For some examples, see John B. Dunlop, *Russia Confronts Chechnya: Roots of a Separatist Conflict* (Cambridge University Press, 1998); Anatol Lieven, *Chechnya: Tombstone of Russian Power* (Yale University Press, 1998); Carlotta Gall and Thomas de Waal, *Chechnya: Calamity in the Caucasus* (New York University Press, 1998); Sebastian Smith, *Allah's Mountains: Politics and War in the Russian Caucasus* (London: I. B. Tauris, 1998); Gail Lapidus, "Contested Sovereignty: The Tragedy of Chechnya," *International Security,* vol. 23 (Summer 1998), pp. 5–49; James Hughes, "Chechnya: The Causes of a Protracted Post-Soviet Conflict," *Civil Wars,* vol. 4 (Winter 2001), pp. 11–48; O. P. Orlov and A. V. Cherkasov, *Rossiia-Chechnia: Tsep' oshibok i prestuplenii* (Russia-Chechnya: A chain of mistakes and crimes) (Moscow: Zveniia, 1998); Vladimir Lysenko, *Ot Tatarstan do Chechni (stanovlenie novogo rossiiskogo federalizma)* (From Tatarstan to Chechnya [the coming of a new Russian federalism]) (Moscow:

Institute of Contemporary Politics, 1995); Oleg Panfilov and Aleksei Simonov, eds., *Informatsionnaia voina v Chechne* (Information war in Chechnya) (Moscow: Prava cheloveka, 1997); Taimaz Abubakarov, *Rezhim Dzhokhara Dudaeva: Pravda i vymysel, zapiski Dudaevskogo ministra ekonomiki i finansov* (Dzhokhar Dudaev's regime: Truth and falsehood, notes of Dudaev's minister of economics and finance) (Moscow: INSAN, 1998).

3. Andrei Shumikhin, "The Chechen Crisis and the Future of Russia," in Roald Z. Sagdeev and Susan Eisenhower, eds., *Central Asia: Conflict, Resolution, and Change* (Chevy Chase, Md.: CPSS Press, 1995), p. 33.

4. Ibid., p. 29.

5. This summary oversimplifies a complicated argument that is found in several versions. See, for example, Rogers Brubaker, *Nationalism Reframed: Nationhood and the National Question in the New Europe* (Cambridge University Press, 1996); Valerie Bunce, *Subversive Institutions: The Design and Destruction of Socialism and the State* (Cambridge University Press, 1999); Fiona Hill, "'Russia's Tinderbox': Conflict in the North Caucasus and its Implications for the Future of the Russian Federation," Harvard University, Strengthening Democratic Institutions Project (September 1995); Georgi Derluguian, "Historical Sociological Interpretation of Nationalist Separatism in the Four Former Soviet Autonomous Republics: Tataria, Chechnya, Abkhazia, and Ajaria" (Ph.D. diss., Department of Sociology, State University of New York at Binghamton, 1995); Ronald Grigor Suny, *The Revenge of the Past: Nationalism, Revolution, and the Collapse of the Soviet Union* (Stanford University Press, 1993); Philip G. Roeder, "Soviet Federalism and Ethnic Mobilization," *World Politics*, vol. 43 (January 1991), pp. 196–232; David D. Laitin, "The National Uprisings in the Soviet Union," *World Politics*, vol. 44 (October 1991), pp. 139–77; Yuri Slezkine, "The USSR as a Communal Apartment, or How a Socialist State Promoted Ethnic Particularism," *Slavic Review*, vol. 53 (Summer 1994), pp. 414–52.

6. This explanation is discussed by Valery Tishkov, *Ethnicity, Nationalism, and Conflict in and after the Soviet Union* (London: Sage Publications, 1997), chaps. 9 and 10; see also the journalistic accounts of Lieven and Gall and de Waal.

7. Abubakarov, *Rezhim Dzhokhara Dudaeva.*

8. Matthew Evangelista, "Dagestan and Chechnya: Russia's Self-Defeating Wars," Program on New Approaches to Russian Security (hereafter PONARS) Policy Memo 95; Georgi Derluguian, "Che Guevaras in Turbans," *New Left Review* 237 (September/October 1999), pp. 3–27. Somewhat more skeptical of personality-based or individual-level explanations is James Hughes, "Chechnya: The Causes of a Protracted Post-Soviet Conflict," *Civil Wars*, vol. 11 (Winter 2001); his article provides an excellent overview of the causes of both wars.

9. Putin, *First Person*, p. 142.

10. I am grateful to Yoshiko Herrera for pressing me to pursue this issue. For further discussion, see her forthcoming work on Russian regionalism. For a discussion of the weak Russian state in the realm of Russian foreign policy, see Matthew Evangelista, "The Paradox of State Strength: Transnational Relations, Domestic Structures, and Security Policy in Russia and the Soviet Union," *International Organization*, vol. 49 (Winter 1995). For an application to the economy, see Hector Schamis, *Re-Forming the State: The Politics of Privatization in Latin America and Europe* (University of Michigan Press, 2001), especially pp. 187–95.

11. Matthew Evangelista, "An Interview with Galina Starovoytova," *Post-Soviet Affairs*, vol. 15 (July–September 1999); Lieven and Gall and de Waal make similar arguments.

12. Matthew Evangelista, "Russia's Fragile Union," *Bulletin of the Atomic Scientists*, vol. 55 (May/June 1999); L. M. Drobizheva, *Asimmetrichnaia federatsiia: vzgliad iz tsentra, respublik i oblastei* (Asymmetrical federation: The view from the center, the republics, and the provinces) (Moscow: Institute of Sociology of the Russian Academy of Sciences, 1998); Gail Lapidus, "Asymmetrical Federalism and State Breakdown in Russia," *Post-Soviet Affairs*, vol. 15 (January–March 1999), pp. 74–82.

13. Rajan Menon and Graham E. Fuller, "Russia's Ruinous Chechen War," and Sam Nunn and Adam N. Stulberg, "The Many Faces of Modern Russia," both in *Foreign Affairs*, vol. 79 (March/April 2000), pp. 32–62. In fact, the articles themselves are somewhat more nuanced than the Council on Foreign Relations press releases that accompanied their publication.

14. Putin, *First Person*, pp. 139–40.

15. Ibid., p. 140.

16. See, for example, in addition to the journalists' accounts cited above, Edgar O'Ballance, *Wars in the Caucasus, 1990–1995* (New York University Press, 1997); Christopher Panico, *Conflicts in the Caucasus: Russia's War in Chechnya* (London: Research Institute for the Study of Conflict and Terrorism, 1995); Olga Oliker, *Russia's Chechen Wars 1994–2000: Lessons from Urban Combat*, MR-1289 (Santa Monica, Calif.: Rand, 2002).

17. Starovoitova quoted in Vladimir Socor, "Critical Voices," Radio Free Europe/Radio Liberty [henceforth RFE/RL] *Daily Report*, no. 236 (December 15, 1994); Putin, *First Person*, pp.141–42.

18. Jessica Eve Stern, "Moscow Meltdown: Can Russia Survive?" *International Security*, vol. 18 (Spring 1994), pp. 40–65.

19. An excellent overview is James Hughes, "Managing Secession Potential in the Russian Federation," in James Hughes and Gwendolyn Sasse, eds., *Ethnicity and Territory in the Former Soviet Union: Regions in Conflict* (London: Frank Cass, 2002), pp. 36–68.

Chapter 2

Epigraph of Yeltsin is from Carlotta Gall and Thomas de Waal, *Chechnya: Calamity in the Caucasus* (New York University Press, 1998), p. 149. Khasbulatov's testimony is reprinted in Glasnost Foundation, *Voina v Chechne: Mezhdunarodnyi Tribunal* (The war in Chechnya: international tribunal) (Moscow: Obshchestvennyi fond "Glasnost,'" 1997), p. 55.

1. Boris Yeltsin, *Midnight Diaries*, trans. Catherine A. Fitzpatrick (New York: Public Affairs, 2000), p. 58. Although called diaries, this book was apparently ghostwritten by Yeltsin's adviser, Valentin Iumashev.

2. Zaidni Shakhbiev, *Sud'ba checheno-ingushskogo naroda* (The fate of the Chechen-Ingush people) (Moscow: Rossiia moldaia, 1996).

3. This summary of the history of Russian-Chechen conflict draws on John B. Dunlop, *Russia Confronts Chechnya: Roots of a Separatist Conflict* (Cambridge University

Press, 1998). Some of the wording comes from my review of Dunlop's book in *Slavic Review*, vol. 59 (Spring 2000), pp. 235–37.

4. Dunlop, *Russia Confronts Chechnya*, p. 23.

5. An excellent summary of the deportations is found in Carlotta Gall and Thomas de Waal, *Chechnya: Calamity in the Caucasus* (New York University Press, 1998), chap. 4. The quotation is from p. 57. For some poignant personal stories, see Sebastian Smith, *Allah's Mountains: Politics and War in the Russian Caucasus* (London: I. B. Tauris, 1998), pp. 58–67.

6. Gall and Waal, *Chechnya*, pp. 57–58.

7. For a discussion of collaboration of a small number of Chechens captured by the Germans, see Dunlop, *Russia Confronts Chechnya*, pp. 58–61. By contrast, more than 17,000 Chechens served with distinction in the Red Army, until, in February 1944, they were withdrawn from their units and deported to the East.

8. Gall and de Waal, *Chechnya*, p. 61. For further discussion of population losses, see Dunlop, *Russia Confronts Chechnya*, pp. 70–71.

9. Dunlop, *Russia Confronts Chechnya*, pp. 75–80.

10. The following documents relate to the decision. They were found in the former archive of the Central Committee of the Communist Party of the Soviet Union (CPSU), later renamed the Russian State Archive for Contemporary History (Moscow): "O vosstanovlenii natsional'noi avtonomii kalmytskogo, karachaevskogo, balkarskogo, chechenskogo i ingushskogo narodov" (On the restoration of the national autonomies of the Kalmyk, Karachaev, Balkar, Chechen, and Ingush peoples), P60/24, from Protocol 60, of the session of the Presidium of the CPSU Central Committee, November 24, 1956; "O vosstanovelenii Chechno-Ingushskoi ASSR i uprazdnenii Groznenskoi oblasti" (On the restoration of the Chechen-Ingush ASSR and abolition of the Grozny region), decree of the Presidium of the Supreme Soviet of the Russian Soviet Federated Socialist Republic, n.d., F. 89, Op. 61, D. 8. Protocol 67, session of the Presidium of the CPSU Central Committee, January 5–6, 1957, item 32, "O territorii Checheno-Ingushskoi ASSR" (On the territory of the Checheno-Ingush ASSR), F. 89, Op. 61, D. 1.

11. Dunlop, *Russia Confronts Chechnya*, pp. 78–79. A series of documents, from 1957 through 1964, have been declassified and published on the return of the Chechens and Ingush to the Caucasus. See the journal *Istochnik* (Source), no. 6 (1996), pp. 89–104.

12. Gall and de Waal, *Chechnya*, p. 73.

13. Taimaz Abubakarov, *Rezhim Dzhokhara Dudaeva: Pravda i vymysel* (The regime of Dzhokhar Dudaev: Truth and falsehoods) (Moscow: INSAN, 1998), p. 49.

14. Shakhbiev, *Sud'ba checheno-ingushskogo naroda*, p. 306.

15. For a discussion of the various political movements in these years, see Timur Muzaev, "Faktor Chechni: Fenomen pobedivshego separatizma" (The Chechnya factor: The phenomenon of victorious separatism), chap. 3 in his *Etnicheskii separatizm v Rossii* (Ethnic separatism in Russia) (Moscow: Panorama, 1999). The Greens eventually joined the radical nationalists and even contributed armed detachments to the new National Guard. See Timur Muzaev, *Chechenskaia Respublika: Organy vlasti i politicheskie sily* (The Chechen Republic: Organs of power and political forces) (Moscow: Panorama, 1995), pp. 129–30.

16. Valery Tishkov, *Ethnicity, Nationalism, and Conflict in and after the Soviet Union* (London: Sage Publications, 1997), pp. 198–201; Dunlop, *Russia Confronts Chechnya*, p. 89.

17. Muzaev, *Etnicheskii separatizm*, pp. 34–35; Tishkov, *Ethnicity, Nationalism, and Conflict*, pp. 200–01.

18. Muzaev, *Etnicheskii separatizm*, pp. 35–36.

19. "Ob obshchestvenno-politicheskoi obstanovke v Checheno-Ingushskoi Respublike" (On the sociopolitical situation in the Chechen-Ingush Republic), Resolution of the Secretariat of the CPSU Central Committee, June 21, 1991, Russian State Archive for Contemporary History, F. 89, Op. 20, D. 69.

20. "O postanovlenii biuro Checheno-Ingushskogo reskoma KPSS" (On the resolution of the bureau of the CPSU Chechen-Ingush Republic committee), Resolution of the Secretariat of the CPSU Central Committee, July 19, 1991, Russian State Archive for Contemporary History, F. 89, Op. 20, D. 75.

21. Tishkov, *Ethnicity, Nationalism, and Conflict*, pp. 200–01.

22. Ibid., pp. 201–02; Muzaev, *Etnicheskii separatizm*, pp. 37–38; Gall and de Waal, *Chechnya*, pp. 95–96. Although Kutsenko is a Ukrainian surname, most sources identify him as Russian.

23. Muzaev, *Etnicheskii separatizm*, pp. 37–38.

24. Shakhbiev, *Sud'ba checheno-ingushskogo naroda*, p. 306.

25. Tishkov, *Ethnicity, Nationalism, and Conflict*, p. 202.

26. Valerii Aleksin, "Obstanovku v Chechne mozhno normalizovat'" (It is possible to normalize the situation in Chechnya), *Nezavisimoe voennoe obozrenie*, no. 21 (June 16, 2000), Internet version.

27. Viktor Baranets, *Poteriannaia armiia: Zapiski polkovnika Genshtaba* (Lost army: Notes of a General Staff colonel) (Moscow: Sovershenno sekretno, 1998), p. 286.

28. Abubakarov, *Rezhim Dzhokhara Dudaeva*, p. 50.

29. Muzaev, *Etnicheskii separatizm*, pp. 37–38.

30. Iu. M. Baturin, A. L. Il'in, V. F. Kadatskii, V. V. Kostikov, M. A. Krasnov, A. Ia. Livshits, K. V. Nikiforov, L. G. Pikhoia, and G. A. Satarov, *Epokha El'tsina: Ocherki politicheskoi istorii* (The Yeltsin epoch: Sketches of a political history) (Moscow: Vagrius, 2001), pp. 585–86.

31. Fiona Hill, "'Russia's Tinderbox': Conflict in the North Caucasus and Its Implications for the Future of the Russian Federation," Harvard University, Strengthening Democratic Institutions Project (September 1995), p. 82; Dunlop, *Russia Confronts Chechnya*, p. 114.

32. Tishkov, *Ethnicity, Nationalism, and Conflict*, p. 202.

33. Hill, "'Russia's Tinderbox,'" pp. 82–83.

34. Gall and de Waal, *Chechnya*, p. 102.

35. Tishkov, *Ethnicity, Nationalism, and Conflict*, p. 202.

36. Abubakarov, *Rezhim Dzhokhara Dudaeva*, p. 8.

37. Ibid., p. 9. For comparable figures, see Michael McFaul and Nikolai Petrov, *Politicheskii al'manakh Rossii 1997* (Political almanac of Russia, 1997), vol. 2, *Sotsial'no-politicheskie portrety regionov* (Sociopolitical portraits of the regions), book 1 (Moscow: Carnegie Center, 1998), p. 291.

38. Abubakarov, *Rezhim Dzhokhara Dudaeva*, p. 21.

39. Tishkov, *Ethnicity, Nationalism, and Conflict*, p. 207.

40. Grachev's order is reproduced in Baranets, *Poteriannaia armiia*, p. 258.

41. Gall and de Waal, *Chechnya*, p. 113.

42. Tishkov, *Ethnicity, Nationalism, and Conflict*, p. 207.

43. Aleksandr Litvinenko and Iurii Fel'shtinskii, *FSB vzryvaet Rossiiu* (The FSB

blows up Russia), excerpts from chap. 1, as published in *Novaia gazeta,* August 27, 2001, http://2001.novayagazeta.ru/nomer/2001/61n/n61n-s01.html, archived with the author.

44. Tishkov, *Ethnicity, Nationalism, and Conflict,* p. 207. For different sets of numbers, but representing the same magnitude of weaponry, see Dunlop, *Russia Confronts Chechnya,* pp. 167–68.

45. David Remnick, *Resurrection: The Struggle for a New Russia* (Random House, 1997), p. 271.

46. Paul Klebnikov, *Godfather of the Kremlin: Boris Berezovsky and the Looting of Russia* (Harcourt, 2000), p. 40. Despite the sensational title, this book, by an editor of *Forbes* magazine, reflects a fairly widespread and uncontroversial understanding of organized crime in Russia and Chechnya.

47. For background on the conflict, see Hill, "'Russia's Tinderbox,'" pp. 47–52; Dunlop, *Russia Confronts Chechnya,* pp. 173–78.

48. Baranets, *Poteriannaia armiia,* pp. 241–42.

49. Ibid., p. 242.

50. For a review of the various efforts, see Muzaev, *Etnicheskii separatizm,* pp. 43–44.

51. Dunlop, *Russia Confronts Chechnya,* pp. 223, 184.

52. Baranets, *Poteriannaia armiia,* p. 299.

53. Gall and de Waal, *Chechnya,* pp. 114–15; particularly good on Khasbulatov's role throughout the conflict with Chechnya is Dunlop, *Russia Confronts Chechnya.*

54. Yeltsin, *Midnight Diaries,* p. 55.

55. Abubakarov, *Rezhim Dzhokhara Dudaeva,* p. 167. He cites particularly remarks Dudaev made at a conference in Grozny in April 1994 and endorses the view of Tatarstan president Mintimir Shaimiev that Yeltsin's opinion of Dudaev hardened at that time.

56. Undated telegram from Dudaev to Yeltsin, VCh-PII-37791, probably from early October 1993, quoted in Gall and de Waal, *Chechnya,* pp. 121–22.

57. Gall and de Waal, *Chechnya,* p. 119.

58. Ibid., p. 121.

59. Baranets, *Poteriannaia armiia,* p. 242.

60. Litvinenko and Fel'shtinskii, *FSB vzryvaet Rossiiu.*

61. Gall and de Waal, *Chechnya,* pp. 122–23.

62. Ibid., p. 154.

63. Kovalev interviewed by Gall and de Waal, *Chechnya,* p. 167.

64. Baturin and others, *Epokha El'tsina,* pp. 586–87.

65. Ibid., pp. 588–89.

66. Abubakarov, *Rezhim Dzhokhara Dudaeva,* p. 28.

67. Baturin and others, *Epokha El'tsina,* p. 593.

68. Gall and de Waal, *Chechnya,* p. 160.

69. Abubakarov, *Rezhim Dzhokhara Dudaeva,* p. 162.

70. Ibid., pp. 30–32.

71. Georgi M. Derluguian, "Ethnofederalism and Ethnonationalism in the Separatist Politics of Chechnya and Tatarstan: Sources or Resources?" *International Journal of Public Administration,* vol. 22, no. 9&10, (1999), pp. 1387–1428, at p. 1417. For an account of the demonstrations that followed Dudaev's closing of the parliament, see Shakhbiev, *Sud'ba checheno-ingushskogo naroda,* pp. 312–14.

72. *Izvestiia,* May 20, 1994, quoted in Dunlop, *Russia Confronts Chechnya,* p. 192.

73. Dunlop, *Russia Confronts Chechnya*, pp. 192–93.

74. Ibid.

75. Baturin and others, *Epokha El'tsina*.

76. Gall and de Waal, *Chechnya*, p. 148.

77. Anatol Lieven, review of John Dunlop's *Russia Confronts Chechnya: Roots of a Separatist Conflict*, in *Europe–Asia Studies*, vol. 51 (June 1999), pp. 720–22.

78. Anatol Lieven, *Chechnya: Tombstone of Russian Power* (Yale University Press, 1998), p. 86. In the review quoted above, he mistakenly dates the last hijacking to June 1995, some six months after the Russian invasion. In fact, it is unfortunately premature to speak of any "last" hijacking. In June 2001, for example, a group of armed Chechens stormed another bus in Mineral'nye Vody, demanding that the hijackers of seven years earlier be released from prison. See Sergei Karpukhin, "Commandos Storm Seized Russian Bus, Kill Hijacker," a Reuters report from July 31, 2001, found at http://ca.news.yahoo.com/010731/5/88o5.html.

79. Lieven, *Chechnya*, p. 85.

80. Gall and de Waal, *Chechnya*, p. 149.

81. Baturin and others, *Epokha El'tsina*, pp. 596–98.

82. For the full listing, see Dunlop, *Russia Confronts Chechnya*, p. 207, n. 39.

83. Aleksandr Gamov, "V Sovete bezopasnosti snachala golosuiut, a potom obsuzhdaiut" (In the Security Council first they vote and then they discuss), interview with former minister of justice Iurii Kalmykov, *Komsomol'skaia pravda*, December 10, 1994.

84. Muzaev, *Etnicheskii separatizm*, p. 44. See also Dunlop, *Russia Confronts Chechnya*, p. 208. The decree was later published in *Novoe vremia* 14 (1995), pp. 6–9. A chronology of government decisions, compiled by A.V. Cherkasov and O. P. Orlov, is found in the Memorial group's collection, *Rossiia-Chechnia: Tsep' oshibok i prestuplenii* (Russia-Chechnya: A chain of mistakes and crimes) (Moscow: Zven'ia, 1998), pp. 23–87.

85. Baturin and others, *Epokha El'tsina*, p. 604. Baranets, *Poteriannaia armiia*, pp. 237–38, reports an abbreviated and slightly milder conclusion to the conversation: "'Nu chto, Dzhokhar, voina?' Dudaev otvetil: 'Voina.'"

86. For a discussion of the meeting, see Gall and de Waal, *Chechnya*, pp. 170–71; and *Izvestiia*, December 8, 1994. Thanks to an anonymous reviewer for reminding me of Grachev's early opposition to invasion.

87. Baranets, *Poteriannaia armiia*, p. 238.

88. Baturin and others, *Epokha El'tsina*, p. 607.

89. Ibid., pp. 625–28.

90. Ibid.

91. Yeltsin, *Midnight Diaries*, pp. 325–26.

92. E-mail correspondence from Nikolai Petrov, September 7, 2001.

93. Baturin and others, *Epokha El'tsina*, p. 624.

94. Abubakarov, *Rezhim Dzhokhara Dudaeva*.

95. Baranets, *Poteriannaia armiia*, p. 266. The growth of Islamic fundamentalist influences in Chechen politics in the wake of the Russian invasion is documented by Muzaev in *Chechenskaia Respublika*, and in *Etnicheskii separatizm*.

96. The quotation is from Nikolai Petrov in e-mail correspondence, September 7, 2001.

97. "Strategicheskie interessy Rossii na Kavkaze" (Russia's strategic interests in the Caucasus), *Izvestiia*, January 12, 1995.

98. For Kovalev's views, see Gall and de Waal, *Chechnya*, p. 167.

99. Baranets, *Poteriannaia armiia*, p. 230.

100. Ibid., pp. 230-32.

101. Ibid., p. 234.

102. Ibid., pp. 226-27. See also "Soldiers Sent to Battle after 8 Days' Training," *Moscow News*, April 10-16, 1997, p. 5.

103. Sergei Iushenkov, chair of the parliamentary defense committee reported these remarks from his conversation with Lobov to Carlotta Gall and Thomas de Waal, *Chechnya*, p. 161. "A Small, Victorious War" was the subtitle of the original British edition of this book. The phrase was earlier used by Russian interior minister Viacheslav Pleve who, in 1904, advocated war with Japan to avert revolution.

104. Baranets, *Poteriannaia armiia*, pp. 232, 240.

105. Remnick, *Resurrection*, pp. 282-83. The account in Gall and de Waal, *Chechnya*, pp. 177-81, also suggests some moral reservations on Vorob'ev's part. For details of the tank troops entering Grozny, see the testimony of Aleksandr Osovtsov in Glasnost' Foundation, *Voina v Chechne: Mezhdunarodnyi Tribunal* (The war in Chechnya: International tribunal) (Moscow: Obshchestvennyi fond "Glasnost'," 1997), pp. 15-16.

106. Lieven, *Chechnya*, p. 106.

107. Baranets, *Poteriannaia armiia*, p. 230.

108. Gall and de Waal, *Chechnya*, p. 176.

109. Ibid.

110. Baranets, *Poteriannaia armiia*, p. 268. Thanks to Mikhail Alexseev for help with the translation.

111. Baturin and others, *Epokha El'tsina*, p. 624.

112. Ibid., p. 622.

113. Glasnost' Foundation, *Voina v Chechne*.

114. Gall and de Waal, *Chechnya*, p. 201.

115. Discussed in ibid., pp. 242-47 and chap. 6.

116. Ibid., pp. 262-75.

117. Ibid., pp. 289-304. For an eyewitness account of the hostage crisis in Pervomaiskoe, see Enver Kisriev's report, "Ethnic Conflict Management in the Former Soviet Union," *Bulletin of the Conflict Management Group*, March 1996, pp. 13-23; see also Michael Specter, "Saying Hostages Are Dead, Russians Level Rebel Town," *New York Times*, January 18, 1996.

118. Gall and de Waal, *Chechnya*, pp. 318-21.

119. Amy Caiazza, *Mothers and Soldiers: Gender, Citizenship, and Civil Society in Contemporary Russia* (New York: Routledge, 2002); Valerie Sperling, "The Last Refuge of a Scoundrel: Patriotism, Militarism and the Russian National Idea," *Nations and Nationalism*, vol. 9 (April 2003, forthcoming); Brenda J. Vallance, "Russia's Mothers—Voices of Change," *Minerva: Quarterly Report on Women and the Military*, vol. 18, nos. 3-4 (2000), pp. 109-28.

120. Lebed' remained an important figure in Russian politics, serving as governor of the Krasnoiarsk region, until his death in a helicopter crash in April 2002.

121. A.V. Cherkasov and O. P. Orlov, "Khronika vooruzhennogo konflikta" (Chronicle of the armed conflict), in the Memorial group's collection, *Rossiia-Chechnia: Tsep' oshibok i prestuplenii* (Russia-Chechnya: A chain of mistakes and crimes) (Moscow: Zven'ia, 1998), pp. 23-87.

122. Ibid., pp. 73, 366–67.

123. Ibid., p. 76. See also Gall and de Waal, *Chechnya,* pp. 326–28.

124. Cherkasov and Orlov, "Khronika," p. 78.

125. Ibid., pp. 80–81.

126. Litvinenko and Fel'shtinkskii, *FSB vzryvaet Rossiiu,* archived with the author.

127. See, in particular, Emil' Pain's comments in *Izvestiia,* April 21, 1998, and *Mezh-dunarodnaia zhizn',* no. 9 (1998), pp. 91–101. Thanks to an anonymous reviewer for this point.

128. Ibid., pp. 85–88. See Gall and de Waal, *Chechnya,* chap. 15.

129. "Printsipy opredeleniia osnov vzaimootnoshenii mezhdu Rossiiskoi Federatsiei i Chechenskoi Respublikoi" (Principles for determining the bases of relations between the Russian Federation and the Chechen Republic), signed by A. Lebed', A. Maskhadov, S. Kharlamov, and S. Abumuslimov, August 31, 1996, Khasaviurt, in the presence of T. Guldimann, head of the OSCE mission in Chechnya. Published in *Nezavisimaia gazeta,* September 3, 1996, and available online at www.cityline.ru:8084/politika/doc/hasavurt.html. For a valuable collection of documents relevant to the end of the first war and ill-fated peace plans, see Diane Curran, Fiona Hill, and Elena Kostritsyna, "The Search for Peace in Chechnya: A Sourcebook 1994–1996," Harvard University, Kennedy School of Government, March 1997.

Chapter 3

Epigraph is from Il'ia Maksakov, "Dagestan ostanetsia edinoi nedelimoi respublikoi v sostave RF" (Dagestan will remain a single, indivisible republic within the structure of the RF [Russian Federation]), *Nezavisimaia gazeta,* May 12, 1998.

1. A detailed study of the role of kidnapping in Chechnya is found in V. A. Tishkov, *Obshchestvo v vooruzhennom konflikte: Etnografiia chechenskoi voiny* (Society in armed conflict: Ethnography of the Chechen War) (Moscow: Nauka, 2001), chap. 13. Stephen Shenfield has provided an English-language summary in his Research and Analytical Supplement 7 to Johnson's Russia List 6191, April 18, 2002.

2. John B. Dunlop, "The Second Russo-Chechen War Two Years On," www.peaceinchechnya.org/paper1.htm, archived with the author.

3. Peter Reddaway and Dmitri Glinksi, *The Tragedy of Russia's Reforms: Market Bolshevism against Democracy* (Washington: U.S. Institute of Peace Press, 2001), p. 613.

4. On the hostage crisis in Pervomaiskoe (Dagestan), January 10–16, 1996, see the eyewitness account of Enver Kisriev, "Ethnic Conflict Management in the Former Soviet Union," *Bulletin of the Conflict Management Group,* March 1996, pp. 13–23.

5. Liz Fuller, "Red Cross Workers Slaughtered in Chechnya," *OMRI Daily Digest* (Open Media Research Institute), no. 242, pt. 1 (December 17), 1996; Liz Fuller, "Red Cross Killings Condemned," and "Raduev Backtracks on Hostages," *OMRI Daily Digest,* no. 243, pt. 1 (December 18, 1996); Liz Fuller, "Raduev Releases Hostages," *OMRI Daily Digest,* no. 244, pt. 1 (December 19, 1996); Sanobar Shermatova and Leonid Nikitinskii, "Chechen Slave Traders," *Moscow News,* no. 14 (April 12–18, 2000).

6. Scott Parrish, "Final Chechen Election Results," *OMRI Daily Digest,* no. 23, pt. 1 (February 3, 1997).

7. Scott Parrish, "Maskhadov Apparent Winner in Chechnya," *OMRI Daily Digest,* no. 20, pt. 1 (January 29, 1997); Scott Parrish, "Maskhadov Warns Raduev," *OMRI Daily Digest,* no. 22, pt. 1 (January 31, 1997).

8. Scott Parrish, "Moscow Welcomes Election Results," *OMRI Daily Digest,* no. 20, pt. 1 (January 29, 1997).

9. Scott Parrish, "Raduev Threatens Terror Campaign against Russia," *OMRI Daily Digest,* no. 21, pt. 1 (January 30, 1997).

10. Scott Parrish, "OSCE Mission Head Expelled from Chechnya," *OMRI Daily Digest,* no. 25, pt. 1 (February 5, 1997); Liz Fuller, "Yandarbiev Puts Screws on Maskhadov," *OMRI Daily Digest,* no. 34, pt. 1 (February 18, 1997).

11. Robert Orttung, "Raduev Troops Parade in Grozny," *OMRI Daily Digest,* no. 44, pt. 1 (March 4, 1997).

12. Liz Fuller, "Udugov Named Chechnya's Chief Negotiator with Russia," *OMRI Daily Digest,* no. 36, pt. 1 (February 20), 1997; Liz Fuller, "Maskhadov Unveils New Government," *OMRI Daily Digest,* no. 56, pt. 1 (March 20, 1997); "Basaev Nominated First Deputy Premier," Radio Free Europe/Radio Liberty (hereafter RFE/RL) *Newsline,* vol. 1, no. 2, pt. 1 (April 2, 1997).

13. Sanobar Shermatova, "Basaev's Left, but He May Be Back," *Moscow News,* July 17–23, 1997, p. 2.

14. Liz Fuller, "Chechen President under Pressure," RFE/RL *Newsline,* vol. 1, no. 5, pt. 1 (April 7, 1997).

15. Paul Klebnikov, *Godfather of the Kremlin: Boris Berezovsky and the Looting of Russia* (Harcourt, 2000), pp. 300–06.

16. Joerg R. Mettke, interview with Chechen President Aslan Maskhadov, *Der Spiegel,* no. 39 (September 27, 1999), JRL.

17. Shamsutdin Mamaev and Nikolai Babichev, "Prestupnye promysly" (The criminal fields), *Kommersant" Vlast',* November 3, 1998, pp. 18–20. In Russian, *promysel* means both "trade" or "business" and "field," as in oil field.

18. El'mar Guseinov, "Pokushenie na Dagestan—ugroza bezopasnosti Rossii" (Attack on Dagestan—threat to the security of Russia), *Izvestiia Ukraina,* December 26, 1997; "Separatism, Islam and Oil," October 9, 1999, Federation of American Scientists website, www.fas.org/man/dod-101/ops/war/2000/02/game/344.htm.

19. Dmitrii Belovetskii, "Salman Raduev: S Pervomaiskim privetom" (Salman Raduev: With May-Day greetings), *Ogonek,* no. 18 (May 5, 1997), www.ropnet.ru/ogonyok/win/199718/18-24-27.html. The Russian subtitle is a play on the term *pervomaiskoe* (May 1), the town where one of Raduev's notorious terrorist actions took place.

20. Timur Muzaev, "Faktor Chechni: Fenomen pobedivshego separatizma" (The Chechnya factor: The phenomenon of victorious separatism), chap. 3 in his *Etnicheskii separatizm v Rossii* (Ethnic separatism in Russia) (Moscow: Panorama, 1999), esp. pp. 54–55. For the earlier development of these organizations, see Timur Muzaev, *Chechenskaia Respublika: organy vlasti i politicheskie sily* (The Chechen Republic: organs of power and political forces) (Moscow: Panorama, 1995), pp. 129–30.

21. Liz Fuller, "Overcoming the Final Barriers to a Chechen Peace Agreement," RFE/RL *Newsline,* vol. 1, no. 26, pt. 1 (May 7, 1997); "Warrant Issued for Raduev's Detention," RFE/RL *Newsline,* vol. 1, no. 25, pt. 1 (May 6, 1997). For some of Raduev's more bloodthirsty threats, see Belovetskii, "Salman Raduev."

22. "Berezovskii Details Russian-Chechen Agreements," RFE/RL *Newsline*, vol. 1, no. 25, pt. 1 (May 6, 1997). The main document is *Soglashenie mezhdu Pravitel'stvom Rossiiskoi Federatsei i Pravitel'stvom Chechenskoi Respublikoi Ichkeriia* (Agreement between the government of the Russian Federation and the government of the Chechen Republic Ichkeria) signed by V. Chernomyrdin and A. Maskhadov, May 12, 1997. Thanks to Vakha Khasanov for giving me a copy.

23. Information from online BBC reports: http://news.bbc.co.uk/hi/english/uk/newsid_125000/125327.stm; http://news.bbc.co.uk/hi/english/uk/newsid_175000/175919.stm.

24. Mamaev and Babichev, "Prestupnye promysly," p. 19.

25. "NTV Journalists Released in Chechnya," RFE/RL *Newsline*, vol 1, no. 98, pt. 1 (August 19, 1997); "Berezovskii, Malashenko on Russian Journalists' Release," RFE/RL *Newsline*, vol. 1, no. 99, pt. 1 (August 20, 1997).

26. Belovetskii, "Salman Raduev."

27. Ibid.

28. "Russia Considering New Oil Pipeline to Bypass Chechnya," RFE/RL *Newsline*, vol. 1, no. 90, pt. 1 (August 7, 1997).

29. "Azerbaijan, Chechnya Discuss Export Pipeline," RFE/RL *Newsline*, vol. 1, no. 103, pt. 1 (August 26, 1997); "Chechnya Doubts Pipeline Will Be Ready by October," RFE/RL *Newsline*, vol. 1, no. 105, pt. 1 (August 28, 1997).

30. "Chechens, Russians Discuss Pipeline Deal," RFE/RL *Newsline*, vol. 1, no. 106, pt. 1 (August 29, 1997); "Russia, Chechnya Fail to Reach Pipeline Agreement," RFE/RL *Newsline*, September 2, 1997, online at http://www.rferl.org/*Newsline*/1997/09/020997.html.

31. "Russian-Chechen Oil Transit Talks again Postponed," RFE/RL *Newsline*, September 8, 1997; "Russia, Chechnya Sign Oil Transit Agreement," RFE/RL *Newsline*, September 10, 1997; "Russia, Chechnya Threaten to Abrogate Oil Transit Accord," RFE/RL *Newsline*, September 11, 1997; "Russia to Build Oil Pipeline Bypassing Chechnya," RFE/RL *Newsline*, September 15, 1997.

32. "Otets chechenskoi mafii dast interv'iu v Moskve" (Father of the Chechen mafia gives an interview in Moscow), June 27, 2001, http://www.lenta.ru/vojna/2001/06/27/nukhaev/. Alberto Farassino, "Il diavolo bianco" (The white devil), *Fucine Mute* web magazine, www.fucine.com/archivio/fm11/farassino-light.htm. Background on Nukhaev is included in Farassino's review of a documentary film, *The Making of a New Empire*, by the Dutch filmmaker Jos de Putter. For a brief biography of Nukhaev, excluding his criminal past and Chechen origins, see "Who Is Who in Azerbaijan," at www.azeronline.com/wiw/nukhayevhoyahmed.htm.

33. Mamaev and Babichev, "Prestupnye promysly," p. 19; "Separatism, Islam and Oil."

34. Mamaev and Babichev, "Prestupnye promysly," p. 19; "Forgiven but Not Forgotten," *Guardian* (Manchester), February 17, 2000, at http://www.guardian.co.uk/chechnya/Story/0,2763,192564,00.html.

35. "Chechen, Ingush Presidents Criticize Berezovskii," RFE/RL *Newsline*, vol. 2, no. 212, pt. 1 (November 3, 1998).

36. Klebnikov, *Godfather of the Kremlin*, pp. 261–64; Mamaev and Babichev, "Prestupnye promysly," p. 19.

37. Evgeniia Borisova, "U.S. Teacher Kidnapped in Dagestan," *Moscow Times*, November 13, 1998.

38. "Four Foreign Hostages Slain in Chechnya," RFE/RL *Newsline,* vol. 2, no. 236, pt. 1 (December 9, 1998); "Chechen President Sheds Light on Hostages' Murder," RFE/RL *Newsline,* vol. 2, no. 237, pt. 1 (December 10, 1998).

39. "Chechen President Calls for Coordination in Combating Crime," RFE/RL *Newsline,* vol. 2, no. 231, pt. 1 (December 2, 1998).

40. "Chechen Opposition Steps Up Pressure on President," RFE/RL *Newsline,* vol. 2, no. 210, pt. 1 (October 30, 1998); "Chechen President, Rivals Reach Agreement," RFE/RL *Newsline,* vol. 2, no. 211, pt. 1 (November 2, 1998); "But Suspends Parliament," RFE/RL *Newsline,* vol. 2, no. 247, pt. 1 (December 28, 1998).

41. "As Moscow Expresses Support for Maskhadov," RFE/RL *Newsline,* vol. 2, no. 217, pt. 1 (November 10, 1998); "Primakov Claims 'Breakthrough' in Relations with Chechnya," RFE/RL *Newsline,* vol. 2, no. 210, pt. 1 (October 30, 1998). On evidence of embezzlement of funds, see Dunlop, "The Second Russo-Chechen War Two Years On."

42. "Moscow Abandons Idea of Power-Sharing Treaty with Chechnya," RFE/RL *Newsline,* vol. 2, no. 232, pt. 1 (December 3, 1998).

43. "Chechens Helped Prevent Chubais Assassination," RFE/RL *Newsline,* vol. 2, no. 227, pt. 1 (November 24, 1998).

44. "Chechen Beheading Suspect Arrested," RFE/RL *Newsline,* vol. 2, no. 238, pt. 1 (December 11, 1998); "Chechnya to Expel Arab Terrorist Group," RFE/RL *Newsline,* vol. 2, no. 238, pt. 1 (December 11, 1998). In March 2001 Russian authorities arrested another suspect they claimed was responsible for the killing of the four engineers. See Amelia Gentleman, "Chechen Held for Kidnapping British Engineers," *Guardian,* March 13, 2001, www.guardian.co.uk/archive/article/0,4273,4151025,00.html.

45. "Confusion over Mobilization of Reservists in Chechnya," RFE/RL *Newsline,* vol. 2, no. 240, pt. 1 (December 15, 1998).

46. "Warns of New North Caucasus Conflict," RFE/RL *Newsline,* vol. 3, no. 9, pt. 1 (January 14, 1999).

47. "Chechen Field Commanders Ignore Parliament Summons," RFE/RL *Newsline,* vol. 3, no. 11, pt. 1 (January 18, 1999).

48. "Chechen President Decrees Introduction of Islamic Law . . . Which Is Seen as Stabilizing Move," RFE/RL *Newsline,* vol. 3, no. 24, pt. 1 (February 4, 1999).

49. "Chechen Opposition Elects Leader," RFE/RL *Newsline,* vol. 3, no. 36, pt. 1 (February 22, 1999).

50. "Chechen Presidential Adviser Abducted," RFE/RL *Newsline,* vol. 3, no. 38, pt. 1 (February 24, 1999).

51. "Stepashin Issues Ultimatum to Grozny . . . ," RFE/RL *Newsline,* vol. 3, no. 47, pt. 1 (March 9, 1999).

52. ". . . As Chechen Leadership Vows to Find Kidnapped General . . . ," RFE/RL *Newsline,* vol. 3, no. 47, pt. 1 (March 9, 1999).

53. ". . . And Opposition Warns of Reprisals," RFE/RL *Newsline,* vol. 3, no. 47, pt. 1 (March 9, 1999).

54. "Chechen President Wants to Meet with Yeltsin . . . ," RFE/RL *Newsline,* vol. 3, no. 48, pt. 1 (March 10, 1999).

55. ". . . Can Count On Moscow's Support," RFE/RL *Newsline,* vol. 3, no. 48, pt. 1 (March 10, 1999).

56. "Stepashin Says Chechen War Was Response to Shpigun Abduction, " RFE/RL *Newsline,* vol. 4, no. 20, pt. 1 (January 28, 2000).

57. "Russian Fighter Planes Buzz Grozny?" RFE/RL *Newsline*, vol. 1, no. 95, pt. 1 (August 14, 1997); "Russia Denies Violating Chechen Air Space," RFE/RL *Newsline*, vol. 3, no. 12, pt. 1 (January 19, 1999); "Chechen President Issues Order to Shoot Down Intruding Aircraft," RFE/RL *Newsline*, vol. 3, no. 62, pt. 1 (March 30, 1999).

58. "Chechnya Halts Export of Azerbaijani Oil," RFE/RL *Newsline*, vol. 3, no. 63, pt. 1 (March 31, 1999).

59. "Stepashin Declares Border with Chechnya Closed," RFE/RL *Newsline*, vol. 3, no. 81, pt. 1 (April 27, 1999).

60. "Chechens, Russians Exchange Fire," RFE/RL *Newsline*, vol. 3, no. 139, pt. 1 (July 20, 1999).

61. "Russia Targets Alleged Chechen Guerrilla Base," RFE/RL *Newsline*, vol. 3, no. 105, pt. 1 (May 31,1999).

62. "As Stepashin Vows to 'Eliminate Bandits,'" RFE/RL *Newsline*, vol. 3, no. 105, pt. 1 (May 31, 1999).

63. "Chechnya Closes Regional Missions in Russia," RFE/RL *Newsline*, vol. 3, no. 139, pt. 1 (July 20, 1999); "Chechnya Closes Moscow Mission," RFE/RL *Newsline*, vol. 3, no. 141, pt. 1 (July 22, 1999).

64. "Russians, Chechens Again Exchange Fire," RFE/RL *Newsline*, vol. 3, no. 144, pt. 1 (July 7, 1999).

65. "U.S. Hostage Released in Chechnya," RFE/RL *Newsline*, vol. 3, no. 127, pt. 1 (June 30, 1999).

66. "Chechen President Appoints Rival New First Deputy Premier," RFE/RL *Newsline*, vol. 3, no. 145, pt. 1 (July 28, 1999).

67. Sergei Stepashin, interview, *Nezavisimaia gazeta*, January 14, 2000.

Chapter 4

Epigraph is from Vladimir Putin, *First Person: An Astonishingly Frank Self-Portrait by Russia's President* (New York: Public Affairs, 2000), p. 139.

1. "Russian Interior Ministry Troops Deployed on Dagestan-Chechnya Border," RFE/RL *Newsline*, vol. 3, no. 152, pt. 1 (August 6, 1999).

2. El'mar Guseinov, "Pokushenie na Dagestan—ugroza bezopasnosti Rossii" (Attack on Dagestan—threat to the security of Russia), *Izvestiia Ukraina*, December 26, 1997. Thanks to Marat Umerov for sharing his newspaper clippings on Dagestan.

3. Enver Kisriev and Robert Bruce Ware, "Conflict and Catharsis: A Report on Developments in Dagestan following the Incursions of August and September 1999," *Nationalities Papers,* vol. 28, no. 3 (2000), pp. 479–522; Il'ia Maksakov, "Dagestan ostanetsia edinoi nedelimoi respublikoi v sostave RF" (Dagestan will remain a single, indivisible republic within the structure of the RF [Russian Federation]), *Nezavisimaia gazeta,* May 12, 1998; Alan Kasaev and Il'ia Maksakov, "Real' naia ugroza Dagestanu" (The real threat to Dagestan), *Nezavisimaia gazeta,* October 6, 1998.

4. On May 15, 1999, State Duma deputies failed to impeach Yeltsin, but the charge that the president initiated the war against Chechnya illegally garnered the most votes, 283 of the 300 needed. "Impeachment Effort Falls Short by 17 Votes," RFE/RL *Newsline,* vol. 3, no. 95, pt. 1 (May 17, 1999).

5. "Chechen Rebels Confirm Arab Warlord Khattab Dead," Agence France-Presse, April 29, 2002.

6. Vladimir Putin, *First Person: An Astonishingly Frank Self-Portrait by Russia's President* (New York: Public Affairs, 2000), p. 139. Putin's account was endorsed by the comparably credible Boris Yeltsin in his ghostwritten memoirs. Boris Yeltsin, *Midnight Diaries*, trans. Catherine A. Fitzpatrick (New York: Public Affairs, 2000), pp. 336–38.

7. Nabi Abdullaev, "Chechen Invaders Capture Dagestani Villages," *Russian Regional Report*, vol. 4, no. 30 (August 11, 1999).

8. "Russian Forces Bogged Down in Daghestan," RFE/RL *Newsline*, vol. 3, no. 158, pt. 1 (August 16, 1999).

9. "Sergeev Denies Bombing Chechnya," RFE/RL *Newsline*, vol. 3, no. 166, pt. 1 (August 26, 1999).

10. "Putin Visits Daghestan," RFE/RL *Newsline*, vol. 3, no. 168, pt. 1 (August 30, 1999); Kisriev and Ware, "Conflict and Catharsis," p. 497.

11. "Chechen Mufti Accuses Moscow of Colluding with Rebels in Chechnya, Dagestan," BBC Monitoring of the London-based Arabic-language newspaper, *Al-Sharq al-Awsat*, January 7, 2000, JRL.

12. Mark Franchetti, "Muslim Warns of Moscow War," *Sunday Times* (London), September 19, 1999.

13. "New Incursion from Chechnya into Daghestan," RFE/RL *Newsline*, vol. 3, no. 173, pt. 1 (September 6, 1999).

14. "Heavy Fighting Continues for Chabanmakhi, Karamakhi," RFE/RL *Newsline*, vol. 3, no. 175, pt. 1 (September 8, 1999).

15. Robert Bruce Ware described the case on Johnson's Russia List, January 25, 2001. See also Simon Saradzhyan, "After One Year, Blast Probe Still Drags On," *Moscow Times*, September 15, 2000.

16. "Islamic Militants Expelled from Daghestan?" RFE/RL *Newsline*, vol. 3, no. 181, pt. 1 (September 16, 1999).

17. Jim Nichol, "Chechnya Conflict: Recent Developments," *CRS Report for Congress* (Congressional Research Service, U.S. Library of Congress, November 10, 1999). Thanks to Milton Leitenberg for a copy of this report.

18. Transcript of BBC Russian Service's telephone interview with Basaev, posted by Tom de Waal to JRL, October 4, 1999 (originally online at http://www.bbc.co.uk/russian/2909_4.htm).

19. Anne Nivat, *Chienne de Guerre: A Woman Reporter behind the Lines of the War in Chechnya*, trans. Susan Darnton (New York: Public Affairs, 2001), pp. 15–16, 250.

20. Joerg R. Mettke, interview with Chechen President Aslan Maskhadov, *Der Spiegel*, no. 39, September 27, 1999, JRL.

21. "Chechen Mufti Accuses Moscow," BBC Monitoring; Paul Klebnikov, *Godfather of the Kremlin: Boris Berezovsky and the Looting of Russia* (Harcourt, 2000), pp. 260–66.

22. Sergei Kovalev, "Can We Believe the Government on Chechnya?" *Russia Journal*, May 8–14, 2000.

23. Interview with the BBC, September 29, 1999, www.bbc.co.uk/russian/2909_4.htm, archived with the author.

24. "Putin Spells Out Terms for Talks with Chechnya," RFE/RL *Newsline*, vol. 3, no. 191, pt. 1 (September 30, 1999); "Moscow Launches Ground Campaign against Chechnya," RFE/RL *Newsline*, vol. 3, no. 192, pt. 1 (October 1, 1999).

25. "PM Says Russia No Longer Recognizes Maskhadov's Legitimacy," Agence France-Presse, October 1, 1999, in JRL; "Exodus from Chechnya Continues," RFE/RL

Newsline, vol. 3, no. 196, pt. 1 (October 7, 1999); Nichol, "Chechnya Conflict: Recent Developments."

26. "'Operation Foreigner' Cleansing Moscow of Caucasians?" RFE/RL *Newsline,* vol. 3, no. 186, pt. 1 (September 23, 1999); also David Filipov, "Moscow's Usual Suspects: Answering Blasts, Police Descend on Dark-Skinned," *Boston Globe,* September 16, 1999.

27. The best work on Islam in Russia is Aleksei Malashenko's *Islamskoe vozrozhdenie v sovremennoi Rossii* (Islamic revival in contemporary Russia) (Moscow, 1998), and *Islamskie orientiry Severnogo Kavkaza* (Islamic orientations of the North Caucasus) (Moscow, 2001).

28. From a profile prepared for the BBC by Tom de Waal and posted by him to JRL, September 7, 1999.

29. Dmitrii Belovetskii, "Salman Raduev: S Pervomaiskim privetom" (Salman Raduev: With May-Day greetings), *Ogonek,* no. 18, May 5, 1997, www.ropnet.ru/ogonyok/win/199718/18-24-27.html.

30. Transcript of telephone interview with Dudaev by members of Harvard University's Russian Research Center, February 14, 1995.

31. Georgi M. Derluguian, "Che Guevaras in Turbans," *New Left Review,* vol. 237 (September/October 1999), p. 10.

32. Timur Muzaev, "Faktor Chechni: Fenomen pobedivshego separatizma" (The Chechnya factor: The phenomenon of victorious separatism), chap. 3 in his *Etnicheskii separatizm v Rossii* (Ethnic separatism in Russia) (Moscow: Panorama, 1999); Timur Muzaev, *Chechenskaia Respublika: Organy vlasti i politicheskie sily* (The Chechen Republic: Organs of power and political forces) (Moscow: Panorama, 1995), pp. 129–30.

33. Sharon LaFraniere, "Moscow Eager to Tie Rebels in Chechnya to Bin Laden," *Washington Post,* September 26, 2001.

34. Viktor Baranets, *Poteriannaia armiia: Zapiski polkovnika Genshtaba* (Lost army: Notes of a General Staff colonel)(Moscow: Sovershenno sekretno, 1998), pp. 277–79.

35. Andrew Bennett at Georgetown University is conducting research on the lessons of the first Chechen War, drawing on the theoretical framework proposed in his book, *Condemned to Repetition? The Rise, Fall, and Reprise of Soviet-Russian Military Interventionism, 1973–1996* (MIT Press, 1999). For an initial consideration, see his paper with Becky Johnson, "If at First You Don't Succeed: Russia's 1999 Intervention in Chechnya," prepared for the International Studies Association annual conference, New Orleans, March 2002.

36. "Few Russians Consider Chechnya Part of Russia," RFE/RL *Newsline,* vol. 3, no. 55, pt. 1 (March 19, 1999).

37. Andrei Piontkovskii, "Life with an Idiot," *Russia Journal,* March 28, 2000. The etymology of the first expression, *mochit' v sortire,* is explained as follows by Catherine Fitzpatrick: *Mochit',* the verb "to soak" in Russian, is based on underworld slang meaning "to make wet or bloody," that is, to kill. And *sortire,* which comes from the French for "going out," is a crude Russian expression for "toilet." See Yeltsin, *Midnight Diaries,* p. 338, fn.

38. Piontkovskii, "Life with an Idiot."

39. Andrei Piontkovskii, "Russia Heaps Nuclear Hate on Chechnya," *Moscow Times,* September 23, 1999.

40. Fedor Gavrilov, "Enemies Are Learning from Each Other," *St. Petersburg Times,* October 22, 1999.

41. Russian First Deputy Prime Minister Boris Nemtsov, quoted on his website, "Ask Boris," www.icem.org/campaigns/no_pay_cc/nemtsov.html.

42. Pavel Fel'gengauer, "Terrorists Didn't Start the War," *St. Petersburg Times,* January 21, 2000.

43. "No Let-up in Dagestan Fighting," BBC Online Network, August 9, 1999, http://news.bbc.co.uk/hi/english/world/europe/newsid_415000/415055.stm.

44. Yeltsin, *Midnight Diaries,* p. 336.

45. Andrei Shukshin, "Putin Thrives on Russians' Pain—Pollster," Reuters report from Moscow, October 22, 1999, on JRL; Gavrilov, "Enemies Are Learning from Each Other"; Sarah Karush, "Chechen War Hits Home in Provinces," *Moscow Times,* December 7, 1999.

46. *Nezavisimaia gazeta,* October 12, 1999.

47. Andrei Piontkovskii, "The Doomed City," *Russia Journal,* April 3–9, 2000.

48. Robert Bruce Ware, "Was There a Kremlin Conspiracy in the Caucasus?" essay posted to JRL, February 6, 2000.

49. This second account would seem inconsistent with Ware's claim from personal knowledge to "affirm the appearance that the invasion caught federal forces by surprise and that they were not at all prepared," in ibid.

50. Ibid.

51. This summary draws on John B. Dunlop, "The Second Russo-Chechen War Two Years On," www.peaceinchechnya.org/paperl.htm, archived with the author. His sources include *Novaia gazeta,* January 24, 2000; a book by former Soviet and Russian military intelligence officers, *GRU Spetsnaz* (Moscow, 2000); and a chapter by Sanobar Shermatova in Dmitrii Furman, ed., *Chechnya i Rossiia* (Moscow, 1999).

52. Rendering this account more plausible is that it coincided with other purported plans to undermine Luzhkov, collectively known as "Storm in Moscow." See Peter Reddaway and Dmitri Glinksi, *The Tragedy of Russia's Reforms: Market Bolshevism against Democracy* (Washington: U.S. Institute of Peace Press, 2001), pp. 608–12.

53. Yeltsin, *Midnight Diaries,* p. 344.

54. Piontkovskii, "The Doomed City."

55. Maura Reynolds, "Moscow Has Chechnya Back—Now What?" *Los Angeles Times,* June 19, 2000.

56. Quoted in Piontkovskii, "The Doomed City."

57. The most detailed Russian account of these events is Aleksandr Litvinenko and Iurii Fel'shtinkskii, *FSB vzryvaet Rossiiu* (The FSB blows up Russia), excerpts from chap. 4, as published in *Novaia gazeta,* August 27, 2001, http://2001.novayagazeta.ru/nomer/2001/61n/n61n-s04.shtml, archived with the author. Several Western journalists have also written about it, and their accounts agree on most points: Will Englund, "Russian Bombs Set off Whispers: Was It Just a Training Exercise or a Plot to Kill Hundreds?" *Baltimore Sun,* January 14, 2000; Maura Reynolds, "Fears of Bombing Turn to Doubts for Some in Russia Terrorism," *Los Angeles Times,* January 15, 2000; Helen Womack, "Did Alexei Stumble across Russian Agents Planting a Bomb to Justify Chechen War?" *Independent* (London), January 27, 2000; John Sweeney, "Take Care Tony, That Man Has Blood on His Hands: Evidence Shows Secret Police Were behind 'Terrorist' Bomb," *Observer* (London), March 12, 2000; Marcus Warren, "Residents of 'Bomb' Flats Are Stars of Poll Drama," *Electronic Telegraph* (London), March 23, 2000.

58. Litvinenko and Fel'shtinkskii, *FSB vzryvaet Rossiiu.* The account in Englund, "Russian Bombs Set off Whispers," draws on comments by Major Vladimir Golev of the Riazan' police and differs only in minor details.

59. Litvinenko and Fel'shtinkskii, *FSB vzryvaet Rossiiu.*

60. Ibid.

61. Ibid.

62. "Ryazan Bomb Turns Out to Be Fake," RFE/RL *Newsline,* vol. 3, no. 187, pt. 1 (September 24, 1999).

63. Litvinenko and Fel'shtinkskii, *FSB vzryvaet Rossiiu.*

64. Ibid.

65. Reynolds, "Fears of Bombing."

66. Womack, "Did Alexei Stumble across Russian Agents Planting a Bomb to Justify Chechen War?"

67. Englund, "Russian Bombs Set off Whispers."

68. Litvinenko and Fel'shtinkskii, *FSB vzryvaet Rossiiu.* Tying Putin to the bombings has also been a major goal of Boris Berezovskii (to whom Litvinenko reportedly has close ties). See, for example, Carlo Bonini, "Mosca, le bombe dei Servizi," and "Quel video di TV6 che accusa il Cremlino," *La Repubblica,* January 29, 2002, pp. 14–15.

69. Englund, "Russian Bombs Set off Whispers."

70. Reynolds, "Fears of Bombing."

71. "Russian Military Releases Detailed Chechen Casualty Figures," RFE/RL *Newsline,* vol. 4, no. 18, pt. 1 (January 26, 2000).

72. Iu. M. Baturin, A. L. Il'in, V. F. Kadatskii, V. V. Kostikov, M. A. Krasnov, A. Ia. Livshits, K.V. Nikiforov, L. G. Pikhoia, G. A. Satarov, *Epokha El'tsina: Ocherki politicheskoi istorii* (The Yeltsin epoch: Sketches of a political history) (Moscow: Vagrius, 2001), p. 786. The figures for the first seven and a half months of the first war were 1,867 dead and 6,481 wounded.

73. "Obstanovku v Chechne mozhno normalizovat'" (It is possible to normalize the situation in Chechnya), *Nezavisimoe voennoe obozrenie* (Independent military review), no. 21, June 16, 2000, web version.

74. Anna Politkovskaia, "Remember Chechnya," *Washington Post,* November 14, 2001. Sergei Iastrzhembskii gave official figures as 3,438 dead and 11,661 wounded. Cited by Dmitrii Muratov, "Generals without a Colonel," *Novaia gazeta,* no. 81 (November 2001), posted on Post-Soviet Armies Newsletter, www.psan.org. The Russian news agency AVN reported somewhat lower figures for the period from August 8, 1999, to March 2002: 2,332 defense ministry personnel killed (plus 118 in Dagestan), 5,898 wounded, 26 missing; 889 Interior Ministry troops killed, 3,074 wounded. See Stephen Shenfield, Research and Analytical Supplement 7 to Johnson's Russia List 6191, April 18, 2002.

75. The Afghan war produced on average 132 deaths and 450 wounded per month on the Soviet side, with a much higher toll among the Afghan civilian population. Baturin and others, *Epokha El'tsina,* p. 708.

76. See the estimates in Dunlop, "The Second Russo-Chechen War." Among the non-Russian civilians killed were numerous journalists and aid workers, such as the American Fred Cuny.

77. Muratov, "Generals without a Colonel."

78. Reynolds, "Moscow Has Chechnya Back—Now What?"; "New Pro-Moscow Chechen Leader Inaugurated," RFE/RL *Newsline,* vol. 4, no. 120, pt. 1 (June 21, 2000).

Chapter 5

Epigraphs are from Boris Yeltsin, *Midnight Diaries*, trans. Catherine A. Fitzpatrick (New York: Public Affairs, 2000), pp. 58–59; Vladimir Putin, *First Person: An Astonishingly Frank Self-Portrait by Russia's President* (New York: Public Affairs, 2000), p. 139.

1. For a good overview, see Joan DeBardeleben, "The Development of Federalism in Russia," in Peter J. Stavrakis and others, eds., *Beyond the Monolith: The Emergence of Regionalism in Post-Soviet Russia* (Washington: Woodrow Wilson Center Press, 1997), chap. 2.

2. Daniel S. Treisman, *After the Deluge: Regional Crises and Political Consolidation in Russia* (University of Michigan Press, 1999), p. 21.

3. David D. Laitin, *Identity in Formation: The Russian-Speaking Populations in the Near Abroad* (Cornell University Press, 1998), p. 191.

4. DeBardeleben, "The Development of Federalism in Russia," p. 38. If all thirty-two ethnically defined units are included (that is, not only republics), they represent over 50 percent of Russia's territory and about two-thirds of the country's natural resources (oil, gas, gold, diamonds, timber, and so forth), another source of concern about separatism. I owe this point to Mikhail Alexseev.

5. Vladimir Socor, "Resistance in Ingushetiia . . . and Dagestan," RFE/RL *Daily Report*, no. 234 (December 13, 1994).

6. See Vladimir Socor's "Ingush Leaders' Warnings," RFE/RL *Daily Report*, no. 232 (December 9, 1994); and "Spillover Effect in Caucasus," RFE/RL *Daily Report*, no. 236 (December 15, 1994).

7. See Vladimir Socor's "More from the Regions," RFE/RL *Daily Report*, no. 235 (December 14, 1994); "Ingushetiia, Dagestan: Resistance to Russian Advance Reported," RFE/RL *Daily Report*, no. 233 (December 12, 1994); and "Spillover Effect in Caucasus."

8. John W. Slocum, "Disintegration and Consolidation: National Separatism and the Evolution of Center-Periphery Relations in the Russian Federation," Occasional Paper 19 (Cornell University Peace Studies Program, July 1995), p. 47.

9. Socor, "Spillover Effect in Caucasus"; Ustina Markus, "Marchuk Warns Ukrainian Nationalists on Chechnya," RFE/RL *Daily Report*, no. 226 (December 1, 1994); Liz Fuller, "Abkhaz, North Caucasians, Crimean Tatars Support Dudaev," RFE/RL *Daily Report*, no. 233 (December 12, 1994).

10. Starovoitova quoted in Vladimir Socor, "Critical Voices," RFE/RL *Daily Report*, no. 236 (December 15, 1994); Vorob'ev in David Remnick, *Resurrection: The Struggle for a New Russia* (Random House, 1997), p. 283; "brushfire" quotation is from Andrei Shumikhin, "The Chechen Crisis and the Future of Russia," in Roald Z. Sagdeev and Susan Eisenhower, eds., *Central Asia: Conflict, Resolution, and Change* (Chevy Chase, Md.: CPSS Press, 1995), p. 29.

11. Carlotta Gall and Thomas de Waal, *Chechnya: Calamity in the Caucasus* (New York University Press, 1998), pp. 223–24.

12. Transcript of my interview with Mikhail Stoliarov, at the office of the permanent representative of the Republic of Tatarstan in Moscow, November 4, 1998.

13. Timur Muzaev, *Etnicheskii separatizm v Rossii* (Ethnic separatism in Russia) (Moscow: Panorama, 1999), p. 75, proposes a figure of 100,000 refugees. The higher estimate comes from the Dagestan office of the UN High Commissioner for

Refugees. Thanks to Robert Bruce Ware, e-mail correspondence, June 6, 2002, for this information.

14. Susan Goodrich Lehmann, "Islam and Ethnicity in the Republics of Russia," *Post-Soviet Affairs,* vol. 13, no. 1 (1997), pp. 78–103.

15. Yoshiko Herrera has pointed out to me that this common ranking of republics, with Chechnya at the bottom, is not founded on very reliable data, however plausible it seems. E-mail correspondence, June 4, 2002. Georgi Derluguian's forthcoming book on Chechnya will explore some of the peculiarities of the Chechen economy—always poor, but nevertheless viable—and how the breakup of the USSR particularly disrupted it.

16. Enver Kisriev, *Respublika Dagestan: Model' etnologicheskogo monitoringa* (Republic of Dagestan: Model of ethnological monitoring) (Moscow: Institute of Ethnology and Anthropology, Russian Academy of Sciences, 1999), pp. 60–61.

17. Transcript of my interview with Mamai Mamaev, Moscow, November 10, 1998.

18. Yoshiko Herrera, "Imagined Economies: Regionalism in the Russian Federation," paper presented to a conference of the Program on New Approaches to Russian Security, Rockport, Mass., May 1999.

19. Taimaz Abubakarov, *Rezhim Dzhokhara Dudaeva: Pravda i vymysel* (The regime of Dzhokhar Dudaev: Truth and falsehoods) (Moscow: INSAN, 1998).

20. Robert Chenciner, *Daghestan: Tradition and Survival* (St. Martin's Press, 1997), pp. 1–2 and jacket blurb.

21. Sebastian Smith, *Allah's Mountains: Politics and War in the Russian Caucasus* (London: I. B. Tauris, 1998), p. 86. The applicability of the "consociational" model to Dagestan is explored in the various works by Kisriev and Ware cited throughout this chapter.

22. Enver Kisriev and Robert Bruce Ware, "Conflict and Catharsis: A Report on Developments in Dagestan Following the Incursions of August and September 1999," *Nationalities Papers,* vol. 28, no. 3 (2000), pp. 479–522, at p. 485.

23. Abubakarov, *Rezhim Dzhokhara Dudaeva,* pp. 79–80, 100–01.

24. Kisriev and Ware, "Conflict and Catharsis," p. 486. See also their chapter, "Political Stability and Ethnic Parity: Why Is There Peace in Dagestan?" in Mikhail A. Alexseev, ed., *Center-Periphery Conflict in Post-Soviet Russia: A Federation Imperiled* (London: Macmillan, 1999), pp. 95–130. In subsequent work, the authors have qualified their emphasis on the *djamaat,* as "*djamaat* connections between leaders and followers did not emerge as a central theme" in interviews and surveys they conducted. They did, nevertheless, find other sources of stability. See Robert Bruce Ware, "Ethnicity and Democracy in Dagestan," report submitted to the National Council for Eurasian and East European Research, Washington, November 2001.

25. See the following articles by Il'ia Maksakov: "V Makhachkale trebuiut otstavki Magomedova" (In Makhachkala, Magomedov's resignation is demanded), *Nezavisimaia gazeta,* September 1, 1998; "Nadir Kachilaev ne nameren skryvat'sia" (Nadir Kachilaev does not intend to hide), *Nezavisimaia gazeta,* September 23, 1998; "Bor'ba s prestupnost'iu ne prekrashchaetsia" (The struggle with crime is not stopping), *Nezavisimaia gazeta,* October 6, 1998; and "V Dagestane rasprostraniaiutsia anonimnye listovki" (In Dagestan, anonymous lists are spread around), *Nezavisimaia gazeta,* October 20, 1998.

26. For a recent overview, see Vladimir Bobrovnikov, "Islam na postsovetskom Severnom Kavkaze (Dagestan): Mify i realii" (Islam in the post-Soviet North Caucasus [Dagestan]: Myths and realities), in Aleksei Malashenko and Martha Brill Olcott, eds.,

Islam na postsovetskom prostranstve: vzgliad iznutri (Islam in the post-Soviet space: A view from within) (Moscow: Carnegie Center, 2001), available at http://pubs. carnegie.ru/books/2001/07am2/.

27. Il'ia Maksakov, "Dagestan ostanetsia edinoi nedelimoi respublikoi v sostave RF" (Dagestan will remain a single, indivisible republic within the structure of the RF [Russian Federation]), *Nezavisimaia gazeta,* May 12, 1998, interview with Magomedsalikh Gusaev, Dagestan's minister of nationality affairs and external relations.

28. The role of religion in Dagestan is more complicated than this summary suggests. For some valuable empirical findings and sensible hypotheses, see Ware, "Ethnicity and Democracy in Dagestan."

29. Kisriev and Ware, "Conflict and Catharsis."

30. Ibid., p. 480.

31. Ibid., pp. 480–81; and Kisriev, *Respublika Dagestan,* p. 60.

32. For these points and the following summary paragraph, see Kisriev and Ware, pp. 480–81.

33. Stephen D. Shenfield, "What Was the 'Tatarstan Model'?" Research and Analytical Supplement, Issue 1, JRL (September 4, 2001).

34. The text of the treaty and many subsequent agreements with Moscow is found in *Suverennyi Tatarstan* (Sovereign Tatarstan) (Moscow: INSAN, 1997), published by the Plenipotentiary Representative of Tatarstan to the Russian Federation.

35. *Chto nuzhno znat' o narodakh Rossii: Spravochnik dli gosudarstvennykh sluzhashchikh* (What one needs to know about the peoples of Russia: A handbook for state officials) (Moscow: Skriptorii, Russkii mir, 1999), pp. 169–70 and appended maps; Muzaev, *Etnicheskii separatizm,* pp. 176–77; Katherine E. Graney, "The Volga Tatars: Diasporas and the Politics of Federalism," in Charles King and Neil J. Melvin, eds., *Nations Abroad: Diaspora Politics and International Relations in the Former Soviet Union* (Boulder, Colo.: Westview Press, 1998), chap. 7.

36. Edward W. Walker, "Negotiating Autonomy: Tatarstan, Asymmetrical Federalism, and State Consolidation in Russia," in Metta Spencer, ed., *Separatism: Democracy and Disintegration* (Lanham, Md.: Rowman and Littlefield, 1998), pp. 227–52, at p. 230.

37. A. V. Gromov and O. S. Kuzin, *Neformaly: Kto est' kto?* (Informals: Who's Who?)(Moscow, 1990); M. Steven Fish, *Democracy from Scratch: Opposition and Regime in the New Russian Revolution* (Princeton University Press, 1995); Vyacheslav Igrunov, "Public Movements: From Protest to Political Self-Consciousness," and Andrei Fadin, "Emerging Political Institutions: From Informals to Multiparty Democracy," both in Brad Roberts and Nina Belyaeva, eds., *After Perestroika: Democracy in the Soviet Union* (Washington: Center for Strategic and International Studies, 1991).

38. Muzaev, *Etnicheskii separatizm,* p. 178; Sergei Kondrashov, *Nationalism and the Drive for Sovereignty in Tatarstan, 1988–1992: Origins and Development* (St. Martin's Press, 2000), pp. 116–17.

39. The concept of ethnic out-bidding comes from Alvin Rabushka and Kenneth Shepsle, *Politics in Plural Societies: A Theory of Political Instability* (Columbus, Ohio: Merrill, 1972); see the discussion in Elise Giuliano, "Nationalism in a Socialist Company Town: Tatars, Russians, and the Kamskii Automobile Works (KamAZ)," paper presented to the MacArthur Foundation CASPIC conference, University of Chicago, May 1–2, 1999.

40. Muzaev, *Etnicheskii separatizm,* p. 178.

41. Uli Schamiloglu, "The Tatar Public Center and Current Tatar Concerns," *Report on the USSR*, December 22, 1989, pp. 11–15, at p. 12.

42. Kondrashov, *Nationalism and the Drive for Sovereignty in Tatarstan*, pp. 92–93.

43. Muzaev, *Etnicheskii separatizm*, p. 179.

44. Lehmann, "Islam and Ethnicity in the Republics of Russia," p. 83, table 2.

45. Schamiloglu, "The Tatar Public Center," pp. 11–15, at p. 12. For a discussion of the regional mobilization of the "haves" against redistribution of economic resources to the "have-nots" during the *perestroika* era, see Philip Roeder, "Soviet Federalism and Ethnic Mobilization," *World Politics*, vol. 43 (January 1991), pp. 196–232; and Donna Bahry, "Perestroika and the Debate over Territorial Decentralization," *Harriman Institute Forum*, vol. 2 (May 1989).

46. Edward W. Walker, "Negotiating Autonomy: Tatarstan, Asymmetrical Federalism, and State Consolidation in Russia," in Spencer, ed., *Separatism: Democracy and Disintegration*, pp. 227–52, at p. 230.

47. Lilia V. Sagitova, "Interesy sotsial'nykh grupp v kontekste etnokul'turnoi i etnopoliticheskoi integratsii Tatarstanskogo soobshchestva" (The interests of social groups in the context of ethnocultural and ethnopolitical integration in Tatarstan society), Institute of History, Tatarstan Academy of Sciences, Kazan', June 2001.

48. Muzaev, *Etnicheskii separatizm*, p. 176.

49. R. S. Khakimov, "Ob osnovakh asimmetrichnosti Rossiiskoi federatsii" (On the bases of the asymmetry of the Russian Federation), in L. M. Drobizheva, *Asimmetrichnaia federatsiia: vzgliad iz tsentra, respublik i oblastei* (Asymmetrical federation: The view from the center, the republics, and the provinces) (Moscow: Institute of Sociology of the Russian Academy of Sciences, 1998), p. 37.

50. Viktor A. Shnirel'man, *Who Gets the Past? Competition for Ancestors among Non-Russian Intellectuals in Russia* (Washington: Woodrow Wilson Center Press, 1996), p. 20.

51. Ibid., pp. 50–51. Nikolai Petrov, in e-mail correspondence, February 9, 2002, points out that Kazan' University has had a strong Department of Economic Geography, suggesting that Shnirel'man's comparison may be somewhat exaggerated.

52. Kondrashov, *Nationalism and the Drive for Sovereignty in Tatarstan*, chap. 8; Michael McFaul and Nikolai Petrov, *Politicheskii almanakh Rossii 1997* (Political almanac of Russia, 1997), vol. 2, *Sotsial'no-politicheskie portrety regionov* (Sociopolitical portraits of the regions), book 1 (Moscow: Carnegie Center, 1998), pp. 236–38.

53. A collection of documents pertaining to these events was assembled by Gorbachev's partisans and published as *Soiuz mozhno bylo sokhranit'* (The union could have been preserved) (Moscow: Izd. Aprel'-85, 1995). Perspectives from the coup plotters themselves I gathered at a conference in Moscow, June 21–29, 1999, with former KGB head Vladimir Kriuchkov, former defense minister Dmitrii Iazov, and Communist Party secretary Oleg Baklanov, among others.

54. *Sovetskaia Tatariia*, August 8, 1990, quoted in *Soiuz mozhno bylo sokhranit'*, pp. 109–110.

55. Kondrashov, *Nationalism and the Drive for Sovereignty in Tatarstan*, p. 105.

56. Ibid., pp. 105–06, 172–73.

57. Ibid., p. 174.

58. Muzaev, *Etnicheskii separatizm*, p. 179.

59. Transcript of my interview with Mikhail Stoliarov, at the office of the permanent representative of the Republic of Tatarstan in Moscow, November 4, 1998.

60. Kondrashov, *Nationalism and the Drive for Sovereignty in Tatarstan*, p. 180.

61. Matthew Evangelista, "An Interview with Galina Starovoytova," *Post-Soviet Affairs*, vol. 15 (July–September 1999), www.vhwinston.com/psa/abstract/af990304.htm.

62. *Sovetskaia Tatariia*, September 18, 1991, cited in Kondrashov, *Nationalism and the Drive for Sovereignty in Tatarstan*, p. 107. For a further development of her own views on the legitimacy of secession, see Galina Starovoitova, *National Self-Determination: Approaches and Case Studies*, Occasional Paper 27 (Brown University, Thomas J. Watson Jr. Institute for International Studies, 1997).

63. Kondrashov, *Nationalism and the Drive for Sovereignty in Tatarstan*, p. 177.

64. Ibid., p. 176; for discussion of Naberezhnye Chelny, site of the Kamskii automobile complex, see R. G. Akhmetov, "KAMAZ—uzel protivorechii mezhdu Moskvoi i Kazan'iu" (KAMAZ—A knot of contradictions between Moscow and Kazan'), in Drobizheva, *Asimmetrichnaia federatsiia*, chap. 6; and Giuliano, "Nationalism in a Socialist Company Town."

65. Khakimov, "Ob osnovakh asimmetrichnosti Rossiiskoi federatsii," p. 39; interview with Mikhail Stoliarov, November 1998.

66. Kondrashov, *Nationalism and the Drive for Sovereignty in Tatarstan*, p. 189.

67. Ibid., pp. 183–84.

68. Pauline Jones Luong, "Tatarstan: Elite Bargaining and Ethnic Separatism," in Timothy J. Colton and Jerry F. Hough, eds., *Growing Pains: Russian Democracy and the Election of 1993* (Brookings, 1998).

69. G. N. Isaev, "Otnoshenie naseleniia k suverenitetu respubliki v Tatarstane" (Attitude of the population toward sovereignty of the republic in Tatarstan), in Drobizheva, *Asimmetrichnaia federatsiia*, pp. 75–80.

70. Sagitova, "Interesy sotsial'nykh grupp."

71. "Zakliuchenie Komiteta po Delam Federatsii i Regional'noi Politike na Dogovor Rossiiskoi Federatsii i Respubliki Tatarstan 'O Razgranichenii predmetov vedeniia i vzaimnom delegirovanii polnomochii mezhdu organami gosudarstvennoi vlasti Rossiiskoi Federatsii i organami gosudarstvennoi vlasti Respubliki Tatarstan'" (Conclusion of the Committee on Federal and Regional Affairs about the Agreement of the Russian Federation and the Republic of Tatarstan "On the delimitation of objects of jurisdiction and mutual delegation of authorities between the organs of state power of the Russian Federation and the organs of state power of the Republic of Tatarstan"), March 22, 1994, reprinted in Vladimir Lysenko, *Ot Tatarstan do Chechni (stanovlenie novogo rossiiskogo federalizma)* (From Tatarstan to Chechnya [the coming of a new Russian federalism]) (Moscow: Institute of Contemporary Politics, 1995), pp. 268–70.

72. Vladimir Lysenko, "Tatarstan, Bashkortostan, dalee bez ostanovok . . . 'Tsepnaia reaktsia' podpisaniia dvustoronnikh dogovorov s sub"ektami federatsii mozhet privesti k rasvalu Rossii" (Tatarstan, Bashkortostan, further without stopping . . . A "chain reaction" of signing of bilateral agreements with subjects of the Federation can lead to the breakup of Russia), originally published in *Rossiiskaia gazeta*, June 26, 1994, reprinted in Lysenko, *Ot Tatarstan do Chechni* pp. 119–21.

73. "Zaiavlenie koordinatsionnogo soveta Respublikanskoi Partii RF 'O tragicheskikh sobytiiakh v Chechenskoi Respublike'" (Declaration of the coordinating council of the Republican Party of the Russian Federation "On the tragic events in the Chechen Republic"), in Lysenko, *Ot Tatarstan do Chechni*, pp. 169–70.

74. *Vneshniaia politika Tatarstana: pretenzii i real'nost'* (Tatarstan's foreign policy; pretensions and reality), special issue of *Panorama-Forum* (Kazan'), no. 16 (Summer 1997); Edward W. Walker, "Negotiating Autonomy: Tatarstan, Asymmetrical Federalism, and State Consolidation in Russia," chap. 10 in Spencer, *Separatism*; Georgi Derluguian, "Historical Sociological Interpretation of Nationalist Separatism in the Four Former Soviet Autonomous Republics: Tataria, Chechnya, Abkhazia, and Ajaria," Ph.D. diss., Department of Sociology, State University of New York at Binghamton, 1995.

75. Georgi M. Derluguian, "Ethnofederalism and Ethnonationalism in the Separatist Politics of Chechnya and Tatarstan: Sources or Resources?" *International Journal of Public Administration*, vol. 22, nos. 9 and 10 (1999), pp. 1387–1428.

76. Ibid., pp. 1393-1399.

77. Kondrashov, *Nationalism and the Drive for Sovereignty in Tatarstan*, p. 127. Derluguian, "Ethnofederalism and Ethnonationalism," also points out the nonethnic character of crime in *Tatarstan*, p. 1404.

78. F. Bairamova, "Nastoiashchii Tatarin ispytyvaetsia na ploshchadi," *Vecherniaia Kazan'*, October 23, 1991, quoted in Shnirel'man, *Who Gets the Past?* p. 53.

79. Hobsbawm's remarks to a meeting of the American Anthropological Association in November 1991 were quoted by Robert M. Hayden, "The Triumph of Chauvinistic Nationalisms in Yugoslavia: Bleak Implications for Anthropology," *Anthropology of East Europe Review*, vol. 11 (Autumn 1993), www.depaul.edu/~rrotenbe/aeer/aeer11_1/hayden.html.

80. Khakimov, "Ob osnovakh asimmetrichnosti Rossiiskoi federatsii," p. 45. On Khakimov's role in the Tatar nationalist movement, see Kondrashov, *Nationalism and the Drive for Sovereignty in Tatarstan*, pp. 125–26.

81. Mary McAuley, *Russia's Politics of Uncertainty* (Cambridge University Press, 1997), p. 80.

82. Jessica Eve Stern, "Moscow Meltdown: Can Russia Survive?" *International Security*, vol. 18 (Spring 1994), pp. 40–65; Robert Orttung, "Tatarstan and Bashkortostan to Unite?" *Russian Regional Report*, vol. 2, no. 29 (September 1997).

83. Leokadiia Drobizheva and Viktoriia Koroteeva, "Social Status and Ethnicity in Russian Republics," Kennan Institute meeting report, vol. 17, no. 16 (2000), on JRL.

84. Dmitrii Nikitin, "Bashkirskie tatary lishilis' iazyka" (Bashkir Tatars are deprived of their language), *Kommersant'*, January 22, 1999; "Bashkortostan Parliament Passes Controversial Language Law," RFE/RL *Newsline*, vol. 3, no. 15, pt. 1 (January 22, 1999); "Tatars Protest Bashkortostan Language Law," RFE/RL *Newsline*, vol. 3, no. 14, pt. 1 (January 21, 1999). On the electoral advantages accruing to Bashkirs, see Henry Hale, "Bashkortostan: The Logic of Ethnic Machine Politics and the Consolidation of Democracy," in Colton and Hough, *Growing Pains*.

85. Muzaev, *Etnicheskii separatizm*, p. 65.

86. Lehmann, "Islam and Ethnicity in the Republics of Russia," p. 83, table 2.

87. Filial' Shaiakhmetov, "Demokratizatsiia Bashkirskogo obshchestva i Islam" (Democratization of Bashkir society and Islam), in A. B. Iunovskii and A.V. Malashenko, *Etnichnost' i konfessional'naia traditsiia v volgo-ural'skom regione Rossii* (Ethnicity and confessional tradition in the Volga-Urals region of Russia) (Moscow: Carnegie Center, 1998), p. 30.

88. "Prilozhenie k Federativnomu dogovoru ot Respubliki Bashkortostan" (Supplement to the Federative Treaty from the Republic of Bashkortostan), March 31, 1992. Thanks to Irek Ablaev for my copy. For some discussion, see Khakimov, "Ob osnovakh asimmetrichnosti Rossiiskoi federatsii," pp. 38–39.

89. Lysenko, "Tatarstan, Bashkortostan, dalee bez ostanovok...," pp. 119–21.

90. On this point, see also R. G. Kuzeev, *Demokratiia, grazhdanstvennost', etnichnost'* (Democracy, citizenship, ethnicity) (Moscow: TsIMO, 1999).

91. "Prilozhenie k Federativnomu dogovoru ot Respubliki Bashkortostan," articles 1–4.

92. "O gosudarstvennom regulirovanii vneshnetorgovoi deitel'nosti v Respublike Bashkortostan" (On the state regulation of foreign trade activity in the Republic of Bashkortostan), March 24, 1998; and "Ob inostrannoi investitsionnoi deitel'nosti v Respublike Bashkortostan" (On foreign investment activity in the Republic of Bashkortostan), December 15, 1997. Both documents courtesy of the Bashkortostan representative to the Russian Federation, Moscow.

93. "Bashkortostan Authorities Consolidate Control over Regional Energy Sector," *Russian Regional Report,* vol. 3, no. 38 (September 23, 1998).

94. Henry Hale, "The Regionalization of Autocracy in Russia," PONARS Memo 42, November 1998, www.csis.org/ruseura/ponars/policymemos/pm_index.htm#1998. For a survey of relations between regional elites and economic interests, including organized crime, see N. Lapina and A. Chirikova, *Regional'nye elity v RF: modeli povedeniia i politicheskie orientatsii* (Regional elites in the Russian Federation: Models of behavior and political orientation), vol. 6 of *Federalizm, regional'noe upravlenie i mestnoe samoupravlenie* (Federalism, regional administration, and local self-government) (Moscow: INION, 1999).

95. Sam Nunn and Adam N. Stulberg, "The Many Faces of Modern Russia," *Foreign Affairs,* vol. 79 (March/April 2000), p. 45.

96. For an engaging political-anthropological account of Sakhalin, see Bruce Grant, *In the Soviet House of Culture: A Century of Perestroikas* (Princeton University Press, 1995).

97. Sakhalin's population declined from 713,000 in 1991 and has continued to do so. Mikhail A. Alexseev, "Sakhalin: The Dying Corner of the Empire," *Russian Regional Report,* vol. 4, no. 39 (October 21, 1999).

98. Steven L. Solnick, "Russian Regional Politics and the 'Northern Territories,'" paper prepared for the 1999 International Symposium, Miyazaki-Tokyo, November 1999.

99. This section draws heavily on the outstanding analysis of Mikhail A. Alexseev and Tamara Troyakova, "A Mirage of the 'Amur California': Regional Identity and Economic Incentives for Political Separatism in Primorskiy Kray," in Mikhail A. Alexseev, ed., *Center-Periphery Conflict in Post-Soviet Russia: A Federation Imperiled* (London: Macmillan, 1999), chap. 6. See also Alexseev and Troyakova, "Watching Out for Regional Separatism in the Russian Far East: Ideological Cueing of Territorial Security, Economic Incentives and Cultural Identity," *Geopolitics,* vol. 4 (Winter 1999), pp. 120–44; Tamara Troyakova, "Regional Policy in the Russian Far East and the Rise of Localism in Primorye," *Journal of East Asian Affairs,* vol. 9 (Fall 1995); and Tamara Troyakova, "Primorsky Republic: Myth or Reality?" *Communist Economies and Economic Transformation,* vol. 10 (September 1998), pp. 391–404.

100. Vladimir Gel'man, "Democratic Gains Reversed in Regional Elections from Moscow to Sakha," *Russian Regional Report,* vol. 7, no. 5 (February 6, 2002).

101. Alexseev and Troyakova, "A Mirage of the 'Amur California'," pp. 208, 210, Nazdratenko quotation on p. 214.

102. Ibid., pp. 216–17.

103. Ibid., pp. 219–20.

104. Michael McFaul, "The Far Eastern Challenge to Russian Federalism: Myths and Realities," in Sherman Garnett, ed., *Rapprochement or Rivalry? Russian-Chinese Relations in a Changing Asia* (Washington: Carnegie Endowment for International Peace, 1999); and McFaul, *Russia's Unfinished Revolution: Political Change from Gorbachev to Putin* (Cornell University Press, 2001), p. 96.

105. Alexseev and Troyakova, "A Mirage of the 'Amur California'," pp. 222–23.

106. Peter Kirkow, "Regional Warlordism in Russia: The Case of Primorskii Krai," *Europe-Asia Studies,* vol. 47 (September 1995), pp. 923–47; and e-mail exchange with Mikhail Alexseev, November 6, 2001.

107. Alexseev and Tamara Troyakova, "A Mirage of the 'Amur California'," pp. 224–26.

108. McFaul, "Far Eastern Challenge."

109. Geoffrey York, "In Russia's Primorsky Region, Corruption Runs Rampant and the Governor Calls the Shots," *Toronto Globe and Mail,* July 11, 1997, quoted in McFaul, "Far Eastern Challenge."

110. Quoted in McFaul, "Far Eastern Challenge."

111. This is a major theme of McAuley, *Russia's Politics of Uncertainty;* and Peter Kirkow, *Russia's Provinces: Authoritarian Transformation versus Local Autonomy?* (St. Martin's Press, 1998).

112. An excellent account of the historical and legal dimensions of this issue is Valentin A. Povarchuk, "The Unresolved Dispute over the Northern Territories/Southern Kurils and Russo-Japanese Relations" (Senior Honors Thesis, Department of Government, Cornell University, May 2000).

113. Alexseev and Troyakova, "A Mirage of the 'Amur California'," pp. 228–30.

114. Andrew Yorke, "Putin and the Oligarchs: More Cooperation than Conflict So Far," *Russian Regional Report,* vol. 7, no. 5 (February 6, 2002).

115. Povarchuk, "Unresolved Dispute," p. 105. For an early and enthusiastic account of Fedorov and his reformist plans, see Francis X. Clines, "Outsider on a Soviet Island Builds a Free-Market Model," *New York Times,* October 15, 1990.

116. See, for example, Vasilii Golovnin, "Sekretnyi protokol ob osoboi zone" (Secret protocol about a special zone), *Izvestiia,* November 4,1998.

117. In Russian: Na Kurilakh u nas khotia i ne rai, no zato i ne samurai! "Oi, Mama, Shikotan!" *Profil',* May 21, 2001, pp. 14–17.

118. Povarchuk, "Unresolved Dispute," p. 106.

119. Solnick, "Russian Regional Politics and the 'Northern Territories'," p. 4.

120. Andrei Ivanov, "Osobaia ekonomicheskaia zona Kuril'skie ostrova" (Special economic zone of the Kuril Islands), *Kommersant* (Daily), January 20, 1999.

121. Floriana Fossato, "Sakhalin: Waiting for Oil but Patience Is Running Out," RFE/RL *Newsline,* vol. 2, no. 203, pt. 1, October 20, 1998; quotation from *Moscow Times,* May 11, 1999.

122. Russell Working, "Sakhalin Is a 'Giant Gas Pump on the Pacific Rim.' So Why Is It Taking So Long to Get Out the Petroleum?" *Vladivostok News*, September 18, 1998, wysiwyg://252/http://vn.vladnews.ru/1998/current/text/sakh1.html, archived with the author.

123. "Sakhalin Oblast," *Russian Regional Report* website, http://archive.tol.cz/ Elections/Russia/Regions/About/Sakhalin.html#History.

124. Mikhail Bugaev, "Sakhalinskii rynok: khronika vzletov i padenii" (The Sakhalin market: chronicle of rises and falls), *Svobodnyi Sakhalin* (Free Sakhalin), September 17, 1998, online version. The economy showed little improvement even a year later. See Alexseev, "Sakhalin: The Dying Corner of the Empire."

125. Transcript of my interview with Vladimir Shapoval, November 4, 1998, Moscow.

126. "Kuril Residents Want Japan to Lease Their Island," RFE/RL *Newsline*, vol. 2, no. 209, pt. 1 (October 29, 1998).

127. Alexseev, "Sakhalin: The Dying Corner of the Empire."

128. Ch. M. Taksami, *Nivkhi: Sovremennoe khoziaistvo, kul'tura i byt* (Nivkhi: Contemporary economy, culture, and way of life) (Leningrad: Nauka, 1967); E. A. Kreinovich, *Nivkhgu: Zagodchnye obitateli Sakhalina i Amura* (Nivkhi: Enigmatic inhabitants of Sakhalin and Amur) (Moscow: Nauka, 1973). In his introduction to Kreinovich's book, D. A. Ol'derogge explains that in the language of the Nivkhi, *nivkhgu* means both "Nivkhi" and "people" in general, the title deliberately reflecting the author's affection for his subjects as human beings. For a discussion of how Russians have studied and interacted with Nivkhi, see Grant, *In the Soviet House of Culture.*

129. The lower figure comes from Peter Rutland, "Sakhalin Waits for Oil and Gas Wealth," *Russian Regional Report,* vol. 4, no. 30 (August 11, 1999); the higher one from my interview with Vladimir Shapoval, November 4, 1998, Moscow.

130. Bruce Grant, "The Nivkhi: Conscience of Sakhalin," *Geographical Magazine,* February 1992, p. 32.

131. Russell Working, "Nivkh Novelist Wants Reparations," *Vladivostok News,* August 21, 1998.

132. Alexseev and Troyakova, "A Mirage of the 'Amur California,'" p. 241.

133. Shapoval interview, November 4, 1998, Moscow.

134. Rafael' Khakimov, ed., *Ekonomika Tatarstana posle 17 avgusta* (Tatarstan's economy after August 17), special issue of *Panorama-Forum* (Kazan'), no. 21 (1999).

135. Stoliarov interview, November 4, 1998, Moscow.

136. Transcript of my interview with Irek Ablaev, plenipotentiary representative of Bashkortostan in Moscow, November 13, 1998.

137. Akhmetov, "KAMAZ," p. 95.

138. Interview with Ablaev, November 13, 1998.

Chapter 6

Epigraphs are, respectively, from Pierre-Joseph Proudhon, *La Fédération et L'Unité en Italie* (Federation and unity in Italy) (Paris: E. Dentu, 1862), p. 25; Agence France-Presse, "Run-Off in Ingush Presidential Vote Poses Test for Russia's Putin," April 29,

2002; Natalia Dinello, "What's So Great about Novgorod the Great: Trisectoral Cooperation and Symbolic Management," report to the National Council for Eurasian and East European Research (Washington, June 3, 2001), p. 8.

1. Quoted in Lilia V. Sagitova, "Interesy sotsial'nykh grupp v kontekste etnokul'-turnoi i etnopoliticheskoi integratsii Tatarstanskogo soobshchestva" (The interests of social groups in the context of ethnocultural and ethnopolitical integration in Tatarstan society), Institute of History, Tatarstan Academy of Sciences, Kazan', June 2001.

2. Quoted in Daniel S. Treisman, *After the Deluge: Regional Crises and the Political Consolidation in Russia* (University of Michigan Press, 1999), p. 15.

3. Interview with Mikhail Stoliarov, at the office of the permanent representative of the Republic of Tatarstan in Moscow, November 13, 1998.

4. Interview with Vakha Khasanov, Chechen "ambassador," Moscow, November 4, 1998. When relations with Russia continued to deteriorate, despite Khasanov's constructive approach, Grozny replaced him with a more recalcitrant representative.

5. Quoted in Mikhail A. Alexseev, ed., *Center-Periphery Conflict in Post-Soviet Russia: A Federation Imperiled* (London: Macmillan, 1999), p. 2.

6. Quoted in Matthew Evangelista, "Russia's Fragile Union," *Bulletin of the Atomic Scientists*, vol. 55 (May/June 1999), www.bullatomsci.org/issues/1999/mj99/mj99evangelista.html.

7. An excellent overview and evaluation of Putin's reform is Nikolai Petrov, "Seven Faces of Putin's Russia: Federal Districts as the New Level of State-Territorial Composition," *Security Dialogue*, vol. 33 (March 2002), pp. 73–91. Highlighting the positive effects of the reforms is Gordon M. Hahn, "Long Arms of Putin's Reform Reaching Russia's Regions," *Russia Journal*, June 14–20, 2002.

8. Matthew Evangelista, "An Interview with Galina Starovoytova," *Post-Soviet Affairs*, vol. 15 (July–September 1999), www.vhwinston.com/psa/abstract/af990304.html.

9. "Russia's Regions: Beyond the Kremlin's Walls," *Economist*, May 20–26, 2000.

10. "Putin Proposes Changes to Parliament, Calls for Stronger State," BBC Monitoring of Russian Public TV, Moscow, May 17, 2000, JRL.

11. RFE/RL Russian Federation Report, no. 17 (May 10, 2000).

12. Quoted in the *Moscow Times*, September 1, 2000.

13. RFE/RL Russian Federation Report, no. 36 (October 4, 2000).

14. Quoted in RFE/RL Russian Federation Report, vol. 2, no. 24 (June 28, 2000).

15. Poll cited in Vitalii Golovachev, "Order at Any Price?" *Trud*, translated by RIA Novosti (June 15, 2000).

16. Evangelista, "An Interview with Galina Starovoytova."

17. Henry Hale, "The Regionalization of Autocracy in Russia," PONARS Memo 42 (November 1998), www.csis.org/ruseura/ponars/policymemos/pm_index,htm#1998.

18. N. Lapina and A. Chirikova, *Regional'nye elity v RF: modeli povedeniia i politicheskie orientatsii* (Regional elites in the Russian Federation: Models of behavior and political orientation), vol. 6 of *Federalizm, regional'noe upravlenie i mestnoe samoupravlenie* (Federalism, regional administration, and local self-government) (Moscow: INION, 1999), esp. pp. 181–86.

19. Georgi M. Derluguian, "A Soviet General and Nation Building," *Chicago Tribune*, October 28, 2001.

20. Ibid.

21. Robert Coalson, ed., *The Silent Regions* (Moscow: Sashcko, 1999), www.gdf.ru/books/books/silence/index.html. The findings are summarized in Stephen D. Shenfield, ed., *JRL Research and Analytical Supplement*, no. 6 (April 2002).

22. This section draws on several sources, including: Iulia Latynina, "Perilous Incompetence in Ingushetia," *Moscow Times*, April 10, 2002; Agence France-Presse, "Run-Off in Ingush Presidential Vote Poses Test for Russia's Putin," April 29, 2002; "Kremlin's Candidate Replaces Aushev in Ingushetiya," *Russian Regional Report*, vol. 7 (May 8, 2002); "Kremlin-Backed Zyazikov Scores 'Surprise' Win in Ingushetia," *Jamestown Foundation Monitor*, April 30, 2002.

23. Cited in "Kremlin-Backed Zyazikov Scores 'Surprise' Win in Ingushetia."

24. "Run-off in Ingush Presidential Vote Poses Test for Russia's Putin."

25. "Aushev Loudly Resigns from Federation Council," RFE/RL Russian Federation Report, vol. 4, no. 15 (April 24, 2002).

26. "Kremlin-Backed Zyazikov Scores 'Surprise' Win in Ingushetia."

27. Andrei Babitskii, testimony before the Commission on Security and Cooperation in Europe on Developments in the Chechen Conflict (Washington, May 9, 2002), JRL.

28. "Politkovskaya: Kremlin Seeks to Create a 'Vainakh Republic,'" *Jamestown Foundation Monitor*, April 18, 2002, citing her article in *Novaia gazeta* of the same date.

29. Robert Bruce Ware and Enver Kisriev, "Russian Recentralization Arrives in the Republic of Dagestan: Implications for Institutional Integrity and Political Stability," *East European Constitutional Review*, vol. 10 (Winter 2001), www.law.nyu.edu/eecr/vol10num1/special/warekisriev.html.

Chapter 7

Epigraphs are from E. H. Carr, *The Twenty Years' Crisis, 1919–1939: An Introduction to the Study of International Relations* (Harper and Row, 1964; reprint of 2d ed., 1946); Carlotta Gall and Thomas de Waal, *Chechnya: Calamity in the Caucasus* (New York University Press, 1998), p. 176.

1. General (ret.) Paul Aussaresses, *Services spéciaux: Algérie 1955–1957* (Paris: Perrin, 2001); Benjamin Stora, *Algeria, 1830–2000: A Short History* (Cornell University Press, 2001); Alistair Horne, *A Savage War of Peace: Algeria 1954–1962* (Viking Press, 1978).

2. My thinking about this issue has benefited from discussions stimulated by Vadim Volkov's comments at a conference of the Program on New Approaches to Russian Security, Nizhnii Novgorod, May 31, 2001.

3. For a compatible account of the problem, see Sarah Mendelson, "Russians' Rights Imperiled: Has Anybody Noticed?" *International Security*, vol. 26 (Spring 2002).

4. Section 1, chap. 1, art. 15, pt. 4. The text is available on many websites, for example, www.russia.net/~oldrn/politics/constitution/.

5. Vladimir Galitskii, "Voina v pravovom vakuume: zakony—ne pomekha, a pomoshch' v bor'be s 'vnytrennim vragom'" (War in a legal vacuum: Laws are not a hindrance but a help in the struggle with the "internal enemy"), *Nezavisimoe voennoe obozrenie* (Independent military review), no. 21 (June 16, 2000), Internet version.

6. Adam Roberts and Richard Guelff, eds., *Documents on the Laws of War*, 3d ed. (Oxford University Press, 2000).

7. In February 1995 members of the Estonian parliament unanimously voted for the Estonian government to recognize Chechnya's independence, but it did not do so.

8. Galitskii, "Voina v pravovom vakuume."

9. Svante E. Cornell, "International Reactions in Massive Human Rights Violations: The Case of Chechnya," *Europe-Asia Studies*, vol. 51 (January 1999), pp. 85–100.

10. See the website of the Parliamentary Assembly of the Council of Europe, http://stars.coe.fr/index_e.htm.

11. Roberts and Guelff, *Documents on the Laws of War*, chap. 16.

12. Ibid., p. 419.

13. Ibid., p. 420.

14. Kadyrov interview with Dmitrii Makarov in *Argumenty i fakty*, February 9, 2000, p. 7.

15. Ibid., p. 245.

16. The human rights group Memorial has been the most active in this sphere. See, for example, *Rossiia-Chechnia: Tsep' oshibok i prestuplenii* (Russia-Chechnya: A chain of mistakes and crimes) (Moscow: Zven'ia, 1998); *Narushenie mezhdunarodnykh norm i rossiiskogo zakonodatel'stva v otnoshenii prav bezhentsev i vynuzhdennykh pereselentsev* (Violation of international norms and Russian law in relation to the rights of refugees and forced resettlers) (Moscow: Zven'ia, 1998); *Pravovye aspekty Chechenskogo krizisa* (Legal aspects of the Chechen crisis) (Moscow: Memorial, 1995). Another particularly active group has been the Glasnost' Foundation. See its *Voina v Chechne: Mezhdunarodnyi Tribunal* (The war in Chechnya: International tribunal) (Moscow: Obshchestvennyi fond "Glasnost'," 1997). On the plight of journalists in the war, see Aleksei Simonov, ed., *Informatsionnaia voina v Chechne: Fakty, Dokumenty, Svidetel'stva* (Information war in Chechnya: Facts, documents, witnessess) (Moscow: Izd. "Prava cheloveka," 1997).

17. Geneva Protocol I of 1977, in Roberts and Guelff, *Documents on the Laws of War*, p. 423.

18. Iu. M. Baturin, A. L. Il'in, V. F. Kadatskii, V. V. Kostikov, M. A. Krasnov, A. Ia. Livshits, K.V. Nikiforov, L. G. Pikhoia, and G. A. Satarov, *Epokha El'tsina: Ocherki politicheskoi istorii* (The Yeltsin epoch: Sketches of a political history) (Moscow: Vagrius, 2001), pp. 622–23.

19. Ibid., p. 625.

20. Ibid., p. 631.

21. Cornell, "International Reactions."

22. David Remnick, *Resurrection: The Struggle for a New Russia* (Random House, 1997), pp. 263–64.

23. Carlotta Gall and Thomas de Waal, *Chechnya: Calamity in the Caucasus* (New York University Press, 1998), p. 186.

24. Elaine Sciolino, "Administration Sees No Choice but to Support Yeltsin," *New York Times*, January 7, 1995.

25. The signatories of the letter (archived with the author), dated March 13, 1995, were A. Belavin, V. Drinfeld, and B. Feigin.

26. An excellent account is found in Gall and de Waal, *Chechnya*, pp. 242–47.

27. Dmitrii Balburov, "Samashki Massacre Shows Grim Reality of War," *Moscow News*, no. 15, April 21–27, 1995, p. 2.

28. *Moscow News*, no. 15, April 21–27, 1995.

29. Quoted in Cornell, "International Reactions."

30. Ken Fireman, "Russian Tactics Wrack Chechnya," *Newsday*, April 17, 1995.

31. Gall and de Waal, *Chechnya*, p. 187.

32. All quotations and figures are from Cornell, "International Reactions."

33. Seymour M. Hersh, "The Price of Oil," *New Yorker*, July 9, 2001, p. 61.

34. "PACE Calls on Russia to Halt Fighting in Chechnya," RFE/RL *Newsline*, vol. 4, no. 20, pt. 1 (January 28, 2000); "Kasyanov Says G-7 Should 'Not Miss Chance' to Support Russia," RFE/RL *Newsline*, vol. 4, no. 21, pt. 1 (January 31, 2000).

35. Gall and de Waal, *Chechnya*, p. 187.

36. Baturin and others, *Epokha El'tsina*, p. 786.

37. Jim Nichol, "Chechnya Conflict: Recent Developments," *CRS Report for Congress* (Congressional Research Service, November 10, 1999). Thanks to Milton Leitenberg for a copy of this report.

38. Pavel Fel'gengauer, "Tactic Simply a War Crime," *Moscow Times*, January 27, 2000.

39. Nina Tannenwald, "The Nuclear Taboo: The United States and the Normative Basis of Nuclear Non-Use," *International Organization*, vol. 53, no. 3 (Summer 1999), pp. 433–68.

40. "Conflict in Chechnya—Implementation by Russia of Recommendation 1444 (2000), Doc. 8700" (April 5, 2000), http://stars.coe.fr/. I thank Mikhail Alexseev for calling this document to my attention.

41. E. H. Carr, *The Twenty Years' Crisis, 1919–1939: An Introduction to the Study of International Relations* (Harper and Row, 1964; reprint of 2d ed., 1946), p. 156.

42. Steven Erlanger, "Russians Step Up Assault on Rebels by Air and Armor," *New York Times*, December 23, 1994.

43. Tim Weiner, "U.S. Officials Muffle Criticism of Russian Attack," *New York Times*, January 18, 1996.

44. Michael Specter, "Saying Hostages Are Dead, Russians Level Rebel Town," *New York Times*, January 18, 1996.

45. Gall and de Waal, *Chechnya*, chap. 13.

46. Boris Yeltsin, *Midnight Diaries*, trans. Catherine A. Fitzpatrick (New York: Public Affairs, 2000), p. 340.

47. "EU Council Chairman: Russian EU Membership Possible in 'Not Too Distant Future,'" *Die Presse*, Vienna, August 28, 2001 (in German), monitored by the BBC on JRL and also available at www.ichkeria.org/a/2001/8/new2908-en85218.html.

48. Agathe Duparc, "L'impossible procès d'un 'héros russe,'" *Le Monde*, April 13, 2001.

49. Ian Traynor, "Russia Prepares to Draw More Blood in Chechnya," *Guardian* (Manchester), June 8, 2001; "Defense Minister Says Budanov 'a Victim of Circumstances,'" RFE/RL *Newsline*, vol. 5, no. 94, pt. 1 (May 17, 2001).

50. Carlo Bonini and Giuseppe D'Avanzo, "Tutti gli uomini del presidente: Così Putin impone l'ordine in Russia" (All the president's men: How Putin imposes order in Russia), *La Repubblica*, July 16, 2001, www.repubblica.it/quotidiano/repubblica/20010716/esteri/12presidunt.html.

51. RFE/RL *Newsline*, vol. 5, no. 107, pt. 1 (June 6, 2001), quoting *Izvestiia*, June 5, 2001.

52. "Kalamanov Says Budanov Case Not Unique," RFE/RL *Newsline*, vol. 5, no. 81, pt. (April 26, 2001).

53. Maura Reynolds, "A War Shrouded in Silence," *Los Angeles Times*, July 16, 2001; also Il'ia Maksakov, "Ideologicheskie posledstviia 'zachistok' v Chechne" (Ideological consequences of the "sweeps" in Chechnya), *Nezavisimaia gazeta*, July 13, 2001, http://ng.ru/events/2001-07-13/2_chechnya.html.

54. Reynolds, "A War Shrouded in Silence."

55. "Russia's 'Dirty War,'" August 9, 2001, BBC, JRL.

56. The next three paragraphs are based on Patrick E. Tyler, "Russian General Admits 'Crimes' in Chechnya," *New York Times*, 12 July 2001.

57. "Russia's 'Dirty War.'"

58. "Rights Activists Mark Chechen Anniversary amid Fears of Russian Crackdown," Agence France-Presse, October 1, 2001, JRL.

59. "Eleven Russian Soldiers Convicted of Crimes in Chechnya," September 25, 2001, http://lenta.ru/english/2001/09/20/federals/.

60. "Russian Prosecutors to Investigate Latest Civilian Deaths in Chechnya," RFE/RL *Newsline*, vol. 5, no. 215 (November 13, 2001).

61. Roberts and Guelff, *Documents on the Laws of War*, chap. 16.

62. "Spain: Don't Ignore Russian Abuses in Chechnya," e-mail report from Human Rights Watch, April 2, 2002, hrwchechnya@topica.email-publisher.com.

63. Ian Traynor, "Kremlin Angered by War Crimes Proposal," *Guardian*, March 23, 2002.

64. Evgeniia Albats, "Putin's Priorities off Target," *Moscow Times*, July 17, 2001. For an overview of the human rights situation in Russia, see Sarah Mendelson, "The Putin Path: Civil Liberties and Human Rights in Retreat," *Problems of Post-Communism*, vol. 47, no. 5 (September/October 2000), pp. 3–12; and Mendelson, "Russians' Rights Imperiled: Has Anybody Noticed?"

65. Viktor Baranets, *Poteriannaia armiia: Zapiski polkovnika Genshtaba* (Lost army: Notes of a General Staff colonel)(Moscow: Sovershenno sekretno, 1998), pp. 287–88. The Olof Palme International Center, according to its website, is "the Swedish labour movement's organisation for international development co-operation and public outreach surrounding international political and security issues." See www.palmecenter.se.

66. Baranets, *Poteriannaia armiia*, p. 288.

67. Quoted in Gall and de Waal, *Chechnya*, p. 237.

68. Baturin and others, *Epokha El'tsina*, p. 696.

69. Nanette Van Der Laan, "Chechens Were Human Shields," *Calgary Herald*, September 21, 1996.

70. Cornell, "International Reactions," pp. 85–100.

71. Baturin and others, *Epokha El'tsina*, pp. 698–99.

72. Ibid., p. 699.

73. Yeltsin, *Midnight Diaries*, pp. 338–39.

74. Anna Politkovskaya, *A Dirty War: A Russian Reporter in Chechnya* (London: Harvill Press, 2001), p. 114.

75. Traynor, "Russia Prepares to Draw More Blood in Chechnya."

76. Ibid., pp. 181–82.

77. Anne Nivat, *Chienne de Guerre: A Woman Reporter behind the Lines of the War in Chechnya*, trans. Susan Darnton (New York: Public Affairs, 2001), pp. 254–55.

78. Ibid., p. 255.

79. On the plight of journalists in the war, see Simonov, *Informatsionnaia voina v Chechne.*

80. Control of the media was evident in the earliest days of the second war. See, for example, "Guerra cecena, parte seconda: il grande silenzio" (Chechen war, part two: The great silence), lettera22 website, October 26, 1999, www.lettera22.com/news/Russia-exURSS/Russia/199910261210.news.shtml.

81. Galia Ackerman, "Tchétchénie: Le témoin gênant" (Chechnya: The embarrassing witness), *Politique Internationale,* no. 87 (Spring 2000), pp. 45–54; Lev Lurie, "The Russian Media Turns," Institute for War & Peace Reporting, Caucasus Reporting Service, no. 14 (January 2000); "RFE/RL Correspondent Reported Missing in Chechnya," RFE/RL *Newsline,* vol. 4, no. 18 (January 26, 2000); "Radio Liberty Reporter Describes Torture in Chechen Filtration Camp," BBC Monitoring of NTV, Moscow, February 29, 2000.

82. Vladimir Putin, *First Person: An Astonishingly Frank Self-Portrait by Russia's President* (New York: Public Affairs, 2000), pp. 171–73.

83. A collection of Anna Politkovskaia's articles appears in *A Dirty War.*

84. Artyom Vernidoub, "Threatened Journalist Flees from Russia," in the online news service, gazeta.ru, 18 October 2001, courtesy of JRL.

85. Anna Politkovskaia, "Grozny under Blockade," *Novaia gazeta,* September 20, 2001, translated by Miriam Lanskoy, www.bu.edu/iscip/digest/vol6/ed0615.html#transcauc.

86. Fel'gengauer, "Tactic Simply a War Crime.

87. Ibid.

88. Maksakov, "Ideologicheskie posledstviia "zachistok" v Chechne."

89. As an eyewitness to several of the early Russian bombing campaigns against civilian areas, Prohazkova had given testimony to a group of Russian human-rights activists seeking a war-crimes tribunal for the first Chechen War. See Glasnost' Foundation, *Voina v Chechne: Mezhdunarodnyi Tribunal,* pp. 41–45.

90. Masha Gessen, "In Russia, Echoes of the Old KGB: Going after Foreign Aid Workers and Others," *U.S. News and World Report,* July 30, 2001.

91. For excellent discussions of these questions, see Sarah E. Mendelson, "Explaining the International Community's Response to the War in Chechnya," PONARS Memo 143 (April 2000); and Kimberly Marten Zisk, "Human Rights Violations in Chechnya: Implications for Western Assistance to Russia," PONARS Memo 142 (April 2000), both available at www.csis.org/ruseura/ponars/policymemos/pm_index.htm.

92. Michael Walzer, *Just and Unjust Wars: A Moral Argument with Historical Illustrations* (Basic Books, 1977).

93. Anatol Lieven, "Why Dagestan Needs the Russians," *New York Times,* August 20, 1999; Anatol Lieven, "Let's Help Russia against the Chechens," *Los Angeles Times,* September 21, 1999; Robert Bruce Ware, "The West's Failure to Understand Chechnya," *Boston Globe,* October 26, 1999.

94. John Ward Anderson, "In Mexico City, Kidnapping Is a Daily Event," *International Herald Tribune,* March 22, 1999; Juan Forero, "Kidnappers in Colombia Branch out to Venezuela," *New York Times,* December 16, 2001.

95. Robert Bruce Ware, "Was There a Kremlin Conspiracy in the Caucasus?" Johnson's Russia List 4092 (February 6, 2000).

96. Robert Bruce Ware, "Russia Could Learn from America's Anti-Terror Campaign," *Moscow Times,* January 11, 2002.

97. Aleksandr Gol'tz, "Schitat' my stali rany, tovarishchei schitat'," *Itogi,* October 12,

1999, pp. 12–14; Fedor Gavrilov, "In Dagestan, It's Déjà Vu All Over Again," *St. Petersburg Times,* September 10, 1999.

98. Nivat, *Chienne de Guerre,* p. 41.

99. Anatol Lieven, "Through a Distorted Lens: Chechnya and the Western Media," *Current History* (October 2000), with a special introduction for readers of Johnson's Russia List 4546 (September 29, 2000).

100. *An Agenda for Renewal: U.S.-Russian Relations,* A Report by the Russian and Eurasian Program (Washington: Carnegie Endowment for International Peace, 2000), p. 35. On p. ii, Lieven is credited as one of several authors, but the discussion of Chechnya closely tracks the views and wording of his *Current History* essay cited in n. 99.

101. Eliot A. Cohen, "The Meaning and Future of Air Power," *Orbis,* vol. 39 (Spring 1995), p. 200, quoted in Ward Thomas, *The Ethics of Destruction: Norms and Force in International Relations* (Cornell University Press, 2001), p. 168.

102. Anatol Lieven, "Soldiers before Missiles: Meeting the Challenge of the World's Streets," Carnegie Endowment for International Peace *Policy Brief,* vol. 1 (April 2001), emphasis added.

103. Anatol Lieven, "The Afghan Terrain," Carnegie Endowment for International Peace Web Commentary, October 25, 2001, www.ceip.org/files/Publications/afghanterrain. asp?from=pubdate.

104. Gol'tz, "Schitat' my stali rany, tovarishchei schitat'," *Itogi,* October 12, 1999, pp. 12–14; Gavrilov, "In Dagestan, It's Déjà Vu All Over Again."

105. Michael R. Gordon, "General in Balkan War Says Pentagon Hampered NATO," *New York Times,* May 21, 2001; Wesley K. Clark, *Waging Modern War: Bosnia, Kosovo, and the Future of Combat* (New York: Public Affairs, 2001).

106. "Interviews: General Klaus Naumann," *PBS Frontline: War in Europe,* quoted in Thomas, *The Ethics of Destruction,* p. 164.

107. Gregory L. Vistica, "What Happened in Thanh Phong," *New York Times Magazine,* April 29, 2001.

108. Quoted in ibid.

109. Walzer, *Just and Unjust Wars,* p. 305.

110. Colin Powell, with Joseph Persico, *My American Journey* (Ballantine Books, 1996), pp. 52, 140.

111. Walzer, *Just and Unjust Wars,* p. 313.

112. I owe several of the points in this paragraph, and some of the wording, to e-mail correspondence with David Wippman, December 11, 2001. On the Kosovo case, see "Final Report to the Prosecutor by the Committee Established to Review the NATO Bombing Campaign against the Federal Republic of Yugoslavia," www.un.org/icty/pressreal/nato061300.htm. For a critique of the report, see Paolo Benvenuti, "The ICTY's Prosecutor and the Review of the NATO Bombing Campaign against the Federal Republic of Yugoslavia," *European Journal of International Law,* vol. 12, no. 3 (2001), www.ejil.org/journal/vol12/no3/ab5.html. Much of the rest of the issue is relevant to this topic as well.

113. Mark Bowden, *Black Hawk Down: A Story of Modern War* (Penguin Books, 2000), p. 225.

114. Lieven, "Through a Distorted Lens."

115. Jack F. Matlock Jr., "Read Their Lips," *New York Times Book Review,* August 12, 2001, pp. 11–12.

116. Leslie C. Green, "War Crimes, Crimes against Humanity, and Command Responsibility," *Naval War College Review,* vol. 50 (Spring 1997), pp. 26–68.

117. A key precedent came in the Tokyo war crimes trials after World War II, when the Japanese foreign minister and others were convicted (Count 55) of having "deliberately and recklessly disregarded their duty" to take adequate steps to prevent atrocities. Green traces the concept back as far as 1439, to an ordinance promulgated by Charles VII of Orleans making commanders legally responsible for the crimes of their subordinates (ibid.).

118. Article 86 of the 1977 Protocol to the Geneva Conventions summarizes the main point: "The fact that a breach of the Conventions or of this Protocol was committed by a subordinate does not absolve his superiors from penal or disciplinary responsibility, as the case may be, if they knew, or had information which should have enabled them to conclude in the circumstances at the time, that he was committing or was going to commit such a breach and if they did not take all feasible measures within their power to prevent or repress the breach."

119. Ibid.

120. "The Chechen Conflict and Russian Democratic Development," Hearings before the U.S. Congress Commission on Security and Cooperation in Europe (March 6, 1996), www.house.gov/csce/chechen.htm.

121. Ibid.

122. "A Free Pass on Chechnya," *Washington Post,* July 21, 2001.

123. Paul Quinn-Judge, "Guerrillas in Grozny," *Time Magazine,* European ed., June 11, 2001.

124. Maura Reynolds, "Moscow Has Chechnya Back—Now What?" *Los Angeles Times,* June 19, 2000.

125. Walzer, *Just and Unjust Wars,* p. 187.

Chapter 8

Epigraphs are from Art Buchwald, "Fighting the Cold Wars of Yesteryear," *International Herald Tribune,* February 8, 2002; Joseph Conrad, *Nostromo* (Oxford University Press, 1984), p. 84.

1. Masha Lipman, "Popularity without Much Else to Show," *International Herald Tribune,* April 25, 2002.

2. Francesco Bigazzi, "Dalla Russia con intelligence," *Panorama,* January 17, 2002, pp. 106–10.

3. For a thoughtful comparison of the role of U.S. hegemony during and after the cold war, see Vittorio Emanuele Parsi, "L'Impero Come Fato? Gli Stati Uniti e l'Ordine Globale," *Filosofia Politica,* vol. 16 (April 2002), pp. 83–113.

4. Several small states, including Austria, Sweden, Finland, and Portugal, refused to sign the agreement during the course of the war. See Bo Svensson, "Integrating Russia: The EU as a Facilitator of FDI," paper for European Forum Seminar, EUI/RSCAS, November 22, 2001, p. 12, n. 12.

5. On framing, see Rodger A. Payne, "Persuasion, Frames and Norm Construction," *European Journal of International Relations,* vol. 7 (March 2001), pp. 37–61.

6. Some specific measures of cooperation that would serve Moscow's interests include "Western support in finding and freezing the funds of pro-Chechen groups abroad, closing their 'information centres', which support terrorist acts and jihad against Russia, and

extraditing Chechen warlords and Arab mercenaries who have found refuge abroad." See Oksana Antonenko, "Putin's Gamble," *Survival,* vol. 43 (Winter 2001–02), pp. 52–53.

7. Roland Eggleston, "Germany: Schroeder Hints at Change in Opinion on Chechnya," and Jeremy Bransten, "Russia: Seeing the Chechen War through Moscow's Eyes," both September 26, 2001, available at www.rferl.org, the website of Radio Free Europe/Radio Liberty.

8. Letter to Chancellor Gerhard Schröder from Elizabeth Andersen and Lotte Leicht of Human Rights Watch, September 21, 2001, "HRW Press Release: Safeguard Rights in Anti-Terror Campaign," September 27, 2001.

9. The transcript of Putin's interview with Barbara Walters is available at http://abcnews.go.com/sections/2020/dailynews/putin_transcript_011005.html.

10. Eggleston, "Germany: Schroeder Hints at Change"; and Bransten, "Russia: Seeing the Chechen War."

11. Francesca Mereu, "Russia: Council of Europe Delegation Urges Negotiations in Chechnya Crisis," RFE/RL report of December 6, 2001, www.rferl/org; Human Rights Watch, "New Killings and 'Disappearances' in Chechnya," March 23, 2002, and "Chechnya: U.N. Rights Commission Must Act, Russian Government Fails to Curb Atrocities for Third Year," March 26, 2002, both available at www.hrw.org/campaigns/russia/chechnya; Patrick E. Tyler, "Police in Chechnya Accuse Russia's Troops of Murder," *New York Times,* January 25, 2002.

12. The attention was comparable to previous years, however, neither much more nor much less (with the exception of the "interwar" years 1997 and 1998). As a rough quantitative measure, consider references to Chechnya or Chechen(s) in each year's report: 1995, 172; 1996, 155; 1997, 31; 1998, 50; 1999, 138; 2000,136; 2001, 150. In fact, each year's report duplicates much of the text of previous years. U.S. Department of State, Bureau of Democracy, Human Rights, and Labor, *Country Reports on Human Rights Practices, Russia, 1995–2001.* The reports are most easily accessible on the website of the U.S. embassy in Stockholm, www.usis.usemb.se/human/.

13. "Russian Military Wants Human Rights Observed during Search Operations," RFE/RL *Newsline,* vol. 6, no. 60, pt. 1 (March 29, 2002); Clara Ferreira-Marques, "Moscow Considers Fresh Talks with Chechen Rebels," Reuters report from Moscow, January 16, 2002.

14. "New Regulations on Chechen Search Operations Violated," *RFE/RL* Newsline, vol. 6, no. 62, pt. 1 (April 3, 2002).

15. "Russia Strongly Criticizes U.S. State Department Report on Human Rights," RFE/RL *Newsline,* vol. 6, no. 44, pt. 1 (March 7, 2002).

16. Testimony of Steven Pifer, Deputy Assistant Secretary for European and Eurasian Affairs, U.S. Department of State, Hearing of the Commission on Security and Cooperation in Europe on Developments in the Chechen Conflict (Washington, May 9, 2002), JRL.

17. This could be an example of what Thomas Risse has called "rhetorical entrapment." See his "'Let's Argue!' Communicative Action in World Politics," *International Organization,* vol. 54 (Winter 2000), pp. 1–39.

18. BBC Monitoring of Putin's annual State of the Nation address to Russian parliament, from Russian television, April 18, 2002, on Johnson's Russia List 6195.

19. Maksim Zorin and Aleksandr Chuikov, "Pankisi Gorge Is no Walk-Over Like in Afghanistan," *Izvestiia,* February 28, 2002.

20. Gennadii Ziuganov, quoted in Robert Cottrell, "Putin's Risky Strategy," *Financial Times,* February 12, 2002.

21. Alan Cullison, "Russia's Left-Wing Politicians Retreat from Their Support of U.S.-Led War," *Wall Street Journal,* February 5, 2002.

22. "Russia Preparing to Boost Oil Exports," UPI report from Moscow, February 4, 2002; Arturo Zampaglione, "Prezzi del petrolio alle stele Wall Street teme l'effetto Kippur," *La Repubblica,* April 3, 2002; "Russia to End Curbs on Oil Exports," RFE/RL *Newsline,* vol. 6, no. 76, pt. 1 (April 23, 2002).

23. Putin's State of the Nation address, April 18, 2002.

24. Alessandra Longo, "Quel feeling tra Silvio e Vladimir: 'Per me é come un vecchio amico,'" *La Repubblica,* April 3, 2002.

25. Gianluca Luzi, "Berlusconi da Putin: prevalgano ragionevolezza e responsabilità," *La Repubblica,* April 3, 2002.

26. Ibid.

27. Hugo Young, "A Welcome for Putin, the Butcher of Chechnya," *Guardian,* April 18, 2000.

28. Longo, "Quel feeling tra Silvio e Vladimir."

29. Paolo Rumiz, "L'Italia in punta di piedi alla conquista dell'Est," *Affari & Finanza,* supplement to *La Repubblica,* April 15, 2002, p. 18.

30. Svensson, "Integrating Russia."

31. "Berlusconi Backs Russia as NATO Member," UPI report, May 14, 2001.

32. Marco Marozzi, "Prodi: la Russia non può entrare nella nuova Ue" (Prodi: Russia cannot enter the new EU), *La Repubblica,* April 14, 2002.

33. Paolo Garimberti, "Nato e Russia: mai più nemici," and Gianluca Luzi, "Questo accordo l'ho voluto io, adesso Mosca entri nella Ue," both in *La Repubblica,* May 29, 2002; Pascal Lamy, "The EU Wants Russia to Make the Grade," *International Herald Tribune,* May 29, 2002.

34. "La lutte contre le terrorisme au menu du sommet OTAN-Russie à Rome," *Le Monde,* May 29, 2002; John Vinocur, "Russia, Oldest NATO Foe, Becomes Limited Partner," *International Herald Tribune,* May 29, 2002; and Garimberti, "Nato e Russia." On Blair's proposal, see Antonenko, "Putin's Gamble," p. 56.

35. "La Tchétchénie ne mobilise pas les eurodéputés," *Le Monde,* April 11, 2002; Breffni O'Rourke, "Russia: European Parliament Concerned over Military Campaign in Chechnya," RFE/RL report, April 11, 2002, www.rfefl.org/nca/features/2002/04/11042002093457.asp; European Parliament Minutes (Proceedings of the Sitting) Provisional Edition, April 10, 2002, www3.europarl.eu.int/omk/omnsapir.so/pvl?prg=calend&langue=en&tpv=prov&file=020410&type=alldoc.

36. The states that voted for were Austria, Belgium, Canada, Costa Rica, Czech Republic, France, Germany, Guatemala, Italy, Mexico, Poland, Portugal, Spain, Sweden, United Kingdom. The states that voted against were Armenia, Burundi, China, Cuba, Democratic Republic of the Congo, India, Indonesia, Kenya, Nigeria, Russian Federation, Sudan, Swaziland, Syrian Arab Republic, Togo, Venezuela, Viet Nam. The states that abstained were Algeria, Argentina, Bahrain, Brazil, Cameroon, Chile, Croatia, Ecuador, Japan, Libyan Arab Jamahiriya, Malaysia, Pakistan, Peru, Republic of Korea, Saudi Arabia, Senegal, Sierra Leone, South Africa, Thailand, Uganda, Uruguay, Zambia. See Human Rights Watch, "Russia: U.N. Chechnya Vote Assailed," e-mail report, April 19, 2002, hrwchechnya@topica.email-publisher.com.

37. Report on the activities of the Joint Working Group on Chechnya (JWG) made up of members of the Parliamentary Assembly of the Council of Europe and of the State Duma of the Federal Assembly of the Russian Federation, Doc. 9415 Addendum I revised, April 22, 2002, available on the PACE website.

38. Steven Levingston, "Rush to Russia: Investors Take Hope in Reform," *International Herald Tribune,* March 25, 2002, p. 9; Anthony DiPaola, "Italy Stands to Gain from NATO-Russia Accord," *Italy Daily,* supplement to *International Herald Tribune,* May 29, 2002.

39. Svensson, "Integrating Russia."

40. Putin's State of the Nation address, April 18, 2002.

41. Theoretical discussions relevant to practice of this sort include Payne, "Persuasion, Frames and Norm Construction"; and Frank Schimmelfennig, "The Double Puzzle of EU Enlargement Liberal Norms, Rhetorical Action, and the Decision to Expand to the East," ARENA Working Papers, WP 99/15 (Oslo, 1999).

42. For example, "Il Consiglio d'Europa avverte: la Lega è razzista e xenofoba," *La Repubblica,* April 23, 2002; and Marco Marozzi, "Dossier Ue: 'Fallaci razzista,'" *La Repubblica,* May 24, 2002.

43. Frank Schimmelfennig, "Conditionality, Costs, and Commitment: Domestic Conditions of Adaptation to Fundamental European Norms in the CEECs and Turkey," paper prepared for European Forum Seminar, EUI/RSCAS, October 11, 2001; Sarah E. Mendelson and John K. Glenn, eds., *The Power and Limits of NGOs: Transnational Democracy Networks and Postcommunist Transitions* (Columbia University Press, 2002), especially Mendelson's conclusion.

Chapter 9

Epigraph is from Robert V. Daniels, "Democracy and Federalism in the Former Soviet Union and the Russian Federation," in Peter J. Stavrakis and others, eds., *Beyond the Monolith: The Emergence of Regionalism in Post-Soviet Russia* (Washington: Woodrow Wilson Center Press, 1997), p. 243.

1. Transcript of Press Conference by President George W. Bush and Russian Federation President Vladimir Putin, Brdo Castle, Brdo Pri Kranju, Slovenia, June 16, 2001, www.whitehouse.gov/news/releases/2001/06/20010618.html.

2. See Sarah E. Mendelson and John K. Glenn, eds., *The Power and Limits of NGOs: Transnational Democracy Networks and Postcommunist Transitions* (Columbia University Press, 2002), p. 243.

3. "Scant Food, Spreading Sickness: Chechen Refugees Face Disaster," Agence France-Presse, 1 January 2001.

4. Testimony of Steven Pifer, Deputy Assistant Secretary for European and Eurasian Affairs, U.S. Department of State, Hearing of the Commission on Security and Cooperation in Europe on Developments in the Chechen Conflict (Washington, May 9, 2002), JRL.

5. "Continuing Torture and Rape in Chechnya," Amnesty International News Release, EUR 46/36/00 (June 8, 2000); John Sweeney, "Cries from Putin's Torture Pit," *Observer* (London), October 15, 2000.

6. Maura Reynolds, "A War Shrouded in Silence," *Los Angeles Times,* July 16, 2001.

7. Katharine Q. Seeley, "Nelle gabbie di Guantanamo per curare i superterroristi," *La Repubblica,* February 5, 2002; Vittorio Zucconi, "I Taliban prigionieri di Guerra," *La Repubblica,* February 8, 2002; Carlo Bonini, "Per tre giorni tra i dannati di Guantanamo," *La Repubblica,* March 17, 2002. Some problems remained, however, as the Pentagon sought to bring charges against 300 of the detainees before special military tribunals "in the absence of specific evidence that they themselves have committed war crimes." See "Guantanamo Mischief," *New York Times* editorial, reprinted in *International Herald Tribune,* April 25, 2002.

8. Overall, the Bush administration's record of sustaining human rights while combating terrorism has been uneven at best. See the critique of Amnesty International reported in "L'après 11 septembre: Amnesty deplore le récul des libertés," and "Amnesty dresse un somber bilan de l'après 11 septembre," both in *Le Monde,* May 29, 2002; and Karen DeYoung, "Group Assails U.S. on Human Rights," *International Herald Tribune,* May 29, 2002.

9. Neil A. Lewis, "U.S. Rejects All Support for New Court on Atrocities," *New York Times,* May 7, 2002.

10. Ibid. In fact, Article 18 of the Vienna Convention does not oblige states to refrain from undermining a treaty if they have made clear their intention not to become a party to the treaty—certainly the case with the Bush administration and the Rome Statute. I thank David Wippman for this clarification.

11. Ibid. Some European writers had already criticized the U.S. standing to make pronouncements on international legality, in light of its failure to ratify the Rome Statute and other agreements. See, for example, the best-selling book by Tiziano Terzani, *Lettere contro la Guerra* (Milan: Longanesi, 2002), esp. p. 54.

12. Clifford Gaddy and Fiona Hill, "Putin's Agenda, America's Choice," Brookings Policy Brief 99 (May 2002), www.brookings.edu/dybdocroot/comm/policybriefs/pb99.htm.

13. Daniels, "Democracy and Federalism," p. 243.

14. For especially persuasive discussions, see Sarah Mendelson, "The Putin Path: Civil Liberties and Human Rights in Retreat," *Problems of Post-Communism,* vol. 47 (September/October 2000), pp. 3–12; and Mendelson, "Russians' Rights Imperiled: Has Anybody Noticed?" *International Security,* vol. 26 (Spring 2002).

15. Paul Goble, "Sovereignty Shared or Suppressed," RFE/RL Russian Federation Report, vol. 3, no. 25 (September 17, 2001).

16. Quoted in ibid.

17. Hans Magnus Enzenberger, *Civil Wars, from L.A. to Bosnia* (New York: New Press, 1994), p. 15.

18. Andrei Babitskii, testimony before the Commission on Security and Cooperation in Europe's Hearing on Developments in the Chechen Conflict (Washington, May 9, 2002), JRL.

19. See, for example, the case studies in Mendelson and Glenn, *The Power and Limits of NGOs.* For a discussion of the record of transnational efforts on arms control during the Soviet and early post-Soviet periods, see Matthew Evangelista, *Unarmed Forces: The Transnational Movement to End the Cold War* (Cornell University Press, 1999).

Index